THE MEDIA WORKS

Joan Valdes
Jeanne Crow

 Pflaum/Standard • 2285 Arbor Boulevard • Dayton, Ohio 45439

Design: Judy Olson
Illustrations: Ralph Mapson
Art Director: Dan Johnson

Acknowledgments

We wish to thank these people for generous assistance:

Lee Moon and Roscoe Kassam, Northwest Magazine Distributing Co., Seattle, Wash.; Gene Estribou, filmmaker and sound studio owner, San Francisco, CA.; Ted Durein, executive editor of Monterey Peninsula *Herald,* Monterey, CA.; Carolyn Fratessa, desk-mate and sounding board, Menlo Park, CA.; Michael Albrecht and Pat Lewis, Pacific Northwest Bell Co., Seattle, Wash.; The Museum of Modern Art, 11 West 53 St., New York, N.Y. 10019; Culver Pictures, 660 First Avenue, New York, N.Y. 10016; John Wayne, 5451 Marathon St., Hollywood, CA. 90038; Dan Faris, The Cinema Shop, 522 O'Farrell, San Francisco, CA.; *Woman's Day* magazine, One Astor Plaza, New York, N.Y. 10036; National Broadcasting Co., 30 Rockefeller Plaza, New York, N.Y. 10020; American Broadcasting Co., 1330 Avenue of the Americas, New York, N.Y. 10019; National Periodical Publications, 909 Third Ave., New York, N.Y. 10022; Marvel Comics Group, 625 Madison Ave., New York, N.Y. 10022; Leo Burnett Co., Inc., Advertising, Prudential Plaza, Chicago, Ill. 60601; Jack Jaxon, Rip Off Press, 1440 Arkansas, San Francisco, CA. 94107; Robert J. Glessing, Canada College, Redwood City, CA.; *Saturday Review,* 380 Madison Avenue, New York, N.Y. 10017; *The New Yorker,* No. 25 West 43rd St., New York, N.Y. 10036; CBS Television Network, 51 West 52 Street, New York, N.Y. 10019; Pyramid Films, Box 1048, Santa Monica, CA.; Phil Buchanan, radio station KMPX, San Francisco, CA.; Canyon Cinema, Sausalito, CA.; Tim, for his strength and support.

J. V.
J. C.

iv

Table of Contents

INTRODUCTION

The mass media include any means through which someone sends out a message to a lot of people.

The medium can be as easily obtainable as a construction fence and a wax crayon:

Or it can be as hard to come by (and to finance) as 15 seconds of prime-time television exposure.

The presentation of the message can be obvious and straightforward:

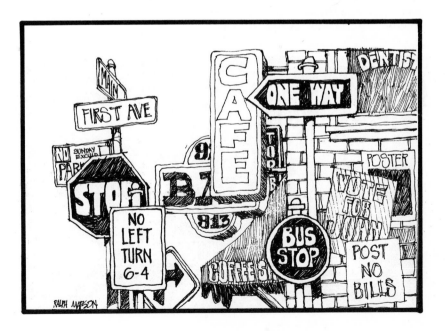

Or it can be subtle or ironic, and so demand some thinking from us.

The message can be tuned in, turned on, or paid for at the magazine stand or movie theater. That is, we can *seek out* messages of excitement, comfort, information, escape, or hope:

Or it can surround us, uninvited, beyond our tuning-in and tuning-out control:

In today's world, message-senders are competing for our attention. This book is designed to investigate the variety of ways each medium suits itself to our needs, works its way comfortably into our lives, and even directs in some measure the way we live them.

SUGGESTED ACTIVITIES: In addition to suggestions labeled DO, the possibilities listed under the following titles will supply action leads. For many of these, your logbook, *Working With The Media Works*, has forms and directions. These are labeled in the logbook with chapter numbers (where the activity is general) and with the textbook page number if the suggested activity is mentioned in the text.

REACT:

Think, form an opinion, listen, tune in, talk, collect examples . . . but you don't have to write anything down to be tuned in.

Dig:

Drudge work—hunt out, write down, be thorough; useful for getting to know the details of a subject and helpful later on as a reference.

Create:

Imagine, produce an original, play a role.

Read:

Suggestions for further reading on a subject. Most titles given will be for paperbacks.

me·di·a, n. a pl. of *medium*
me·di·um, n., pl. -*diums*, -*dia*, adj.
—n. 1. a middle state or condition; mean. 2. something intermediate in nature or degree. 3. an intervening substance, as air, through which a force acts or an effect is produced. 4. the element that is the natural habitat of an organism. 5. surrounding objects, conditions, or influences; environment. 6. an agency, means, or instrument: *Newspapers are a popular advertising medium.* 7. *Biol.* the substance in which specimens are displayed or preserved. Also called *culture medium.* 8. *Bacteriol.* a liquid or solidified nutrient material suitable for the cultivation of microorganisms. 9. *Fine Arts.* a. *Painting.* a liquid with which pigments are mixed. b. the material or technique with which an artist works: *graphic medium; sculpture as a medium of artistic expression.* 10. a person serving, or conceived of as serving, as an instrument through which another personality or a supernatural agency is alleged to manifest itself: *a spiritualistic medium* . . .
—Syn. average, mean, middling, mediocre.

"I just invented a new concept. It's called media."

Drawing by Joseph G. Farris. © 1971 Saturday Review, Inc.

With mass media as envoys of democracy and optimism, messages are quickly relayed from New York or Hollywood to all citizens. Communications is no respecter of tradition or of social conservation. The preservation of values is anathema to the great god of data, whose pleasure it is to spit out most of the information received before digesting it. Only the new is newsworthy, and the new is by nature better than the old. Last year's eye was pretty, *Cosmopolitan* admits, but it will no longer serve. To gaze with an outdated eye is as bad as praising last year's pop singer. To appear at a college reunion as the same self who graduated would be tasteless and would indicate to others that you are "alienated."
—Kathrin Perutz, *Beyond the Looking Glass, Life in the Beauty Culture,* Pyramid, 1971, $1.25

In this book, *me·di·a* means . . .

MOVIES

TELEVISION

ADVERTISING

Magazines

COMICS

RADIO

Newspapers

THE WORKINGS

CHAPTER 1

Locally Speaking...

In this chapter, we will take a look at each medium at its local outlet: the magazine stand, the movie theater, the local radio stations, the local TV channels' offerings, the advertisers' products on your home shelves, and your town's newspapers. While reading this chapter and the next one, which concerns itself with the message-*makers* of each medium, think of an "inside man" (or woman) in each field that you know or would like to get to know. In other words, find someone to talk to about each of the media. Consider him or her your personal source of information and ask him (by phone, letter, or in person) any questions that come up in class throughout the year.

Dig:

Make a list of your people-in-the-know, for Comics (cartoons), Newspapers, Magazines, TV, Radio, Advertising, Movies, Recordings. Describe their connection with the medium (record distributor? sports editor for a newspaper? filmmaker? comic artist? record store owner? fashion editor for a magazine? weather girl at a TV station? deejay? advertising agency copywriter?) and give the address of the company they are associated with. They can be local or far away. Reach for the sky!

The activities in these first two chapters will involve a lot of "digging out" of information. The more thorough your investigation is, the more examples you will have at hand when testing out the ideas in this book.

Newspapers

I. TRADITIONAL FORMAT

Go out and buy a *daily* newspaper, the one most read by the adult members of your community. See if it conforms to the following portrait of "Your Average, Run-of-the-Mill, Traditional Daily."

Front Page: The newspaper's name at the top, flanked on each side by "ears" or boxes in which weather news, index of contents, special feature items are indicated. A "banner" or headline in large letters running across the entire width of the page. The most important news story of the day, in the last column to the right (in the hope that the reader's eye "drops down" there after it scans the headline from left to right). Other important news stories or at least the "lead" for each (introductory generalized summaries of the detailed article to follow). Pictures. A "feature story" or human interest story, usually boxed-in or bordered, emphasizing emotional content rather than factual news. Much of the front page news is from the two major news services: AP (Associated Press) or UPI (United Press International). For a reporter to get his article, with his own byline at the top, onto the front page is big stuff!

Editorial Page: The one page devoted to opinion. Usually the "masthead" (information about title, ownership, management, as well as subscription and advertising rates) is on this page, as well as names of the newspaper staff. Letters to the Editor are the reader's way of speaking out on local and national issues. There are syndicated columnists as well as local editorials taking a stand on current issues. It is often on this page that the "personality" of a newspaper can be most readily seen. Many people subscribe to a paper because they *agree* with the editors. Most newspapers figure their editorial page will contain 60% local-issues and 40% national-issues commentary.

Entertainment Page: TV, radio, movies, art, music: logs and calendars of events, movie ads, critics' columns.

Sports: Scores, "feature" articles, syndicated columnists who report background material, human detail, opinion.

Women's Page: Fashion, food, social events, advice to the lovelorn.

Business & Finance: Stock reports, local promotions, and new assignments.

Vital Statistics: Marriages, divorces, deaths, births, funerals.

Comics: Self-explanatory

Classified Ads & "Filler" (stories with little news value, used only to fill up space).

Advertisements: Usually about 60% of the paper, prepared and placed on the page before news stories are laid out.

"In-between" pages: News items—local, national, and international.

REACT:

Note any radical departures from traditional format your local newspaper exhibits.

DIG:

Everyone reads the paper differently. Some people have only a few sections which they check in on every day; others read a paper cover to cover ("getting into it like they would into a warm bath" in McLuhan's words). Most people, in fact, have a newspaper reading ritual—a place they sit and a plan of attack. Interview a housewife, a businessman, a teacher, and an elderly person and report on their reading "rituals."

II. KNOW YOUR EDITORS: They Make "Quality" Newspapers Possible (or Impossible).

Distinguish between syndicated columnists (who might be commenting on events 1,000 miles away from your home base) and local columnists. Then do a little research on the local ones. What is their background? Are they qualified to cover their assignments? For instance, is there one entertainment editor, or are there many to cover radio, TV, art, movies, etc.?

Dig:

List the editors and annotate their approach to their subjects as the year goes on. Also list reporters whose bylines appear frequently.

React:

Write a letter to the editor of your choice if you wholeheartedly approve or disapprove of his work.

III. NEWSPAPER CHAINS: Who Owns What

As of 1967, there were 73 communities where one person or company owned or controlled all of the local newspaper and broadcast outlets. Even more communities are "one-newspaper towns." Such media monopolies generate fears. Is it not dangerous when the power to inform, misinform, or omit to inform rests in one group? Another fear, often groundless, is that a one-newspaper town is somehow "controlled" by the policy-making editors of that paper. The only way to fight such control, if it does indeed exist, is to subscribe to other news sources. This is often difficult on the local level.

Dig:

Compare your newspaper with those from other cities in its coverage of one major event within the past year.

React:

Comment on the possible abuses of power in the following situations:

1. The *Los Angeles Times,* the property of the Chandler family and Republican in its influence, is a joint owner of the *LA Times-Washington Post* News Service.

2. Scripps-Howard newspaper chain owns 95% of the UPI news service and publishes the *World Almanac.*

3. One man, Donald W. Reynolds, owns two newspapers in Fort Smith, Arkansas, and its only TV station and uses them as weapons of war against legislation he dislikes and politicians he opposes.

Dig:

Who owns your town's newspaper (s)? What else do they own?

Magazines

I. CHECKING OUT YOUR TOWN'S MAGAZINE STANDS: A Look at the Vendors

Consider the following descriptions of magazine types as you go "on the road" with your next assignment:

General Circulation: Aimed at the widest possible readership, its format shows a considerable range of subject matter—a "something for everyone" approach. In news coverage, it emphasizes personality more than issues, people more than abstract ideas. Its language is non-technical so that it can be understood by the average reader.

Life
Reader's Digest

Also included in the general circulation category are those magazines aimed specifically at the woman/girl and man/boy

True
Argosy
Sports Illustrated

groups. They are instructional (with how-to-do-it type articles); they often offer escape (through fiction, looks at other people's lives, and intimate first-hand accounts); and especially in the hobby/pastime types, they show a distinct consumer-orientation (it is sometimes difficult to distinguish between their instruction and their ads).

Playboy
McCall's
Good Housekeeping
Ingenue

Popular Mechanics
Horse & Rider
Guns & Ammo
High Fidelity

Comics

Entertainment: The movie magazines and any others which register the pulse of the people in the entertainment world; appeal to our curiosity about people's private lives.

Modern Screen
TV Guide
TV Radio-Mirror
Photoplay

News—Departmentalized: Classifies news events (national, international, education, etc.). Format is tightly structured and the editor's job is to fill the compartments. Reading the departmentalized news magazine is like going through a familiar ritual.

U.S. News & World Report
Time
Newsweek

News—Extended: Selects a few events and treats them in depth and in detail; not so much current events as significant ones. The magazine can be politically oriented according to its editor or it can have a recognized affiliation with a specific pressure group, business, religious, or social organization.

The Nation
The New Republic
The Commonweal
Christian Century
American Legion

Cultural—Literary: These magazines assume a sophistication in their readership. Articles in depth on the great issues of the day, fiction by established writers, and any other stimuli for reflective thinking compose their format. "News" is just as often of the Fine Arts as of the Political Arts.

Atlantic
Harper's
New Yorker
Esquire
World Commentary

Trade Journals: Those magazines read by the members of a specific trade or business or discipline. Technical language usually puts off the lay reader. They are meant to be tools for "keeping up" on the research in one's particular field. For those outside the profession, there are the popularized trade journals, which keep the laymen informed about specialized worlds. These magazines are sometimes criticized for over-simplifying and over-dramatizing their subject.

Broadcasting
AMA Journal

Psychology Today

Confessions: These magazines claim to be collections of people's "true" stories, but are actually stories written to a strict formula. Stories, which are written to appeal to women, fall into two categories: sin and suffering—the sensational and the poignant.

True Story
Modern Romance
True Confessions
Love Stories

React:

1. In checking out the magazine stand, are any patterns of magazine display evident? For instance, was *True* magazine very often displayed next to *Playboy*? (There are such things as publisher's representatives whose job it is to go around from vendor to vendor and see if he can get his publisher's magazines "preferential display," for instance, right next to a best seller, etc.).

2. Do most of the magazine stands in your town carry approximately the same titles? Or are there some who seem to cater to a specialized readership?

II. TRACKING THE PATH OF THE UNSOLD MAGAZINE: A Look at the Distributor

Have you ever wondered how the magazines get from their publisher's stapling machines to the racks of your local magazine stand? Or what happens to those that don't sell? Both tasks belong to the distributor

It is the distributor's job to destroy the "bulk" of an unsold magazine (in the old days, it was tossed into a vat of dye to guarantee the obliteration of its contents) and to return only the covers to the publisher as proof of non-sale. Both vendor and distributor are credited for those magazines which they bought but were unable to sell.

(usually one for every major city and its major vendors, and another for outlying areas and small vendors within the city). With names such as Select Magazines, Curtis Circulation Co., Publishers' Distribution Corp., and Northwest Distributing Co., the distributors' role is to get copies to dealers throughout the U.S. and Canada; to shift copies from places where they are selling slowly to places where they are sold out; and to recall copies that dealers are unable to sell. To get a clearer picture of the whole process, here is a picture-history of the route of an unsold 25¢ magazine.

Dig:

Look in the Yellow Pages of your telephone book under "Magazine Distributors." Copy exact name, address, phone number. Then plan either an interview, field trip, letter, or phone-call approach to his operations. What questions would you ask in order to find out more information about a distributor's world? Compare your suggestions with your classmates', and then carry out all those which seem practical. You might begin by asking him what territory his operation covers, what problems he has, which magazines are in most demand, etc.

III. CHECKING OUT THE HOME COFFEE TABLE: Just Which Publishers Are You Supporting?

The histories of magazine publishing houses are as colorful and dramatic as the contents of the magazines themselves. Here are some informal histories of some of the biggest ones.

Condé Nast Publications: Condé Nast, a St. Louis boy, started with *Collier's* at $12 a week, worked up to $40,000 a year, and decided to become a publisher for himself in 1909 by buying *Vogue* and *House*

& Garden. He aimed at the elegant and upper class. Today, among its 30 publications are *Bride's Magazine, Glamour, House & Garden, Mademoiselle, Vogue,* and *Analog Science Fact and Science Fiction.*

Dell Publishing Co.: A record-setter in the mass publications world ever since George Delacorte founded it in 1919. "We've published more magazines under more titles than any publisher in the United States," Delacorte asserts. Its distribution warehouses throughout the country do a fast and furious business. Of their high circulation "Dell Modern Group," *Modern Romance* and *Modern Screen* are perhaps the best known. *Ingenue* is directed toward the early teen-age girls. *Inside* and *Frontpage Detective* are successes in the "Dell Men's Group." The titles of Dell Comics would make too long a list.

Fawcett Publications, Inc.: Capt. Wilford H. Fawcett started a joke book, characterized by "rough humor," shortly after World War I. Its success got him going in the publishing world. Since its time, *True Confessions* (now a Macfadden-Bartell publication), *Mechanix Illustrated. True,* and *Woman's Day* have added mightily to the four Fawcett sons' spending money.

Hearst Corporation: Besides newspapers and radio-TV properties, the Hearst family has a sizable list of prospering magazines under its ownership. In the general magazine category, there are *Comopolitan* and *Good Housekeeping.* Specialized publications include *Motor, Motor Boating, Sports Afield, Eye, Science Digest, Harper's Bazaar, House Beautiful, Town & Country,* and *Popular Mechanics.*

Johnson Publishing Co., Inc.: Ethnic magazines, in this case for blacks, have always had to struggle for financial support from advertisers, but John H. Johnson changed all that. His first effort, *Negro Digest,* went well, and *Ebony* (a *Life*-type publication) attracted the big advertisers with its success and circulation. Since then, *Tan* and *Jet,* concentrating on women and news-picture format respectively, have been good sellers.

Macfadden-Bartell Corp.: Bernarr Macfadden, the poor Illinois farm boy, went from rags to riches via the super-sensationalism express. His *True Story* and *True Detective* formulas were hits and were imitated countless times (by himself, even) bringing success each time. The Depression was hard on him and the Bartell Broadcasters, Inc. took control, adding magazines to their radio and TV holdings. Titles aimed at the "working class woman . . . who brings to her problems and conflicts an emotional rather than a logical approach" (those are Macfadden-Bartell words) include *True Confessions, Motion Picture, True Romance, True Experience, True Love, Photoplay, TV Radio-Mirror, Silver Screen. Sport, True Detective,* and *Master Detective* are among their magazines for men. *Pageant* is their publication which comes closest to "mass circulation" format.

Magazines for Industry, Inc. (Cowles Communications, Inc.): Basically in business for specialized industries (*The Candy Marketer, Modern Medicine, Nursing Homes,* and *Dental Industry News*), this publishing house operates *Venture, Family Circle* (and operated *Look* until it went defunct in September, 1971), as well as many newspapers and radio-TV stations.

Marvel Comic Group (Goodman Publishing Co.): Stan Lee, editor-in-chief of Marvel Comics, changed the whole idea of comics from "a mass vehicle for children of all ages" to a "specialized art form for sophisticates." Deciding in 1961 that comic superheroes should resemble real people and not just be cardboard characters, he created a whole new set of "sympathetic" heroes. Other, more conventional (and highly successful) comic groups produced by Goodman are the Complete Adventure Group, Complete Men's Group, Complete Women's Group, My Romance Group, and Screen Stars Group.

Meredith Corporation: Beginning its publishing life with a farming magazine, *Successful Farming,* in 1902, publishing under the Meredith name has continued into the present with *Better Homes and Gardens,* with its 78 regional editions, at the head of its circulation list. Meredith Corporation has pushed its boundaries beyond the farm fence in other ways, too: besides magazines, it owns Consumer Books, AM, FM, and TV stations in four states, a cable TV operation, and Appleton-Century-Crofts' educational operations. Keeping its image of friend to the farmer, the company gives substantial support to the 4-H program for farm youth.

Petersen Publishing Co.: The ascent of Robert Petersen in the publishing world was accomplished on four wheels. Beginning with the magazine *Hot Rod* in 1947, he is now publisher of 11 titles, 10 of them in the car-hobby-recreation field. *Skin Diver Magazine, Guns & Ammo, 'Teen,* and *Hot Rod Cartoons* are but a few of the titles. Petersen also publishes books and annuals, holds stock in an automotive racetrack, runs a film production company, and owns a 470,000-acre cattle ranch.

Ziff-Davis Publishing Co.: *Skiing, Boating, Flying, Popular Photography, Stereo Review, Popular Electronics,* and *Car and Driver* are among the Ziff-Davis titles which reflect their interest in the reader with hobby and recreation interests.

Dig:

Look for the publisher of those magazines to which your family subscribes (or which you regularly read and have a supply of). List the name of each magazine, its single-copy price, the number of copies you get in one month, and the name of its publisher. Then draw your conclusion, by simple multiplication, about which publisher should be thanking you the most for sending your pocket money his way. (If you do not find the publisher's name among those described above in the informal histories, look for it on the Table of Contents page of the magazine.)

❧RADIO❧

| AM Tuner | 54 | 60 | 70 | 80 | 90 | 100 | 120 | 140 | 160 | KC |

Did you ever wonder what those numbers on a radio dial stood for? Why does the AM dial start at "54"? (Why not simply "1"?) Why is the last number "160" and not a nice round "100"? For the same reason a thermometer doesn't start at "1" and end at "100"—something *specific* is being registered, that doesn't fit neatly on a 1-100 scale: in the case of the thermometer, body temperature by degrees; in the case of the AM radio dial, sound wave *frequencies* by *kilocycles* (so many thousand cycles per second). Each radio station has its own frequency, assigned (or "allocated") to it by the FCC (Federal Communications

Commission). In fact, the FCC was created because broadcasters were jumping their allocated frequencies and increasing their power at will, causing chaos on the airwaves. (In 1971, a young amateur radio operator in the U.S. was faced with a heavy fine and possible jail sentence for broadcasting over a frequency he was not licensed to use; he had been jamming radio communication between airplane and airport and could have caused a disaster.)

Once a radio station has its frequency allocation, it is legally ready to broadcast. Financing the venture—setting up such monumental items as a *sound studio* (at the radio station), a *transmitting station,* and its *antenna*—is quite another matter. These are the bare essentials for the successful transmission of a disc jockey's voice from his microphone to your radio, or tuner:

In the *sound studio* of a radio station, the deejay's voice becomes part of an equalized program signal which is fed from the telephone line to an audio amplifier and then on to the . . .

Transmitter, where it is converted into a radio frequency signal. If you have ever been driving and found the radio station you were listening to "overpowered" temporarily by a louder one, you must have been driving past a transmitter station. Power from the transmitter is radiated into the surrounding area by the . . .

Antenna. This is usually a grounded metal tower, either guyed or self-supporting, often located near soil of high electrical conductivity (salt-water marshes are especially good; WCBS in New York is on a tiny man-made island in Long Island Sound). The higher the antenna tower, the lower the frequency.

If the station is AM, it has one of a possible 107 frequency channels (each covering 10 kc of the radio band). AM (amplitude modulation) has to do with the way the sound wave registers a change in pitch or loudness; AM waves vary in height. For some reason, this makes them susceptible to static, but it also allows them to travel longer distances than the static-free FM waves. If a station is FM, it has one of a possible 100 allocated frequency channels, ranging along an 88 . . . 108 mc (megacycles) band. It looks like a tight squeeze until you realize that megacycles are registering the number of *million* cycles per second. So the FM dial is, in fact, quite spread out.

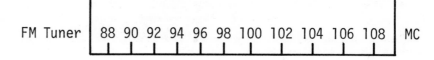

| FM Tuner | 88 | 90 | 92 | 94 | 96 | 98 | 100 | 102 | 104 | 106 | 108 | MC |

Chris Edwards, popular deejay of station KYA, San Francisco

Walter Cronkite of CBS News

Arthur Godfrey, "Mr. Radio"

React:

Go home tonight and see how many frequencies you can tune in on your radio. List them by station number and call letters. (Don't peek at the radio log in the newspaper yet.) Which stations have the clearest signals? Which are coming from farthest away? Do this for both AM and FM, if possible.

Dig:

After the members of the class have pooled their findings, make up a master chart for AM and FM, listing local frequencies, in order, station call letters, and the general type of programming for each. Use as a guide the example given here, which happens to be for the Seattle, Washington, area. Consider the labels "Top 40," "Easy Music," "Country Western," "Classical," "Pacifica," "All-News," "R & B," "Religious," and "Educational" (described below) to describe the type of programming. Feel free to make up your own labels if a station does not fit into any of these categories.

Top 40 (Rock & Roll, "foreground" music): Never a moment of silence between music and talk; news never more than five minutes and never in depth. Announcers tend to use a high level of volume and excitement and are billed as personalities. Frequent use of station call letters, jingles, and other "sounds" to identify the station quickly. Commercials, according to the Drake-Chenault formula, are "clustered," four an hour, not to exceed 2 minutes 10 seconds each cluster. American Independent Radio format (Drake-Chenault) had 50 stations signed up in 1971 for either their "Solid Gold" or "Hit Parade" syndicated program services. These services establish the station's sound, then record master tapes to suit it.

Easy Music (Conservative Popular, MOR: Middle-of-the-Road): Also referred to as "elevator music," "dentist office music," and "background music," it specializes in the non-offensive, non-obtrusive instrumentals (Montovani, Percy Faith, Ray Conniff, Bert Kaempfert, Paul Mauriat) and "mellowed-out" vocals

Weekday Radio -- AM -- Seattle, Washington

Frequency	Station Name	Its Specialty
1590	KUUU	"Superstar Radio," memory tunes
1540	KFKF	Homemakers programs, softball games, fights
1510	KURB*	
1460	KYAC*	R & B
1400	KTNT*	Popular Music
1380	KRKO*	Pop Standards and Top 40
1360	KMO *	Country Western
1300	KOL	"Golden 1300" -- Top 40
1250	KTW	Religious
1230	KWYZ*	Easy Music/Country
1150	KAYO	Entertainment/Country
1090	KING	
1050	KBLE	Christian Radio
1000	KOMO	
950	KJR	Home of Fab 50, Top 40
910	KIXI	
850	KTAC*	Top 40/Rock & Roll
800	KQIN*	"Golden Music"
770	KXA	"Full Concept Music"
710	KIRO	
630	KGDN	Inspirational/Religious
570	KVI	Husky Sports

*Local stations

Weekday Radio -- FM -- Seattle, Washington

Frequency	Station Name	Its Specialty	
92.5	KFKF-FM	Hit Parade (Day) Rock & Roll (Night) STEREO	
93.3	KBLE-FM	Nashville Northwest Sound After 7:00 p.m. Religious	
94.1	KOL-FM	Progressive Rock STEREO	Rare, good music; old and new; often plays entire album without interruption. "Earth News" every hour.
94.9	KUOW-FM	Educational Classics Student Rock 6-mid.	NPR News -- National Public Radio affiliate University of Washington, continuing education. Interviews and debates.
96.5	KLSN-FM	Pop Standards 8-8 STEREO 8-mid. Classics	
97.5	KTNT-FM	Popular Music 12-7 Country Music	
98.1	KING-FM	Classic King	
98.9	KBBX-FM	Instrumentals STEREO	
99.9	KISW-FM	Progressive Rock STEREO Classics too	
100.7	KIRO-FM	Pop Standards	
101.5	KETO-FM	Pop Standards	ABC News
105.3	KBIQ-FM	Instrumental Standards STEREO	
107.7	KRAB-FM	Ethnic Music Conversation Commentary, Jazz, Classics	NPR affiliate. Old- fashioned radio serials. Subscriber-supported. Currently fighting an obscenity suit.

(Beatles' songs without the Beatles singing them). The announcers usually don't push themselves strongly as personalities. Programming is almost exclusively music, with five minutes of syndicated news on the hour; it lends itself to automation.

Country Western (Modern Country): Self-explanatory.

Classical: Announcers must be experts in pronunciation of musical composers and titles in all languages. Symphonies, concertos, chamber music, opera, and other works of the great masters make up the programming. Such stations command a devout following; some even encourage "listeners' guilds" whose members pay $3 per year to back the station's projects.

Pacifica: Sometimes referred to as "radical weirdo" by those who fear free expression of strong opinion, the Pacifica station claims only that it is in existence solely as a "carrier of opinion." The fact that the conservative elements do not appear on the format makes its voice a liberal one.

All-News: Some all-news stations (Group W) count on "random tune-in" by listeners and broadcast news, in one form or another all day long ("the ultimate refinements of the global village"?). Others are simply "information-oriented" (and older-audience-oriented at the same time) with a 15-minute newscast every hour, four or five Top Forty tunes an hour to keep the sound contemporary. Still others have news from conservative viewpoint to liberal with a personality news at noon and an ombudsman service to help citizens cut through bureaucratic red tape. At times, they will broadcast 24-hour specials on some controversial subject.

R & B (Rhythm & Blues): Oriented to black culture.

Religious: Underwritten by some church, usually Protestant or Evangelical, these stations broadcast much transcribed material. Local churches sometimes do live programs.

Educational: Originating at a nearby university, these stations often make use of an educational program exchange and broadcast informational fare for adults, students, and the general public. Often, they'll switch to Rock & Roll late at night. The Corporation for Public Broadcasting offers money ($25,000 in a 1971 appeal) to groups interested in beginning a full-service public radio station. Universities often take up the offer and become an NPR (National Public Radio) affiliate and an outlet for NPR programs.

CREATE:

If you were the writer for a newcomer's guidebook to your city and your assignment were to write a chapter on radio stations, indicating which ones would appeal to which types of people, how would you write it up? Choose *one* audience.

> *Example:* In the Seattle, Washington, area, in a book called *The Hedonist: An Unconventional Guide to Seattle Entertainment,* the following comments, directed at the young, "with-it" audience, are made:
>
> KIXI: With a minimum of comments and commercials, they broadcast blah, wishy-washy music right into your ear.
>
> KIRO: Thrill your friends with the Beatles' favorites done by a thousand strings or such travesties as Crosby, Stills, and Nash hits done as saxophone instrumentals.

Feel free to take a more positive approach.

REACT:

Donald West, Managing Editor of **Broadcasting Magazine,** said in an article in the June 21, 1971, issue: "Radio is a ubiquitous, one-to-one medium, with virtually all tastes, biases, likes and dislikes represented somewhere on an AM or FM dial." What does he mean? Is he right?

> For the better part of my life I was a daytime serial star in what is now nostalgically called the Golden Age of Radio. Nobody called it that then. It is only when a thing is dead that it becomes golden.
> —Mary Jane Higby, *Tune In Tomorrow,* Ace, 1968. $.95

TELEVISION

I. THE BIG THREE: Network TV and Your Local TV Station

The three commercial television networks are private business enterprises, under no form of control (except tax laws). They are basically money-making institutions answerable to no one. The Big Three are:

> ABC — American Broadcasting Company
> CBS — Columbia Broadcasting System
> NBC — National Broadcasting Company

REACT:

Identify each of the three network channels available in your town. In other words, *what* channel fits *which* local call letters and what is the network affiliation for each?

This is how a commercial TV network operates:

1. Each year (with continual adjustments throughout the year) the network selects a program schedule for nationwide distribution. This schedule is made up of programs actually produced by the network (college and professional football, World Series, Olympics, political conventions, space flights, daily news—in other words, *news, special events,* and *sports*) and programs provided by program packagers, TV film companies, and feature film distributors, who sink thousands of dollars into pilot films and story-lines that they hope the networks will accept and develop into a series.

2. The network selects about 200 local stations throughout the United States for its *affiliates* (CBS leads in affiliate strength, feeding 241 local stations with its programs; NBC is next with 217; and ABC is third with 171) and it rents from the telephone company interconnecting facilities to transmit simultaneously to each affiliate the programs and ad messages the network has chosen (although no network can force a station to take particular programs). It is in this way that the network advertiser is assured that his message is being received nationwide.

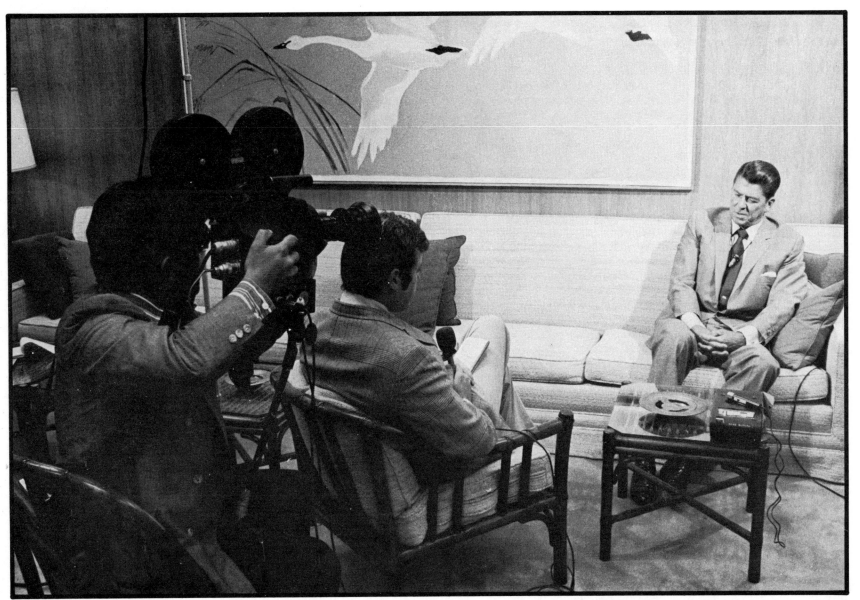

San Francisco's KRON news team interviews California's Governor Reagan

Affiliate stations pay networks anywhere from a few hundred dollars in small towns for an hour of prime-time programming to $10,000 or more in New York City, the number-one market.

3. The network contracts with national advertisers through advertising agencies to defray program or time costs and supply advertising "plugs" (time segments available to advertisers). The cost of advertising time depends on the Nielsen rating of the program the ad interrupts. For instance, during the prime time hour of 9:00-10:00 p.m. on a Wednesday night, the 18-minutes' worth of advertising (six minutes on each network) brings the networks about a million dollars from the advertisers. Some of this money the networks share with their affiliates in return for the affiliates' transmitting network programs.

4. Non-network activities of local TV stations are limited to before- and after prime time news shows (including weather and sports), films produced for TV and distributed by independent syndicators, feature films, and local experiments. Critics of the network system think that at least 50% of programming in prime time should be done by *independent* producers, who produce for advertisers, who have in turn bought time from the networks in the customary way. Costs are high. A one-hour situation comedy or spy drama can run $300,000. But the independents are confident that shows of quality and audience appeal can be turned out for a great deal less than that.

To encourage *local* programming during the 7:00-11:00 p.m. prime time hours, the FCC has adopted a rule that no local station may devote more than three of these four hours to network shows.

5. Network *ownership* of TV stations is under attack. Although the networks are limited by law to five VHF-TV stations each (plus two UHF-TV, seven AM radio and seven FM radio stations), they generally own their stations in the biggest and richest markets. These stations are known as O&Os (for owned and operated). The 15 TV O&Os owned by the three major networks are immensely profitable.

Besides the three major networks, other important independent station owners are Capital Cities Broadcasting, Corinthian Broadcasting, Cox Broadcasting, Gross Television, Lin Broadcasting, Metromedia, Reeves Telecom, Scripps-Howard Broadcasting, Sonderling Broadcasting, Storer Broadcasting, and Taft Broadcasting.

The FCC may move against chain broadcasters and require that owners hold only one television, AM or FM station per market.

Criticism of the network system runs along the same lines as Rep. John Moss's statement, made in 1967 as a reaction to the networks' giving only a few prime hours to independent producers: "The networks apparently look upon the public airwaves as a giant money tree to be shaken until all but few barren leaves are left as a token."

In spite of such criticism, the network system continues to enjoy overwhelming public acceptance because its spending power enables it to hire talent and resources which would be beyond the reach of small local stations. The Big Events are covered well (by a smooth-working team of veteran newsmen and technicians) and can be telecast *live* (because of the networks' nationwide hook-ups).

Dig:

Log the three networks' prime time (3 hours between 7:00 p.m. and 11:00 p.m.) programming, and classify each program according to type, such as . . .

Law and Order Series: Cowboy, cop, detective, Fed, or lawyers vs. crime.

Inside World of . . . . . . hospital, Hollywood, magazine publishing, medicine, etc.; any in-group other than law and order.

Situation Comedy (or Formula Families): Light-hearted laughter bouncing back and forth among the members of a frolicking family unit.

Smart/Daffy Career Girl Series: Oh, the scrapes, the misunderstandings, the embarrassments, the triumphs—and all lived through while dressed in a fantastic wardrobe. Situation comedy without the family element.

Variety: Little bit of song, dance, comedy, or whatever is booked.

Talk Show: Conversations with celebrities and other "interesting people."

Panel/Quiz Show.

Feature Film: A movie that has done the movie theater rounds or movie-for-TV.

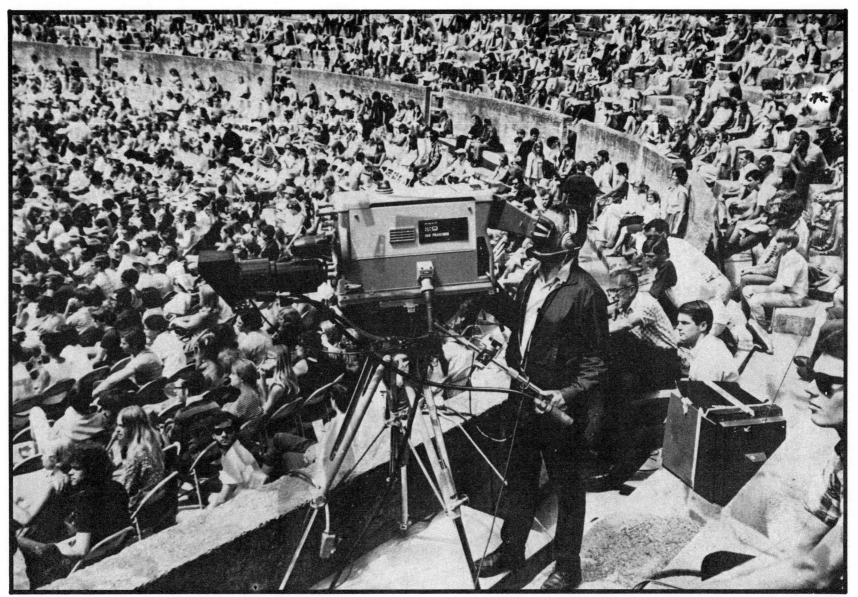

San Francisco's PBS station, KQED, covers a special event

News: Current events *live,* the day they happen, introduced by the "anchor-man" and reported by the network's news correspondents on location.

News Feature: Mostly recorded events of the recent past; live announcers set stage and introduce film and tape units.

Sports Event/Feature.

Personal Information Programs: Farming, grooming, cooking, gardening.

Non-personal Information Programs: Science, travelogs, documentaries.

React:

1. Are the networks distinguishable from one another in the programming they offer?
2. Is there any one type of program that heavily outweighs the others in weekly hours?
3. Does any one network show a willingness to experiment with new types of programs?

Dig:

Finally, show how you "typed" each program by listing program titles under one of the 13 "type" headings.

II. GETTING LOCAL: How Does Your Town Fill the Time Slots Before and After Prime Time? What Are Your Non-Network Local Stations?

The owner of a local TV station depends for his economic survival on his affiliation with a big network, which commands talent and resources that the local station could not get on its own. The only other thing as crucial as a network affiliation to a local station is the renewal of its FCC (Federal Communications Commission) license. Citizens' groups have challenged the renewals of FCC licenses lately on the grounds that the TV station was not adequately serving "public interest, convenience, and necessity." And in some cases, the FCC has revoked the license,

after investigation, and turned the frequency over to another broadcasting group. The local station, then, has two sets of standards to meet: the network's and the commission's.

Most of the 600 local, network-affiliated stations throughout the United States have a programming load that includes about 60% of network supplied material, 15% of programs produced by the local station, and the remaining 25% from suppliers, which prepare and sell programs for local broadcast. The quality of the locally originated shows varies a great deal.

Dig:

Consider the sources for programming that a local station has:

Network-produced: Originating at the national network, produced by their staffs.

Syndicate Programs, network: Networks often underwrite series which are produced by others (Ziv, MCA, Desilu). Sometimes you will see in the program credits: "Produced by XYZ in cooperation with ABC network" in which case it is both a network and a syndicate production.

Local Station Programs: Produced by the local station's staff.

Network and Syndicate Film or Tape, played locally: Stations use recorded syndicate programs when they subscribe to a library or buy a series, or when an agency places them on the station in behalf of an advertiser. Also, network programs are often made available on a rerun basis. In these cases the films or tapes are played locally.

Other national sources: Recorded programs are sometimes produced by church groups, military services, health and safety organizations, etc.

Other local sources: Local schools, civic groups, churches, political organizations.

For this investigation, either visit a local, network-affiliated station or watch one full weekday's programming for such a station and determine the source of each of its offerings. Name the show and figure out where it came from, in other words.

REACT:

1. Is there a qualitative difference between the station you studied and those your classmates studied?
2. Do the local offerings of one station show greater community interest and involvement than the others?
3. Does one station give more attention to segments of the audience, such as farmers, children, liberals, conservatives?
4. What amount of non-network time is devoted to live, anything-might-happen programming, as opposed to syndicated, pre-recorded material?

Diq:

Consult the TV section of your newspaper or just flip channels of your set in the middle of the day and make a note of the non-network affiliated local stations your set receives. Where do they originate? What type of programming do they carry?

III. CABLE TV AND PUBLIC TV

Cable TV (or CATV—Community Antenna TV) began innocently enough as a means of getting good television reception to communities "beyond the hills" or behind tall apartment buildings within cities; to areas, in other words, where line-of-sight radio relay was blocked. By means of huge antenna towers, amplifiers, and a *coaxial cable* running directly into these blocked homes (or into a nearby community antenna), near-perfect reception was made possible. Not only did cable transmission avoid the hills and building obstacles of conventional TV, it also bypassed atmospheric interference (to which color is especially susceptible).

Soon people who got satisfactory reception on line-of-sight transmission wanted the perfect picture they heard a cable could give them. And word got out that a cable, because it was not a victim of the shortage of space on the radio spectrum, could mean a selection from dozens of viewing channels as opposed to the three or four that most people have to choose from. The fee of $4-$6 per month seemed a fair price to pay for such advantages.

But Cable TV has caused considerable controversy. Regular stations complain that it "fragments" audiences and thus makes the mass advertiser's dollar harder to get. Others fear that Cable TV will turn into pay TV, especially if it continues its connection with sports events. What if, so the fear runs, a fantastic heavyweight fight is scheduled to be broadcast over Cable TV only, and those hooked up to the cable are asked to pay $5 to have the picture "unscrambled" for viewing? Not much to pay per family or gang, but just think, if a half million homes participated, the Cable TV owners stand to make $2½ million for just pushing a few buttons!

The FCC has ruled that CATV systems will have to provide at least one channel as a public access channel and one as an educational channel. It also released the freeze on cable TV entering some large cities, thus clearing the way for the growth of CATV.

REACT:

If you do not have CATV, question someone who does have it, as to quality of reception, number of channels received, programming, and monthly fees. Keep informed of the changes and controversies growing out of CATV by clipping articles about it from newspapers and magazines.

Public TV, formerly known as educational TV, has broadened its scope. In 1967, Congress established the CPB (Corporation for Public Broadcasting) to bring money and direction to the growing field of public TV and radio. The CPB in turn created a network, the PBS (Public Broadcasting System) to select, schedule, and distribute shows nationally. New York-based NET (National Education Television), which used to produce most of the shows, is now one of at least eight producers for PBS programs. It is up to the program manager at each of the 200 local PBS stations to decide which of the nationally produced material his station will show.

What *is* Public TV? Basically, it's *non-commercial* television; that is, it does not depend on the advertiser's dollar for support. Instead, it waits for Federal grants (put into motion by Congress each year; a dependency that bothers both PBS and Congress because it looks like governmental control), foundation grants (Ford, Carnegie Corp., etc.), citizen contribution, and funds from companies who also spend money

Students learn to operate video equipment at San Carlos' cable Channel 12.

for commercial network TV time (e.g., Mobil Oil Corporation, Xerox, Polaroid, and Sears). Unlike their exposure on commercial TV, their only mention on PBS usually consists of pre- and post-show identification billboards.

Public TV's problems are mostly monetary; it's hard to survive without the advertiser's lavish dollar. Most producers are committed to quality, yet without a reliable source of funding, it is hard to entice talent away from more lucrative jobs. Experimentation is Public TV's life blood, and yet very few people gamble their dollars on experiments. Big spenders often do not want to be identified with anything "far out." Reliance on government funds cramps new style, some critics say.

Dig:

Log one complete day of programming on the PBS channel in your town. Describe each program as to type, special presentation, and effectiveness. If possible, jot down any mention of the source of funds and the producer for each program. Finally, make a rough guess about the amount of locally produced shows vs. the nationally produced shows for the one day you watched.

The only way to get "local" about advertising (unless, of course, you live on Madison Avenue) is to take a look at the products around your house and see which ad messages you (or whoever does the shopping for your family) believed. Consider Procter & Gamble and General Foods, who in 1970 spent $265,000,000 and $170,000,000 respectively on the advertising of their many products. (Their *sales* amounted to over $3,000,000,000—Procter & Gamble, and $1,975,000,000—General Foods, so don't feel sorry about all the money they spent.)

React:

Here are some of their products. Check the cupboards at home and see how many you have.

Procter & Gamble: Detergents & Cleansers—Bold, Dreft, Duz, Cheer, Oxydol Plus, Salvo, Tide XK, Biz, Gain, Cascade, Comet, Ivory, Joy, Lava, Mr. Clean, Safeguard, Spic & Span, Thrill, Top Job, Zest, Camay, Downy. *Food*—Bigtop Peanut Butter, Crisco, Duncan Hines cake mixes, etc., Fluffo, Jif Peanut Butter. *Toilet Articles*—Crest, Gleem, Head & Shoulders, Hidden Magic, Lilt, Pampers Diapers, Prell, Scope, Secret. *Coffee*—Folger's. *Household Paper:* Charmin Paper, White Cloud Bathroom Tissue, Puffs, Bounty.

General Foods: Shake 'n Bake, Maxwell House, Sanka, Yuban, Maxim, Jell-O, Dream Whip, Whip 'n Chill, D-Zerta, Minute Rice, Baker's Coconut, etc., Birds-Eye frozen foods, Good Seasons Salad Dressing, Open Pit Barbecue Sauces, Kool-Aid, Twist Lemonade, Toastems, Danka Pastry, Burger Chef Systems, Inc., Viviane Woodard Cosmetics, D. Atlee Burpee Seeds, Post Cereals, Gaines Pet Foods, Tang, Start, Orange-Plus, Awake, Log Cabin Syrups, La France Whiteners, Brighteners, Cool 'n Creamy Frozen Puddings, Thick 'n Frosty Frozen Shake Concentrate.

Dig:

Notice that one company will produce two toothpastes. Wouldn't *one,* claiming to be the *best,* be enough? What accounts for this duplication? Is "brand loyalty" a factor? Compare advertising pitches for Crest and Gleem—do they appeal to a different audience? Answer the same questions for the Bold-Cheer-Duz-Dash-Oxydol Plus-Salvo-Tide XK-Gain duplications among the Procter & Gamble products.

"Sesame Street" is one of PBS' most popular shows.

"Masterpiece Theatre" is another popular PBS show.

As an in-class exercise, try to translate the "foreign" text below without consulting the crib information given after each report. (Hint: the reports are from *Variety,* a daily trade paper of the entertainment world. The excerpts here are from the "Picture Grosses" section.) Important "foreign" vocabulary words are in bold face.

'Sweetback' Sizzling 20G, Seattle; 'Miller' Loud 9G, 2d, 'Carnal' Hip 10G, 6th Seattle.

SEATTLE.–**Firstrun houses** this week have a solid **holdover** front with exception of "Sweet Sweetback," smash in Coliseum **opener** . . .
Topping the holdovers is "Carnal Knowledge," in sixth week at the Music Box. "McCabe and Mrs. Miller" is big in second Blue Mouse round while "Hellstrom Chronicle" is moderate at the Fifth Avenue, also in second . . .
Estimates for This Week: Blue Mouse **(SRO) (739; $1.75-2.50)** "McCabe & Mrs. Miller" (2nd wk) Big $9,000. Last Week, $12,200. Coliseum **(NG) ($1,870; $2-2.50)** "Sweetback" **(Cinemation)** Smash $20,000. Last Week, "Big Doll House" **(New World)** (3rd wk) $5,800

Seattle article: "Firstrun houses" refers to those theaters which get the films first in a town. After it's run at a firstrun theater, the film either becomes a "move-over" to another theater in town, or ships out to another city for another chance at a first-run showing. "Holdover" and

"opener" refer to the length of time a movie has been at a theater: "opener" is the first week, "holdovers" the weeks that follow.

"Blue Mouse" is the name of a theater in Seattle; SRO (Sterling Recreation) is the name of the chain the theater is a member of; 739 is the seating capacity of the theater; and $1.75-$2.50, the ticket price range.

"Cinemation" and "New World" are distributors' names. The theater manager reading this page and desiring to "book" a successful movie would contact the distributor's representative in his area.

'Darkness' Bright $30,000, Hub; 'Doc' Rousing 15G, 'Shadows' Slick $4,500 Boston.

BOSTON.–Hot weekend hit the city again, but biz held up remarkably well although rain would have built grosses. Firstrun trade continues generally good as strong **preemers** and **longruns** garner solid **takes.** Horror and sex combo broke big with Gemini Pictures prexy hometown boy Howard Zuker in to kick off "Daughters of Darkness" looming lofty at the **Music Hall** . . .

Boston article: "Preemers" are those shows which are premiering (in their first week); "longruns," those successes which are still pulling in viewers' money ("takes") at the box office after many weeks.
"The Music Hall" refers to Radio City Music Hall in New York, the most prestigious "showcase" theater in the country. (See the Los Angeles entry for definition.)

'Sunday' Brisk 6G, Pitt; 'Miller' $9,600 Pittsburgh.

PITTSBURGH.–"On Any Sunday" shapes strong in first week at the King's Court as **sock product** and all types of promotion keeps **exhibs** in business . . .

Director Joseph Losey

Director William Wyler

Pittsburgh article: Who knows, except those in Pittsburgh during August of 1971, what the "sock product" promotional gimmick was at the King's Court Theater. Whatever it was, it worked; it got people talking . . . and paying. Such gimmicks are part of the *press book* that National Screen Service compiles for every motion picture released. It contains materials necessary to advertise and promote a picture, from which theater managers order what they want (ad matrixes to send to the local newspapers, for instance). "Exhibs" are exhibitors, or theaters.

'Pinocchio' Leads L.A. by Nose, 260G; 'Klute' Terrific 235G; 'Strain' $85,000; 'Jake' 60G; 'McCabe' 38G; 'Carnal' 35G

LOS ANGELES.–In **showcase situations,** "Andromeda Strain" is likely hefty $85,000 eighth **in 19**; "Willy Wonka" trim $30,000 second in 19; "Big Jake" handy $60,000 second in 11 . . .
Los Angeles firstruns display strong potential this week, sparked by flock of money pix to boost overall outlook. "McCabe and Mrs. Miller" sights a fine $39,000, teeing at Pacific Pantag and "Last Run" a sock $30,000 at the Village among exclusives . . .

Los Angeles article: "Showcase situations" are special in the movie world. Radio City Music Hall in New York is *the* showcase theater in the United States. A movie shown there has so much promotion and advertising behind it that the reverberations are felt, not only in the New York area, but throughout the states. The task of "booking" a picture after it has been well received at the Music Hall is easy work. Everybody has heard about it and everybody wants it. Los Angeles theaters are, of course, Hollywood's closest showcases. Count them: "in 19" means showing in 19 theaters simultaneously; 19 + 19 + 11 = 49 showcase showings. These movies have been released in a "multiple situation," that is, given simultaneous openings at several theaters. The opposite practice is a single situation release where one outstanding theater in a metropolitan area is chosen as the showcase. Often such a showing is by "hard-ticket" only (two shows a day; high priced admission; reserved seats only).

'Pinocchio' Smash 37½G, Denver; 'Hand' Quiet 6G, 'Tapes' Snappy $14,500 Denver.

DENVER.–**Reissue** of "Pinocchio" is topping the newcomers with a smash take in three **hardtops.**

Denver article: "Reissue" is re-releasing an older picture that is considered a classic (*Pinocchio, Fantasia, Gone With the Wind*). "Hardtops" are the walk-in theaters, as opposed to the drive-ins (which usually get the re-issues, not-so-classic). It has been estimated that there are 10,000 hardtops in the U.S. and 3,700 drive-ins.

'Clowns' Mild 6G, Det.; 'Jake' 13G Detroit.

DETROIT.–The blast of publicity attending Ann-Margret's local nitery show helped keep "Carnal Knowledge" among top grossers in its sixth week at Northland . . .
"Clowns" opened mild in Studio North. "Last Run" is slow in third lap at Quo Vadis I. "Brain of Blood" is anemic in second week at Fox.

Detroit article: And don't think Ann-Margret (or perhaps the booker) planned it that way!

A look at two pages of *Variety* is enough to see that a movie's "greatness" is gauged by its ability to haul in the coins at the box office. The "good" movies are described in the same terms as one would describe an aggressive, powerful, extroverted man: sizzling, loud, hip, bright, rousing, slick, brisk, smash, snappy, solid, strong, lofty (many were chosen by the *Variety* writers for their pun value, of course). The "bad" ones are described in terms of the All-American washout: mild, quiet, anemic, slow, moderate, and thin. There seems to be no recognition that a poorly-attended movie might be artistically beautiful, and that a box office smash might be tasteless and morally distorted.

This equation of greatness with profit has plagued the movie industry for years. It can't seem to shake the notion even when faced time and again with criticism. John Hartl, movie critic for the *Seattle Times,* pointed out in his August 15, 1971, column:

Director Bruce Brown

Director Kenneth Loach

It does seem that, to those in the movie business, commercial success can legitimize anything. Even such a universally deplored film as *The Stewardesses* is beginning to draw some defenders, now that it is a box office hit. After originally reviewing it as a 'sub-standard' sex movie, *Variety* wrote a follow-up story that found new virtues: 'Campy soap opera . . . good humor . . . epic provides a real visual trip.' A similar pattern can be seen in the reception given *Sweet Sweetback's Song,* an incredibly inept low-budget fiasco that has been treated seriously ever since it became one of the top grossers of the year. A writer for *The New York Times* found that 'technically, the film dazzles, as a rough diamond glittering in inquisitive light . . .' Adulatory interviews with its creator in *Time* and *Life* have followed.

Does this worshipful attitude toward the Hit, the thing that dazzles and attracts on the surface, reflect a broader ill in American life—namely, the loss of appreciation for *excellence,* which often appears in mild, moderate, and quiet forms?

DIg:

Find out which are the first run theaters in your area. List them. What movies are currently playing at each one and how long have they been there?

What do you know about these movies? Where did you get your information? Do you want to see any of them? How many of them are geared to the youth-audience? (Summer is considered the prime release time for youth-oriented pictures. What were last summer's offerings at these theaters?) And while we're on the subject of release-timing, keep your eyes open this fall for the big movies that studios consider Academy Award possibilities. They'll produce them and release them by December to meet the deadline, show them in a few "showcase situations," and then wait until after the awards ceremony to give the movies a broader release.

CREATE:

Using *Variety* vocabulary and format, report on the movie situation at the first-run houses in your locality. Make up a headline (unless you can somehow find out, you'll have to guess at the "take") and date-line. Distinguish between openers, holdovers (what week); indicate "showcase situations" if any; show number of theaters playing the same movie; mention distributor's name, theater, theater chain, seating capacity, ticket price range just as shown on the *Variety* page. Use the entertainment section of your newspaper, a copy of *Variety* if you can get it, and some ingenuity in getting the information you need.

DIg:

See if you can talk a theater manager into showing you National Screen Service's press book. Copy some of the "suggestions for advertising the movie" that you find in it (the more bizarre the better).

REACT:

1. Do you think the movie-rating system is a good idea?
   G—for general audiences (including children)
   PG—for general audiences with parental guidance suggested
   R—restricted; no one under 17 unless accompanied by an adult
   X—no one under 18 allowed in theater
2. What aspects of the big movie business would an independent theater owner resist? In other words, what would be the ingredients of a healthy "underground film" movement?

> Making motion pictures is a blending of the creative artist with the technician. A writer's description of an interior sparks a visual idea for an art director, and then a blueprint for a carpenter. An actor's terror on screen becomes a musical note for a composer. A producer's first enthusiasm for a story eventually goes into heavy cans of film to be rented to theatres. The parts and pieces of movie-making are often as intriguing as the whole.
> —Theodore Taylor, *People Who Make Movies,* Avon, 1967, $.75

Chapter 2

What It's Like Behind the Scenes

Newspapers

Early Colonial Newspapers In a sense, the first newspapers in America were ancestors of the present-day Underground Press. Their editors, often impassioned and impatient, sought to extend their single voices and by so doing bring about change. Not content with reporting what was happening, these activists wanted to make things happen. One such editor, Benjamin Harris, in the first issue of his *Publick Occurrences Both Forreign and Domestick,* 1690, voiced anti-government views. There was no second issue; the government stepped in and halted further publication, on the technicality that he had failed to obtain a license.

1791 The freedom of the press was guaranteed in the Bill of Rights. The 1734 John Peter Zenger Case, in which a New York newspaper publisher was freed of a libel charge because it was proved that he wrote the truth, must have helped along this right to print the truth.

1830s: The New York Scramble Taking advantage of improvements in the printing press that accelerated production and decreased costs, Horace Greeley introduced New York to its first penny newspaper (the *Morning Post)* on New Year's Day, 1833. If it hadn't been for a snowstorm that day, the paper might have lasted more than one issue. (Greeley, in 1841, launched the *New York Tribune* on its long and illustrious career, attracting early readers with its high intellectual and moral tone and its strongly individual editorial voice.) But an enterprising 23-year-old man, Benjamin Day, took up the banner in the same year and, with a news coverage of police activities, courtroom decisions, human interest stories, crime, and fires (no politics or finance), made a tremendous success of his *New York Sun.* Competition came fast, in 1835, from James Gordon Bennett and his *New York Herald,* which included a top quality Wall Street report; spicy news from the theater, society, race tracks, sports, public happenings, ships' arrivals, and foreign reports.

Expansion The format of newspapers was greatly affected by a variety of inventions and technical improvements after

1830. For one thing, the telegraph was perfected and helped newspapers develop foreign coverage. (In 1845 the Mexican war front reports were way ahead of the U.S. mails.) Photographs began to enliven the printed page. And the perfection of a more efficient cylindrical press (1847) and the use of wood pulp in newsprint cheapened and sped up production. In the 1890s, color was added.

In 1860, the Westward expansion greatly increased the need for news until there were 3,000 newspapers to meet the demand.

1895 to the 1900s Newspapers became Big Business. William Randolph Hearst began his empire with the acquisition of the *New York Journal* (1895) and his rivalry with Pulitzer's *New York World* resulted in "yellow journalism" (sensationalism in order to sell), so named because each of the newspapers used the color in decorating their comic strips. The profiteering motives of this era led Charles A. Dana to say, "Journalism consists in buying paper at two cents a pound and selling it at ten cents a pound."

Wire Services emerged (AP—Associated Press, 1900; UP—United Press, Scripps-Howard, 1907; INS—International News Service, Hearst, 1909) with the aim of sharing their news and news-gathering expenses. What began as a convenience soon became a substitute for actual news-gathering on the spot, a corporate necessity, resulting in the "rip and read" standardization of reported events straight from the wire service copy. What was once the extension of the individual voice became anonymous and impersonal statements attributable to no one.

1920-40 and 1960s Consolidations and mergers increased standardization of news. Again in the '60s increased reliance on news service copy inspired Spiro T. Agnew to say, "How is network news determined? A small group of men, numbering perhaps no more than a dozen, decide what forty to fifty million Americans will learn of the day's events in the nation and the world."

Journalism in the U.S., except in a surviving handful of cities, consisted of one ownership per town. Monopolies, desiring to offend no one, hired syndicated columnists to give forcefulness to their newspapers (and to accept the consequences).

Even though the Hearst empire diminished (from twenty-odd dailies to eight), other chains were going strong: Newhouse, Scripps-Howard, Gannett, Cowles, Copley, and others.

Recent Developments UP and INS merged to form UPI. CNS—Community News Service—began in 1970 to provide day-to-day (rather than crisis) coverage of New York's inner city, minority community activities and issues. Its subscribers, which include radio and TV stations as well as newspapers, report that it is invaluable as a "tip service" and as a resource for hard-to-get information.

To broaden news coverage, newspapers hired *stringers,* part-time reporters who are stationed out-of-town or abroad. Stringers send in articles only when something of interest occurs in their locations.

Underground Press Hundreds of these newspapers (circulation, 3 million), with the Berkeley *Barb* as their prototype, extended the definition of "freedom of the press" to include the use of direct, shocking language to assault the sensibilities, unchecked use of profanity, scatology, pornography, obscenity; the going to extremes to catch the attention of the ear, the eye, the emotions. It was an answer to the objective, uncommitted, offend-no-one newspaper; but also to the corporate, anonymous statement brought on by Bigness in the newspaper business. For whatever else it is, the underground paper is human. (See Chapter 10 for a more thorough discussion of the underground press.)

Monterey Peninsula Herald

Letter from an editor:

Abraham Lincoln said "Let the people know the facts, and the country will be safe."

Alexander Hamilton said "The liberty of the press consists, in my idea, in publishing the truth, from good motives and for justifiable ends, though it reflect on the government, on magistrates, or individuals."

Thomas Jefferson said ". . . were it left to me to decide whether we should have a government without newspapers, or newspapers without a government, I should not hesitate a moment to prefer the latter."

Nothing much has changed over the years. We live with the belief that the free competition of ideas has made this Republic the audacious and independent country that it is.

A good newspaper prints the important news and provides information, comment and guidance that is most useful to its readers.

It reports fully and explains the meaning of local, national and international events which are of major significance in its own community. Its editorial comment provides an informed opinion on matters of vital concern to its readers.

By reflecting the total image of its own community in its news coverage and by providing wise counsel in its editorials, a good newspaper becomes a public conscience. It also must be lively, imaginative and original; it must have a sense of humor and the power to arouse keen interest.

To implement these principles of good editing requires a skilled staff, an attractive format, and adequate space for news and comment. The staff must possess the professional pride and competence necessary to breathe life and meaning into the daily record of history.

Good writing must be combined with an effective typographical display of copy and pictures to capture the full drama and excitement of the day's news. Good printing is essential.

A good newspaper should be guided in the publication of all material by a concern for truth, the hallmark of freedom, and by a concern for human decency and human betterment.

Walter Lippmann has said, "The theory of a free press is that the truth will emerge from free reporting and free discussion, not that it will be presented perfectly and instantly in any one account."

The newspaper has been described at its worst as a mirror of community smugness. At its best, the newspaper is a community alarm clock.

Most readers have never stopped to think of their first association with a newspaper. It probably started before they could read, by scanning the comic page. In any event they grew up with their newspaper, accepting it as a part of life as they would any familiar article in their household.

A newspaper recorded their birth; it hovered backstage as they were graduated from school; it ushered them to the altar of matrimony; it listened as they may have pleaded a cause in a divorce court; and it will serve as the ex-officio pallbearer at their funeral.

In between it will write the history of the reader's triumphs and tragedies if they affect his neighbors in any way.

But how often have these readers viewed their newspaper as a stout defender of their liberties, a voice against injustice, a tireless prober into the acts of public servants and a constructive influence in their community?

Now how does all this come about?

A newspaper is made up of four parts. They are:

1. The news department
2. The advertising department
3. The mechanical and press departments
4. The circulation department.

In the newsroom, there is usually a managing editor who oversees the entire news-gathering process, a city editor who runs the city room where the local news is gathered, and a wire editor who edits the news that comes in over the leased wires from the Associated Press, United Press International, and *The New York Times* and other services.

The opinion columns, comic strips, and other material such as bridge columns and chess columns are syndicated services used by many papers.

In the newsroom there are specialists: the sports editor and writers, the women's editor and her staff, and among the reporters, "subject specialists," or people who write about schools, the courts, space technology, urban affairs, and other specialized segments of community life.

The news that comes in over the wires now also comes into the newspaper office on tape, which is fed directly into typesetting machines without human assistance. Even the local news is "punched" on tape and run through a computer that adjusts the words to fit the line width of the newspaper, and even hyphenates words automatically.

There are also machines on which the editor can "call up" stories on a viewer, much like a television screen, and edit them on the screen. The stories are stored in the memory bank of computers. Few newspapers are set in type manually now.

Eventually the stories are gathered—local, national, international, sports, society, syndicated columns—and, after being set in type and put into page form, go to the press room to be printed.

The huge presses of a city daily are very expensive, and turn out papers at 60,000 copies an hour and sometimes more. From the press, these copies go to the circulation department where they are bundled for the area of town or district they go to, and delivered by truck to the newspaper boys who distribute them door-to-door. Some of the papers are delivered in outlying areas door-to-door from trucks.

An editor is an easy man to meet. Do not hesitate to do so. If you have an opinion, write a letter to the editor. These letters are always welcomed.

Or just go to his office and tell him what you think. You may want to contribute an article, or do press relations for your club, or otherwise get involved.

Radio and television bring news and opinion as well. But after a fleeting second the image and words are gone.

More and more newspapers are trying to be something different from what they once were. "The scoop," or trying to beat somebody else to the news, is old hat. Now the idea is that newspapers provide what the other media can't, that is, the detailed background information on local and world affairs that the reader needs in order to make wise decisions as a citizen.

This digging out of relevant background detail is sometimes quite a long and complicated process, but since the reader can keep his newspaper around as long as he wishes—to reread the article, to clip an item and send it to a friend, to take it to a public meeting—the effort is worth while. This type of in-depth commentary role is new to newspapers in recent years, and it gives them an importance that is much greater than the old service of merely giving the spot news.

Remember, the newspaper is part of your life. Make the most of it.

Ted Durein, Executive Editor
Monterey Peninsula Herald
Monterey, California

CREATE:

Draw a floor plan of a small newspaper office, using as a guide the information in the letter above (concerning major departments and operations) and the newspaper material you have already dealt with in Chapter 1. You'll want to show the four distinct departments: News (with desks for reporters, editors; space for wire service machines), Advertising (drawing boards for layout work, office to keep the accounts in, etc.), Mechanical and Press Departments, and Circulation. Give everyone enough light and easy access to the coffee machine. Consult someone-in-the-know about newspaper operations if you want your plan to be really workable.

Take the best results from the class and compare them with an *actual* newspaper office floor plan. Who knows, maybe they'll hire you to redesign the building!

Magazines

Before 1776 There were only fifteen periodicals in the Colonies. A periodical's average life was about ten months. The most famous editors were Benjamin Franklin and William Bradford, with Thomas Paine writing revolutionary editorials for *The Pennsylvania Magazine* in 1775 and 1776.

Post-Revolution The infant nation saw the birth of many magazines, the most important of which was *The North American Review* (1815 to 1940), whose editors included James Russell Lowell and Henry Adams.

1830-1850 Magazines, supported mainly by advertising, began to be circulated nationally. Some of the magazines begun during this period and still being published are *Atlantic,* Boston, 1857, and *Harper's,* New York, 1850. *The Saturday Evening Post* was started in 1821 and was one of America's favorite magazines until its death on February 8, 1969, at the ripe old age of 148 years. (In 1971, it was resurrected as a "nostalgia magazine.") It was during this period that Edgar Allan Poe edited several magazines and contributed to them his stories, poems, and literary criticism.

Collier's Like *The Saturday Evening Post, Collier's* was a popular family magazine with a long history. It was founded in 1880 and lasted until 1957.

Reader's Digest The country's most successful single magazine was started by De Witt Wallace in 1922. Written for the broad middle class, the magazine collected articles from other magazines and rewrote them into short, easier-to-read versions. Today, though, most of its articles are originals. *All* articles are selected for their optimistic outlook.

Look Magazine *Look* Magazine, which was founded in 1937 by Gardner Cowles, Jr. only a few months after *Life* Magazine, folded in 1971. Owner Cowles blamed the increase in postal rates and competition from TV advertising. Now, of all the "family" magazines, only *Life* remains.

Women's Magazines Among the earliest magazines was one that was strictly for women. It was called *Godey's Lady's Book* (1830-98). Since then, there have been several big magazines which cater to this large segment of the population: *Harper's Bazaar* (one of the first to emphasize style in woman's wear), *Cosmopolitan, Ladies' Home Journal,* and *McCall's* (started in 1873 by a New York garment maker hoping to sell his tissue-paper dress patterns through mail orders).

Men's Magazines The history of *Playboy* magazine is the Cinderella story of magazines. Begun in 1953 as an idea of Hugh Hefner, it has developed into a multi-million dollar business, involving other enterprises such as publishing and nightclubs. Prior to *Playboy,* the big men's magazine was *Esquire,* which changed its editorial policy in the 1950s to devote itself to current issues and popular culture.

Little Magazines Usually little in size and number of pages, these magazines grew up outside the great literary centers and devoted themselves to a specialized readership. The best known editor of a little magazine was H. L. Mencken, who founded *The American Mercury* in 1924 and edited it until 1933, filling it with his biting criticism of the American scene. Others are the liberal *Nation, New Republic,* and the conservative *Common Sense* (1932-1946) and William F. Buckley's *National Review.*

Recent Developments With 67% of its revenue coming from advertising, the magazine competes with TV for the advertiser's dollar. Yet in 1969 both circulation and advertising revenues hit all-time high figures. With TV also providing mass entertainment, the way for a magazine to survive in the 1970s is to appeal to a specialized readership, as *Psychology Today, National Geographic,* and *Saturday Review* have done. Editorial "formula"—adhering to a combination of features which readers like and come to expect—replaces the brilliant, autocrat editor whose magazine was an unpredictable product of his far-wandering genius.

"Big" magazines go small. Due to increased postal rates, *McCall's* and *Esquire* changed to a smaller page size. *Saturday Review* was purchased by the founders of *Psychology Today,* who planned to expand *Saturday Review's* operation. *Saturday Review's* longtime editor, Norman Cousins, resigned and started his own magazine, *World.* Women's libbers started a magazine entitled *Ms.*

Have You Always Wanted Your Own Magazine??

The most successful and longest-lasting magazines have been those which have had a strong editor . . . so that the magazine is but an expression of his powerful voice.

Wouldn't you like to see your own voice in print? Delivered to millions of homes every week, or every two weeks, or every month? Or quarterly? An Ego Trip? No, an Ego Vacation!!

Others have done it . . .

*   Look at Hugh Hefner, who began with a unique idea—to make looking at pictures of nude women respectable—and has built his magazine *Playboy* into a multi-million dollar industry which has subsidiary businesses that have multiplied like, well . . . like rabbits!

*   The success of *Psychology Today* has encouraged the publishers to create a brand new magazine for yet another specialized audience. The magazine? *Sexual Behavior.*

*   Before taking the plunge, review the life and death of *Life* Magazine, which passed away Dec. 29, 1972, with a circulation of seven million.

*   *Rolling Stone* was started in 1967 with $10,000 and after four years was finally operating with a profit and an income of over $2,000,000! Its success has inspired the creation of *Rags, Clear Creek, Earth,* and other "counter culture" magazines.

ALL YOU NEED TO GET STARTED besides yourself, of course, and your staff is one million dollars.*

All that really leaves is the *reader*. Decide the person you want to buy your magazine and then write what he wants to read. It's that simple!

*Of course, you want a slick magazine with photographs in full color.

"I guess I *am* a genius."**

**from "The Most," a short film documentary about HH.

Setting Up Shop

As you can see by the chart below, there are several different departments in the organizational set-up of a magazine, each one necessary but vastly different from the other.

Here's what you'll need in the way of staff; better start writing letters to all those friends of yours who are good at this sort of thing.

Getting Organized

Schedule an editorial conference to plan each issue. Everybody agree what should go in and where? GOOD! Got the writing and photographic assignments firmed up with the staff? Oh, you got some unsolicited material and "freelance" stuff that looks good? GREAT! (But how does that make your *staff* writers and photographers feel?) Get those schedules for deadlines made out and in everyone's view!

After the "dummy," showing relative positions of copy, illustration, and ads, is completed, send it to the printer. They'll send back proof sheets of it to look over, so all your editors can get together and talk it up again. Give it final approval, send it for its final press run. It's out of your hands—printed, assembled, and stapled. Congratulations!

React:

Try to figure out what the responsibilities of each of the staffers is. Check your guesses and revise your descriptions if necessary.

Create:

Make up a magazine staff out of your classmates and friends.
Decide on the magazine's NAME;
Audience it will be directed toward;
Contents by department.
Do a "dummy" for the cover of the first issue, and the Table of Contents.

COMICS

Early Days "The Yellow Kid," a single cartoon, appeared in the *New York World* newspaper in 1896 and was so successful that it became a regular. Early cartoons, such as "The Katzenjammer Kids" (1897), "Buster Brown" (1902), "Mutt and Jeff" (1907), "Bringing Up Father" (1913), and "Gasoline Alley" (1919), which had a laugh in each installment, were used as circulation builders for newspapers.

1925 *The New Yorker* magazine introduced the one-line-caption cartoon, the subtlety of which left the interpretation up to the reader. Peter Arno, James Thurber, Otto Soglow, Charles Addams, and Whitney Darrow, Jr. were regular contributors of this type of cartoon. Saul Steinberg had his beginnings with *The New Yorker.*

"Tarzan" A comic strip based on the popular novels of Edgar Rice Burroughs started a new kind of comic, the continuity strip, which told a story in serial form. Naturally the stories were filled with adventure and each had its special kind of "superhero" . . . Dick Tracy (1931), Terry & the Pirates (1934), Buck Rogers (1929), and Superman (1938).

"Blondie" Begun in 1931 by Chic Young, this strip about average American family life has long been a favorite. Dagwood Bumstead, the bumbling, "boss-pecked" nice guy, is the prototype of the image of the American husband that abounds in popular culture. Like "Tarzan," "Blondie" was the inspiration for a series of popular movies in the '30s and '40s.

"L'il Abner" Another long-time favorite strip is "L'il Abner," begun in 1934 by Al Capp, about a family that lives in Dogpatch, a long way from the big city. "L'il Abner" was a successful Broadway musical in the '60s.

The Comic Book Experiments with publishing comic strips in book form in the early '30s proved a huge success, and the popularity of the comic book continued through the '40s. The biggest comic book distributor is National Comics (DC), which has 47 different titles, the most popular of which are *Superman, Wonder Woman,* and *Batman.* DC sells 75 million copies a year.

A close second to National is Marvel Comics, headed by Stan Lee, who tries to make his strips relevant. His super-heroes—like Captain America, Spider-Man, the Fantastic Four—are shown as real people who sometimes feel insecure, who suffer, and who mature and age. They are concerned with real issues, but take a rather liberal viewpoint. (Their fans may counter that they only balance such establishment figures as "Little Orphan Annie" and "Dick Tracy.")

"**Peanuts**" Everybody loves Charlie Brown and his friends, Snoopy, Lucy, Linus, Schroeder, Peppermint Patty, and Pigpen. In the 20-some years since Charles Schulz' strip was purchased by United Features Syndicate, "Peanuts" has become an American institution. It appears in over 1,000 newspapers in the United States and Canada and in another 100 or so throughout the rest of the world. It is read by 60 million people. It has been the basis of several television specials, a popular movie, and a musical, "You're a Good Man, Charlie Brown." Snoopy has been adopted by NASA as a mascot. Minister Robert Short sees in the strip an expression of fundamental Christian theology and has written two books on the subject, *The Gospel According to Peanuts* and *The Parables of Peanuts*. There are other "Peanuts" books, greeting cards, sweatshirts, dolls, pillows, lunch kits, toys, and so on. Schulz, who still does the strip himself, is very selective about who gets licenses. "Peanuts" has become a multi-million dollar business.

Walt Disney On December 16, 1966, *The New York Times* ran the headline.: "WALT DISNEY, 65, DIES ON COAST: FOUNDED AN EMPIRE ON A MOUSE."

Mickey Mouse was first seen by the American public in 1928 in a sound cartoon called "Steamboat Willie." Everyone was delighted with this new form of animation, in which each movement was carefully matched with the sound (then a new element in movies). At the time of his death, Walt Disney had come a long way from the man who with a couple of assistants created this short simple film and who was once the voice of Mickey. He was the overseer of a vast "magic kingdom" that produced motion pictures, television shows, books and magazines, recordings, comic strips, educational films, toys and other Disney-licensed merchandise, and his own private playroom—Disneyland. Although he had long since ceased to draw cartoons, Disney maintained a careful control over everything that carried his name, coloring each with his own simple, almost childlike, philosophy.

Dig:

Go out and buy a comic book. Read it. Give your eyewitness account of what you saw . . .

Name of comic, publisher, group conventions of the comic book art: List some of the words used to represent noises (imitate the printing, draw bubbles). How are the following represented: thought, explanations from the editor, time passing, shouting, emphasis? Is there a variety of "camera angles"? Which is used most often—from above? below? or on a level with the subject? What are the comic ads for? Who are the artists and writers? Is there any attempt at personal communication between the comic book staff and the readers?

Example: "You and I have always known where comics were at, and now it's a kick to see that the rest of the world has finally caught up with us. Excelsior!"—Stan Lee's Soapbox.

React:

In Pierre Couperie's *A History of the Comic Strip,* he says, "The American comic strip is not an incoherent series of pictures, but the most authentic form of the dreams, hopes, splendors, and miseries of our century."

And Jim Steranko, one of Marvel's artists, said in an interview:

"I think if you decide to be an artist or a writer, you automatically accept the responsibility of being alone. However, after your 50 or 60 years are up you'll be able to look back and see this output that you've done that will endure long after you've gone, and will continue to fill the minds of millions of people."

Both men take a pretty sober view of the comic world. In your reading of comics, do you find evidence for their statements? *Is* there something important and enduring offered?

Captain Marvel © 1972 Marvel Comics Group

If you walked into the "bullpen" of Marvel Comics at 625 Madison Avenue, New York, you might meet Stan the Man Lee (editor), Ring-a-Ding John Romita (artist), Happy Herb Trimpe (artist), Adorable Art Simek (letterer), James Steranko (artist), or Gary Friedrich (scriptor), to mention only a few of the Merry Marvel Marching Society. All of them are people who believe pictures are great for communicating. You also might see Daredevil, Thor, Sub Mariner, Captain America, Iron Man, Sergeant Fury, Invisible Girl, the Human Torch, the Think, the Avengers, Spider-Man, the Black Panther, the Falcon, Nick Fury—Agent of SHIELD—to mention only a few in the gallery of characters these men work with every day.

In an article in *Rolling Stone* (September 16, 1971), Robin Green talks of the loyalty and devotion of fans who write letters to the bullpen if they have discovered the slightest error or inconsistency in the characters' whereabouts or actions "because they keep track, they know everything that's happened in that strange world."

> The People at Marvel are paid to be professional children, and the atmosphere around the office is correspondingly chaotic, moody, riotously emotional.
>
> Roy Thomas, Associate Editor
> Marvel Comics
>
> Marvelmania is a subculture, a living-breathing-changing-happening art form, a fantasy world in which millions live, some of them most of the time.
>
> Robin Green
>
> Some people think that everything should be relevant, but I think you should be able to escape.
>
> Roy Thomas

Sometimes, the reader must wonder if he really *is* escaping when he looks at Lee's "superheroes." For instance, he has made Spiderman a neurotic, guilt-ridden, insecure fellow with romantic problems, financial difficulties, sinus attacks, and fits of insecurity (he's embarrassed about appearing in public in a costume!). At least, they're someone *else's* insecurities.

The Comic's Trip

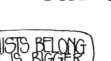

1. Artist develops an entire episode for his family of characters, penciling out rough sketches and balloons for dialogue.

2. Artist begins drawing (usually India ink on bristol paper ¼ or ⅓ larger than finished size), correcting mistakes with opaque white. He notes which area he would like shaded, or in the case of a Sunday color strip, which colors he would like where. At this point, some artists bring in specialists to fill in such things as the landscape, the balloons, or the script. The artist mails his batch of drawings to his syndicate.

3. The comic editor of the syndicate (King Features, Field Enterprises, United Features, Publishers-Hall, etc.) rereads the strip to catch errors in spelling, lapses in taste, consistency (doorknobs on doors, etc.) and passes it on to the syndicate's photo-engraver.

4. The photo-engraver makes an engraved zinc plate from a photograph of the drawing, then applies a special cardboard (like papier-maché) to it, under great pressure. The result is a mold, or "matrix" of the original drawing. Any number of these matrices can be made.

5. The syndicate then mails one matrix to each of the newspapers carrying the strip.

6. The local newspaper adapts the matrix to its own rotary presses, and the strip appears, about one month after the artist drew it, in the Comic Section.

CREATE:

- Make up a new superhero. Give him a snazzy name and think up a few characteristics (of speech, costume, personality) that will distinguish him from other superheroes. Dream up a few episodes in which he reveals his heroic nature as well as his human nature.

- Get the Sunday comics and create your own comic strip, using the pictures but not the dialogue of one (or more) of the regular Sunday features. Use only the frames you need; change the sequence if you wish; add characters from other strips (Mary Worth in Snoopy's dog house?!); change the character's image (a *hip* Dick Tracy?!); borrow some noise words from other pages; add a frame or two of your own, if necessary—in short, create an original comic effect out of second-hand materials. Pay attention to the expressions on the characters' faces when assigning them dialogue.

❧RADIO❧

1278 Roger Bacon talked about using electricity for communication and was put in prison for dealing in black magic.

1835 Samuel F. B. Morse demonstrated that signals could be transmitted by wire and was ridiculed by the public and rebuffed by his colleagues. Five years later, the surprise nomination of James Polk over the favorite Martin Van Buren at the Democratic National Convention was telegraphed to a skeptical Washington. When the train arrived hours later with people to confirm the telegraphed message, dramatic proof was made of the speed of communication by telegraph.

1876 In his tiny Boston laboratory, inventor Alexander Graham Bell told his assistant in the next room, "Come here, I want you," using a device he had developed for transmitting the human voice by wire. The public thought his device, called the telephone, was fascinating, but saw little practical use for it. By the end of the century, the tangle of overhead wires had become such an obstacle that overhead cables were constructed. In 1902, the first long-distance underground cable was placed in operation between New York and Newark, New Jersey.

1901 Marconi demonstrated the wireless telegraph by sending the letter "s." The way had been paved for wireless communication. Developments such as the vacuum tube and audion tube (a three-element tube which detected radio waves and amplified them) made the transmission of music and speech over long distances possible.

1920 The first commercial broadcasting station was formed in Pittsburgh, Pennsylvania, by the Westinghouse Electric and Manufacturing Company. KDKA went on the air by broadcasting the Harding-Cox election returns. Soon after, it broadcast the Harding inauguration ceremonies, then the Dempsey-Carpentier fight, and then the World Series. By this time, the public was abandoning its "crystal set" or "cat-whisker" radios (so-called because of the sharp, thin wire used to make electrical contact with the crystal detector) which required headphones, and was scrambling to buy the Westinghouse home radio receivers (which sold for $60 without headsets or loudspeakers). By 1930, nine percent of American homes had radios.

The Golden Age The '30s and '40s were the heyday of radio. It was America's favorite form of entertainment and families sat in their living rooms listening to the voices of their favorite entertainers coming out of the big box: Jack Benny, Fred Allen, Amos 'n Andy, Bing Crosby, Bob Hope, Burns and Allen, Fibber McGee and Molly, Ozzie

An early radio station set-up.

William Conrad played the role of Matt Dillon on radio's "Gunsmoke" series.

& Harriet, Henry Aldrich, Edgar Bergen and Charlie Mc-Carthy. They heard the voices of their favorite movie stars doing adaptations of movies on the *Lux Radio Theater.* And bobby-soxers thrilled to the sound of Frank Sinatra singing the Top Ten on the Lucky Strike *Hit Parade.*

Soap Opera Advertisers sold a lot of household cleansers and housewives forgot their own troubles with *Helen Trent, When a Girl Marries, Ma Perkins, Stella Dallas, Our Gal Sunday; Road of Life,* and other 15-minute, crisis-packed stories that went on five days a week, year after year, with nothing ever really resolved (except that the particular soap that sponsored each show was claimed the best). America followed the trials of *One Man's Family,* the only nighttime "soap opera," from 1932 until it went off the air in 1959.

Children's Shows If the afternoons were for mother and the evenings for dad and the family, the time in between was "the children's hour." Their favorite comic strip characters came to life . . . or, at least, found their voices: Skippy, Little Orphan Annie, Buck Rogers, Dick Tracy, Captain Midnight, Superman, The Green Hornet, and the Lone Ranger. Children were urged to eat Wheaties and grow up straight and strong like "Jack Armstrong, the All-American Boy." And, as two lines of actual script show, he *was* a hero:

Billy: Jumpin'-jiminy'gee'whiz, Jack . . .
Jack: Quiet, Billy, there's no time for that . . .

The whole family turned out the lights and eagerly awaited the chilling stories of *The Shadow, Inner Sanctum, Lights Out, Suspense,* and *I Love a Mystery.*

1950s Radio as family entertainment was dying. Television, the new audiovisual medium, was commanding everyone's attention during the "prime-time" evening hours. Gradually TV became what radio had been, and radio, in order to survive, had to economize and to change its programming. It did so by providing music as background for everyday activities such as housecleaning and driving and by taking advantage of its mobility by offering on-the-spot news coverage, traffic, and weather reports. It emphasized the things that it could do that television could not, and so remained an important part of everyone's life.

Famous Radio Shows "A day that will live in infamy." From the time of his inauguration to his announcement of the attack of Pearl Harbor on December 7, 1941, Franklin D. Roosevelt used the radio to speak to the American people, to raise their hopes during the Depression and to calm their fears during the war years. It was the first time that there was such personal contact between a President and the public.

"The woman I love." In 1936, the world heard the man who the day before had been King Edward VIII explain why he had given up the throne to marry an American divorcée.

The Hindenburg explodes. In 1937, broadcasting a routine coverage of the arrival of the German dirigible, Herbert Morrison of WLS, Chicago, broke into tears as he described the explosion and burning of the passenger-carrying airship.

The War of the Worlds. A nationwide panic was very nearly set off during the Halloween broadcast in 1938 of the H. G. Wells story of a Martian invasion of earth. Orson Welles presented the play by imitating the technique that gives radio its power—on-the-spot, instantaneous news coverage.

Read *The Panic Broadcast* by Howard Koch, which contains the original script of Orson Welles' famous broadcast.

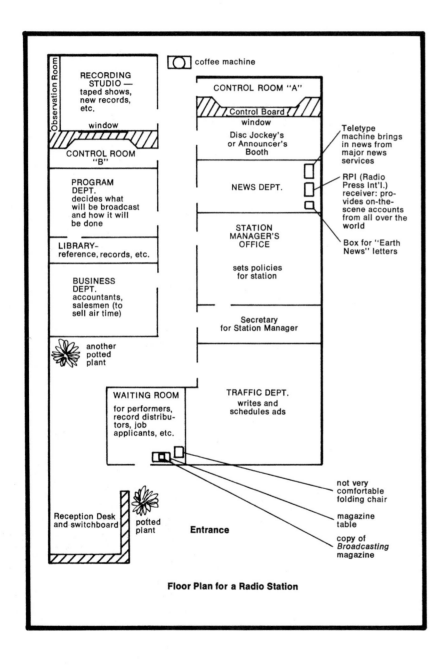

Floor Plan for a Radio Station

React:

- Look at the floor plan of the radio station and decide which office you would want to get into if you were able to bypass the uncomfortable folding chair in the waiting room . . .

  If you were:

  a. A hungry record salesman intent on getting your distributor's record "aired."

  b. An FCC man waiting to read the records of one day's broadcasting to track down a rumor that there were "offensive elements."

  c. An agent of ASCAP, BMI, or SESAC, the performing rights societies who collect money *every time a copyrighted song is performed* (even a 1920s one!). (The stations, once a month, take a cross section of their programming and log every song, its publisher, the performing rights association that the publisher is connected with, and they figure out the fee due to the society. This information is often obtained by the laborious process of sitting with a week's worth of playlists, pulling the records for each song, and then copying the appropriate information from each label.)

  d. A student wanting publicity for your Senior Carnival.

  e. A disc jockey looking for the position advertised in *Broadcasting*.

  f. A prospective station owner, looking to add this station to his media conglomerate.

  g. The chief engineer about to start his 6-10 shift.

  h. The media buyer for an ad agency, intent on buying and scheduling wisely 20 minutes of time slots a week, and in need of looking at the station's current "rate card."

  i. A fanatic about "Space-Out-Spud-Spittin' Sam," the 2:00-6:00 p.m. deejay.

- You're thinking about becoming a station manager, and you read in an article that only one fourth of all the radio stations in the United States make money; one third of them lose money (2,790 reported profits; 1,328 reported losses).

  The article goes on to discuss the finances of a station with a staff of 122 employees: personality announcers that get paid as high as $100,000 (Dick Whittinghill at KMPC-AM in Los Angeles) and $350,000 (John Gambling at WOR-AM in New

York); services such as traffic helicopters, mobile units for "on-the-spot" news, etc.; and rights to sport attractions ($1.5 million for Rams, Angels, and UCLA Sports was paid by KMPC). Would you take the job? How would you meet such horrendous expenses?

deejays wanted

It isn't always comfortable on the leading edge, but it's an exciting place to be. All that energy is what makes it. It's just as dangerous as surfing, as being out in front of a really good wave. It's the fastest ride. It's the best ride. You have more control over the board at any time and you're almost dead at any second. It's the same situation with us.—Doug Cox, General Manager, KPPC-FM, Pasadena, California

HELP WANTED, announcer; Soul jock, must be clean for Drake type black format, please send tape, resume, photograph, and salary requirement. Box . . .

We are knocking off the strict rock format and retaining the best of the contemporary music with modern MOR. To complete the package we need bright, communicative announcers who can project personal appeal to young adults as well as the 30 group. Box . . .

Major east coast rocker seeks experienced jock heavy on production.

Great opportunity for stable, dedicated professional. Send current tape, resume and picture to . . .

SITUATION WANTED: San Francisco Bay area only—top rated California rock jock, first phone, college degree, 30, references. Will consider other formats. Box . . .

"It's a hard life. Very few owners of radio stations look at these guys (deejays) for what they do, what they supply. I believe in them. I put up with them kicking holes in my door with those tantrums because I believe in them. It's a hard job being behind an FM microphone, being on the edge you talk about, that's what the edge does to them. It leaves them with nothing. Nobody records it. They don't have anything to sell. They don't have any estate when they get old and their kids are growing up and they want to put them through college." Doug Cox, General Manager, KPPC-FM, Pasadena, California

All quotes from *Broadcasting,* June 21, 1971.

In 1877, Thomas Edison invented a machine that music came out of. And then we had . . .

VICTROLA
PHONOGRAPH
HI-FI
STEREO
SURROUND SOUND

A Hit Record: Journey From First Groove to Center Label

AGAC— American Guild of Authors and Composers. Twenty percent of publishing companies use their contract, which is considered standard.

ASCAP—American Society of Composers, Authors, and Publishers

BMI— Broadcast Music, Inc.

SESAC—Specializes in religious and sacred

The World of ... Records

We have seen how a songwriter's song gets published and made into a record (opposite). Perhaps the most crucial factors in that record's success are the performers chosen to present the song, the producer chosen to pull everything together, and the quality of the sound studio where the recording session takes place.

A good recording group usually has considerable experience with live concerts and dances, where they have acquired a certain professional polish. When they feel ready to record and to sign contracts, they usually expect some sizable advances and a healthy percentage of sales. Gone are the days when the artist goes unpaid or poorly paid for his efforts, thanks to lessons learned from groups such as the Beatles, the Rolling Stones, and the Jefferson Airplane—all of whom realized that the record companies who owned the contracts were making far more than the performers and artists.

Some of the things which are now negotiated in the recording contract are the amount of advertising, artistic control (who decides which performers will be used and how their material will be recorded), amount of time allowed for recording (budget), which sound studio, what producer. Yesterday's performer went to a studio, did his thing, let everyone else do his job, did a few takes, and left. It was all over in a short amount of time. Now we have musicians who want to get involved in every stage of the recording process—producing, arranging, engineering the new advanced equipment (many tracks, 16 and 24, mixing down, and mastering). Every job has become more sophisticated and the performers want to be involved in all of it, thereby completely shaping the "Art" that is the finished product. Thus, all of these steps in the recording process are subject to negotiation between the recording companies and the performers.

In preparation for the recording session, the producer will get together with the performing group and they will discuss material to be recorded on the album (usually a combination of their own and other songwriters' material). They then start rehearsing and the producer starts making changes in instrumentation, voicings, and arrangements until he gets the "sound" that he thinks will sell (after all, his job is to make gold records). Producers come and go. One will be popular for a while, then the record companies and groups will go elsewhere. Chances are that if a producer has done a best selling album, groups will flock to him, hoping that his "magic" will help them turn out a best seller. Still, some groups want to produce their own music.

The equipment available for use in a recording session nowadays is so versatile as to allow recording techniques quite different from 10 years ago. With as many as 24 different tracks on tape, you can record some instruments and voices, go back, add more, change some and symphonically approach the *construction* of a record and then mix these tracks together—through all sorts of blending, echo, perspective and frequency changing devices—to make the end product quite unlike anything that could be done live, simultaneously, by that same group in performance. All of this equipment misused, say for sheer novelty of effect, can lead to disaster.

The sessions themselves are an exchange (sometimes heated) of ideas between musician and producer and are approached like a montage —part built upon part until the final results are agreeable. This takes a lot of time, and studio time is expensive. Record companies and producers will not tolerate indecision and "messing around" once the recording stage is reached. So if you are about to embark upon your first recording venture, pull yourself together beforehand. If you blow that first opportunity, it's almost impossible to get another.

There was a time . . . when the music business was a simple arrangement between authors, composers, and publishers. AGAC President, Edward Eliscu

The merging of large corporations has created super holding corporations that have come to be called conglomerates.

The bounty in the recording field is so rich that the Schwann Catalog, printed on thin paper in small print, takes on biblical dimensions.—Hans W. Heinsheimer, "Music from the Conglomerates" *Saturday Review,* February 22, 1969.

Dig:

Get a favorite record and translate the information on the album cover.

    Name of record
    Artist (singer or group)
    Publisher
    Sound studio/location
    Engineer
    Songs—who wrote the ones you like (give title and songwriter)?
    Producer—is there any mention of him? What other records has he produced?
    Record company or label

Example:
Clouds
Joni Mitchell   *Chelsea Morning*
                    Song to Aging Children Come
                    Both Sides Now
Composer, Arranger—Joni Mitchell
Recording studio: A & M Studios, Hollywood
Engineer: Henry Lewy
Producer—mentioned only for song *Tin Angel*—Paul Rothchild
Label: "Reprise Records" (a division of Warner Brothers)
      Seven Arts Records
      4000 Warner Boulevard   488 Madison Avenue
      Burbank, California   New York, New York

Read:

Rolontz, Robert, *How to Get Your Song Recorded,* New York, Watson-Guptill Publishers, 1963. Includes in its appendix the names and addresses of record companies, music publishers, distributors (listed by state), recording studios, and pressing plants. Wise, Herbert H. (ed.) *Complete Guide to the Electric Band: Professional Rock and Roll,* New York, Collier Books, 1967. Gives information on how to form your own band, on sound systems, on how to write rock music without reading music, and so on.

ADVERTISING

500 BC Advertising began when the first Babylonian merchant hung a sign above his shop. As civilization grew more complex, advertising became more persuasive, pervasive, and powerful.

1300s European law decreed that merchants display signs above their establishments. These signs became more and more artistic until they developed into the poster, forerunner of our modern billboard, a multi-million dollar business.

1450 Gutenberg invented movable type. After this, advertisers did not have to rely on the posted bill alone; handbills could be printed and distributed throughout cities to advertise products and services.

1797 Lithography was perfected. Pictures and drawings could be printed on the advertisements, making them attractive and appealing in themselves, regardless of what they advertised.

1850s Modern advertising really began. Increasing industrialization created the need for manufacturers to reach a larger market for their products. They advertised through newspapers. As this process became more complex, agencies were formed to handle such newspaper advertising. They were the forerunners of modern ad agencies.

1864 *Carlton & Smith* was formed to represent religious weeklies and farm journals. In 1878 a man named J. Walter

Thompson went to work for the agency and in 1890 controlled it. Today the *J. Walter Thompson* advertising agency is the biggest in the world, with a multi-million dollar billing. Other agencies, begun in the 1890s and now very powerful, are *B.B.D. and O.* (Batten, Barton, Dursten, and Osborne) founded by George Batten and *Foote, Cone & Belding,* once known as Lord & Thomas before Albert Lasker assumed control.

1891 Richard W. Sears founded a new industry totally dependent on advertising and sent out his first mail-order catalogue.

1911 The Advertising Federation of America convened in Boston to adopt a code of advertising ethics and came up with the slogan "Truth in Advertising," in response to protests against fraudulent sales pitches (especially for patent medicines). This organization later developed into the Better Business Bureau.

1925 Half-tone engraving was perfected and four-color printing was introduced, both of which made art work more expensive. Ad agencies now had to take on the supervision of production and printing, in addition to their basic job of placing ads.

1931 Outdoor Advertisers Inc. was formed, standardizing outdoor poster sizes and developing other regulations.

Market Research As civilization grew more complex, its people more diverse and its products more specialized, the agencies needed to become expert at locating prospective purchasers for particular products. Market research developed —the technique of finding the right buyers for a proposed product.

New Media As the numbers of newspapers and magazines grew and as new media, such as radio and television, developed, the work of the ad agency became even more complex. The advertising potential of each of the media, from national network broadcasting to the simple matchbook cover, had to be analyzed.

Madison Avenue The blocks between 200 and 650 on this New York street comprise a mile of office buildings, which house the biggest ad agencies in the world. This mile is surrounded by the offices of station representatives who sell advertising time for radio and TV and by the sales offices of magazines and newspapers. It is a "communications belt" which is responsible for billions of dollars' worth of advertising a year, or about half the money spent on advertising in the United States. Through its branches it controls almost half of the rest.

1970 The most recent development in the world of advertising is the merging of agencies.

According to the U. S. Bureau of the Census,* the following millions of dollars were spent on advertising in 1970. Notice that TV advertising expenditure is almost *twice* that of any other medium.

Magazines	$162,000,000
Network radio	104,000,000
Network TV	249,000,000
Newpapers	127,000,000
Outdoor	109,000,000
Business papers	126,000,000

*U.S. Bureau of the Census Statistical Abstract of the U.S.: 1971 (92nd ed.) Washington, D.C., 1971.

How are ads created?

Have you ever wondered how the same outdoor ad can be seen painted on a ramshackle barn in Podunk and also on a well-lighted billboard in downtown Metropolis? How the newspaper version will appear in both a small city weekly and a large city daily? How the theme of the ad will be picked up by radio and TV spot commercials?

As you may have guessed, the advertisements for a certain product comprise a well-thought-out and well-organized *campaign*—a coordinated attack on the customer calculated to make him feel a need for the product and encourage him to purchase it. The people who create these campaigns work for *advertising agencies,* whose success or failure rest on how many *accounts* (products) they handle. The ad agency's income is 15% of its *billing.* That is, it gets 15% of the amount all its clients spend on advertising. Because of the sensitive and shadowy nature of advertising, the business is a precarious one. For example, three or four people may form an agency founded on one or two million-dollar accounts. Should one of these accounts take its business to another agency (anything to increase sagging sales), the bottom drops out of the agency—literally.

How is a campaign created?

First, *market research* is conducted—to see what kind of people (if any) will buy the product. Second, *motivational research* is done. Experts analyze the psychological reasons people may or may not buy the product. Third, a *theme* is created based on the findings of the research. Sample ads are created around this theme and tested to see which are more effective. Fourth, once the ads are decided upon, the agency must decide the best places to run them, in which *medium,* and how frequently. Fifth, the agency *tests* the results of the ad placement, the most intangible phase of the campaign. For the client, though, the test is simple: if sales go up, the ad campaign is good.

CREATE:

Imagine that you have inherited a small manufacturing company or have just invented a fantastic new product. In order to sell your product, you need to advertise. Write an account of what you might have to go through to bring your product to public attention. The following is an example.

STORY of AN Ad CAMPAIGN OR "DIARY of AN Ad HOUSE LIFE"

March 3, 1981.

I have found it! The ultimate in carving knives! No longer will host and hostess have to leave a dinner table full of guests in order to wrestle with the roast turkey in the kitchen. No longer will the head of the family have to practice carving, awkward and embarrassed, in front of his impatient children who, alas, will no longer settle for the easily-removable drumstick. No more will the appliance buzz of the *electric* carving knife intrude upon the dinner-table conversation. My *electronic* knife looks like a finely tempered antique. It allows the carver to work masterfully. For, in my knife, tiny, thin scanning beams of light (invisible to the eye) seek out and define the contours of the hidden bones and joints of the roast to be carved. Then, automatically, the blade receives the message from the beam and adjusts its slant and downward pressure accordingly. The result: thin, uniform slices—a carver's dream! Tomorrow I will approach General Eclectic to see if they will manufacture it; they'll decide on the best ad agency to advertise it.

March 4.

They have taken to my idea and have selected the agency of Durdston, Dudston, Daffney, and Dollnap to develop the campaign. (I wonder, out of 4,200 ad agencies in the United States, why they picked one with *that* name?)

March 10.

Called General Eclectic to ask why I hadn't seen any advertisements for my knife. They said that the agency was undertaking some preliminary "market research" to determine if there was a true consumer need for my knife, and if so, in which parts of the country and by which types of people.

April 1.

Market Research has concluded that there is a sizable market for the knife. The ad agency has appointed an "account executive" to be in charge of planning the entire advertising campaign. His name is Dudley. He will present his ideas to the Planning Board first thing next week to map out basic strategy.

April 6.

The Copy Department of DDD&D has written out several slogans and sales pitches. Dudley told me some of them: "Don't be a chicken any longer when it's time to carve the turkey," and for the youth market, "Let's get it all together—on the serving platter, instead of the tablecloth!" and for the executive with sophisticated tastes, "Feeling embarrassed by that electric carving knife that looks like a kitchen appliance on your heirloom linen tablecloth?" (Dudley said that a major part of the campaign would concentrate on convincing the public that the *last* innovation in carving knives was obsolete.)

April 11.

Dudley told me that the copy is now in the Art Department of the agency, getting illustrations to accompany the written word. Next stop, the Layout Department (which puts the ad copy and the illustrations together in a striking way) and then I get to sit in on the presentation of the tentative campaign to General Eclectic.

April 15.

I was impressed by the presentation. The typographer had some fun experimenting with printing: ELECTRIC to make the electric knives look uncomfortable to hold and hear, and *Electronic* to emphasize the ease with which my knife operates. The Media Department is still working out a plan for the best possible representation in the various media. In the meantime, various "pre-testings" are going on. One pre-test, called the "consumer-jury" type, involves getting a bunch of consumers together, presenting them with alternative ads to see which they like best and which are most clear and convincing.

June 14.

I saw the first ad for my knife! It was in a men's magazine in the barber shop. The picture showed a suave young man carving a barbecued roast in front of admiring friends. The copy read, "Keep your cool while the meat keeps its hot." I guess they wanted to hit the California backyard summer barbecuer's market.

June 15.

My friend Bob from New Jersey called last night to tell me he saw an ad in the same men's magazine, same issue, same page, but different picture—the carver was *inside,* in a richly panelled dining room. This must be an example of the agency's "split-run test"—two different copies in the same issue to test the effectiveness of the pitch. There was a little address card in the lower corner of each ad if the reader wanted to send for more information on the knife. Smart move, Dudley! You can find out which ad produced the greater response by checking the different code numbers on those address cards.

September 21.

Well, I've seen my knife in newspapers, magazines, on TV and even heard a disc jockey mention it casually on commute-time radio. DDD&D tells me that Starch service has begun gathering "readership figures" from consumers to see which ads were actually read, listened to, or viewed with attention by the public. All this "post-testing" will help the agency plan the big impact push around Thanksgiving (turkey-carving time) and Christmas (gift-giving, mail-ordering time).

January 1.

In spite of competition from pre-sliced frozen turkey, the vegetarian's lobby, and women's liberationists insisting that "No Hens Shall Be Cooked," I made a million dollars last year on my knife.

**Durdston, Dudston, Daffney, and Dollnap
Advertising Agency**

Inter-Office Memo   March 15

TO: Bill Dudley, Account Supervisor

FROM: Market Researchers

RE: Electronic Knife. General Eclectic
             Account

    Report on in-depth interview with
women asked to compare notes on Thanksgiving
Day turkey carving problems.

Quotes taken from tape:

"We <u>bought</u> one of those electric knives, but they're for the birds! They're too noisy ... they smell like a vacuum cleaner ... and they're dangerous!! One of my kids (you know how restless kids get at family dinners) tripped over the cord and poor Harry almost sliced his fingers instead of the turkey."

"I haven't gotten one ... they just don't look right at the dinner table with the linens, the china, the extra special attention you give to details for holiday dinners ... things should be elegant!"

**Durdston, Dudston, Daffney, and Dollnap
Advertising Agency**

Inter-Office Memo   March 17

TO: Copy Writer, Creative Department

FROM: Bill

SUBJECT: Electronic Knife (Gen. Eclectic Account)

        Attached is Market Research report. Suggest you pick up these themes for the women's market:

1. The convenience of the electronic knife, but also <u>silent</u>, <u>safe</u>, and <u>quiet</u>

2. Luxury look ... in the <u>traditional</u> manner

3. <u>Accuracy</u>, but also <u>speed</u>

4. Appeal to <u>male</u> <u>ego</u>

5. Ideal as a <u>gift</u> (Father's Day, Christmas).

CREATE:

You work for an advertising agency. You have just been given an account and are to plan the advertising for a one-month intensified campaign. Your budget is $350,000.

1. Decide how you would spend the money. How much would you spend on each: TV, radio, newspaper, magazine, billboard, other? Keep these (not accurate) figures in mind:
   $50,000—the cost of creating an ad for any *one* of the above media.
   $ 1,000—the cost of running *one* ad in any medium.

2. Decide on an overall theme or slogan, such as Pepsi's "You've got a lot to live," or Taryton cigarettes' "I'd rather fight than switch," or the idea of "law and order" for a political candidate.

3. Make a general plan for a one-minute TV commercial, a one-minute radio spot, a half-page newspaper ad, a full-page magazine ad, a billboard.

4. Decide which TV show you want your commercials to appear on, which radio station, which newspaper, and which magazine.

Here is a list of your sponsors. Select one.

1. A new product "Zitsaway—a new pimple cream."
2. A new model car, the Numbat.
3. Proposition 39—change the draft age from 18 to 26 to 45 to 60.
4. Proposition 17—revoke the compulsory education law: going to school would be strictly voluntary.
5. A teenage candidate for President (you name him).
6. A rock group.
7. PEACE.
8. Long hair on men.

MOVIES

Zoopraxiscope A disc displaying a series of still photographs or drawings which, when revolved, gave the illusion of motion. The idea of the gadget went back to ancient times.

Peep-shows A popular attraction of the penny arcades in the 1890s featuring a very short motion picture sequence of a very simple and quite unsensational human action. The projector used was the *kinetoscope,* showing pictures taken by the *kinetograph,* the first motion picture camera. Both were invented by Thomas Edison.

Nickelodeon A nickel in the early years of 1900 admitted you to a makeshift theater and five minutes of the fascinating sight of people seeming to move on a screen! If you were lucky, you saw a film with a story, like George Melies' *A Trip to the Moon* (1902), the first science fiction movie. (It was done strictly for laughs!) Or Edwin Porter's *The Great Train Robbery* (1903), the first Western, an exciting eight minutes long.

Hollywood Because it was so near the Mexican border, many independent film producers moved to Southern California to escape the injunction over pirating and patent rights disputes. The great expanses and the fine weather made the area perfect for making movies, and Hollywood became the glamorous movie capital of the world. Sir Cedric Hardwicke, in his memoirs (1961), remarked, "I believe God felt sorry for actors so he created Hollywood to give them a place in the sun and a swimming pool. The price they had to pay was to surrender their talent."

D. W. Griffith Because of his experiments with motion picture technique, introducing in his films nearly every cinematic device used today, he is recognized as the undisputed genius of movie directors. His best known films are *The Birth of a Nation* (1915) and *Intolerance* (1916). Other famous early directors were Mack Sennett, who made the Keystone Cops films, and William Ince.

Charlie Chaplin The most popular star of the silent era, who to this day is claimed by many to be the comic genius of the movies. Critics judge his *Gold Rush* (1925) and *City Lights* (1931) his two best films. Other famous silent stars were Mary Pickford, America's Sweetheart; Douglas Fairbanks, the swashbuckling hero; the Gish sisters, who played in many of Griffith's films; William S. Hart, who brought realism to the Western; Theda Bara, the original vamp; John Barrymore, the "Great Profile"; Greta Garbo, the "Most Beautiful Woman of the Movies"; Valentino, the "Latin Lover"; Clara Bow, the "It" girl; Will Rogers, the rope-twirling satirical comedian from Oklahoma; Lon Chaney, "Man of a Thousand Faces"; and Pearl White, heroine of the melodramas.

1927 Sound was introduced to the movies (in the film *The Jazz Singer* with Al Jolson), bringing a radical change in motion picture technique (some say for the worse). Dialogue and music were emphasized, resulting in filmed plays and the extravagant musicals of Busby Berkeley. The stars of this era were Clark Gable, Jean Harlow, Mae West, W. C. Fields, and the Marx Brothers.

The Marx Brothers in ''Go West,'' an MGM-TV release.

1932 Technicolor, a three-color process, was seen for the first time. It was used in the film *Gone With the Wind* (1939), one of the most popular and profitable movies of all time.

The Golden Age The '30s and '40s were the movies' "Golden Age" in the sense that people went to a "double feature" once or twice a week for escape entertainment. The Western, the gangster film, sophisticated comedies, romantic or adventure dramas, and war films made stars of Bette Davis, Humphrey Bogart, Ingrid Bergman, Cary Grant, Gary Cooper, James Stewart, Gregory Peck, Spencer Tracy, Katharine Hepburn, and Joan Crawford, among others.

1948 The advent of television "knocked the movies for a loop" (to use a favorite movie expression).

1950s Moviemaking experimented with wide-screen techniques —CinemaScope with stereophonic sound, Natural Vision (3D, requiring the audience to wear special glasses), Cinerama, Todd-AO, and Vista Vision—to try to entice the public back to the movie theaters. But, as Samuel Goldwyn remarked in 1956, "A wide screen just makes a bad film twice as bad." The drive-in movie became popular during this period.

1960s With TV providing the function that the movies had earlier—that of furnishing the general public with pap— the motion picture became more of an art form, developing film techniques introduced by the television commercial and taking on controversial and realistic themes that heretofore had been the province of the foreign film. Considering the frankness of language and the explicitness of sexual scenes in the movies of the '60s, it is strange to think that Clark Gable's last line in *Gone With the Wind* ("Frankly, my dear, I don't give a damn.") created a furor of shocked indignation and that the Hays Office (founded in 1922 to "clean up" the movies) ruled that, in an acceptable movie, a man and woman, even though married, could not be shown in the same bed.

Charlie Chaplin in *City Lights*

November 3, 1971

Dear Mom and Dad,

Greetings from Hollywood—how are things in Michigan—cold, I bet! It's sunny here, as usual (ha! ha!). Well, your daughter is in the movies! My agent (get that) got me a part in this big movie they're making at Mogul-Golden-Magnate... I'm just an extra, but look what happened to Marilyn Monroe! She played a bit part in a Bette Davis movie and practically overnight she became a superstar!

Wait'll you hear what movie—but don't get shook up, because what really happens is nothing like it says in the book—Quiet on the Set by Amy Dargent!! Remember that book that Mrs. Mundaney across the street read you all the dirty parts out of? Don't laugh—they paid half a million $$ for the rights! (Maybe after I'm out here for awhile I can write a book like that and make a million, huh? Tell Dad I'm only kidding.)

Anyway, the part I'm in is the scene when Raff, the star's husband, comes looking for her at this wild Hollywood party—she used to be this top star but then she becomes an alcoholic and starts running around (those are the parts you read, Mom)—and he can't find her and he leaves. Oh, have you read who's playing the leads? Tory Peck and Barbara Bovine! They wanted Liz Lusher but she costs too much. Bovine took a lower salary for a percentage of the gross. She's not as dumb as she acts!

Anyway, Mom, the whole scene lasts about 30 secs. and they've been shooting it for a week! And that doesn't even count all the time they spent fixing up the set and setting up the shots. All I'm supposed to do is to hang my arms around this guy's neck and laugh with my head thrown back. I think I've done it a million times already. Always something goes wrong—not so's you'd notice, you know. But the director—he's so perfectionist! I should complain—I get $35 a day just for that. And if they decide to give me a line, I'll get a hundred more! 'Course, when you count what I pay to the union, my agent, and for clothes (Mr Leitch, my agent, says it pays off to look like a starlet), I'm lucky I can pay my rent. Don't worry, Dad, I'm not going to ask for more money. You'd think they'd buy me a dress to wear for the scene, or at least loan me one from wardrobe, but no—we have to watch the "budget," the assistant director says. That's about all he says, "Budget, budget, budget." It's really crazy—they spend I don't know how many umpteen millions on a movie and they're always pinching pennies on the set.

In a way, I can understand it, though—you wouldn't believe how many people they've got working around here. This so-called wild party is nothing compared to the people just around the set! But don't think it's a party for real—cause it isn't. When I'm not handing and laughing, I just sit around waiting for the next take. All anybody talks about is the job, too (tell Dad—just like at work). And the worst of all, I didn't even get to see Tory Peck! You think they'd have him waiting around at the money they pay him? They use a stand in, and the shot where he opens the door and looks around, they shoot later. (You'd never notice when you see the movie.) That's the really hard part about acting—when

you have to shoot a scene and you don't
even know what it's about. You know, sometimes they shoot two parts of the same
scene months and sometimes miles apart!

I'll write more tomorrow — I'm dead tired —
slaving all day over a hot set — ha! ha! That's
no joke — with those lights, it is hot!

g'night

Hi, again. Well, we finally finished the scene
today. I'm glad but now I have to start
hustling for another part. Or, my agent
does — he'd better. I finally saw Tory Peck —
in the flesh. What a disappointment! You
wouldn't believe it, mom, those wrinkles...
and the bags under his eyes. All he's got
is the flashy caps on his teeth and
fabulous clothes, of course. Even Dad looks
better, honest.

There's a rumor going around the set that
they're going to sneak the movie in minneapolis
(not for another few months though — it has
to be edited and scored and all that and
besides they want to make it for the Oscar
deadline). maybe you and Dad could drive
over and catch it. Then you could write on the
cards how great that extra was at the wild
party. (No kidding, they read those things like
their life depended on them. And I guess it does,
when you sink umpteen million $$$ into a movie,
you hope the audience likes it.) You never know,
look what happened to marilyn monroe...

Love,
D—

P.S. I was thinking of looking for a job in Hollywood
TV, but then I read Look magazine's (Sept 7, 1971)
article "Would You Let Your Daughter Do It?" and
thought, "No thanks!"

Sincerely,
Marion Davies

Dear Mr. Alexander,
   Here is the "story" you wanted of how we made
<u>Report from Mars</u>. I hope it's what you want.

Jason

A FILM IS
BORN...

Once upon a time there were two high school students
named Rick and Dave, who had to do a term project
for Social Studies. They had never made a film, but
they <u>had</u> done term projects before, and all they
knew was that it was time for them to progress from
research papers to film production. After several
brainstorming sessions, when they considered every
stupid idea each other came up with, they finally
agreed on an idea--to film the account of the first
colony on another planet (Mars, they thought, would
be okay) in the style of a documentary. The film
would look like a documentary for television made by
a journalistic team covering the colony in the first
few months of its development.

   After the excitement of figuring out the idea
wore off, Rick and Dave were faced with some nitty-
gritty problems ... like: Where would they get the
movie equipment? Where would they get the money for
film? <u>Where</u> would they film? What about costumes?
etc. etc. etc. They went to their Social Studies
teacher, Mr. Crow, for help. He suggested that they
contact the Film Club to see about equipment and film.
They did. The Film Club sponsor, Mr. Alexander,
listened to their idea with great interest. (He
really digs film.) He said that the club would lend
the boys a camera (a fancy model with automatic zoom
lens and electric-eye exposure meter), a tripod,

editing equipment, PLUS furnish them with 12 rolls
of film (enough for nearly 50 minutes of film before
editing) if they met certain conditions. First, they
had to show him a shooting script (he's a real
stickler about that) and second, they had to agree
to show the film at the Film Festival the club put on
every spring, and also to show it as a noon movie for
the student body in order to make some money for the
club treasury. This was only fair because he <u>was</u>
giving them about $60 worth of film. To the second
part of the agreement, Rick and Dave agreed without
hesitation; but as for the first part, they were
doubtful. They didn't know <u>how</u> to write a movie
script. It was at that point that Mr. Alexander
suggested that they join the Film Club and get some
of the members to help them out on their film. (This
was Mr. A's sneaky way to get them into the club and
also to get more members involved in filmmaking.)

   They joined the club and that's when they met
me. I had been involved in four films already, and
one of them had won second prize in last year's
Film Festival. Which is why they asked me to help
them with the script. Rick and Dave were really into
Utopian societies and communes and all that stuff and
what they wanted to do was to compare the Martian
colony to American colonies and to show how it was
like a second chance for the United States and all
that. <u>Really.</u>, they wanted it to show all their ideas
about the "Ideal Society," about which they went on
and on. I had to keep interrupting them to explain
that, in a movie, you have to <u>show</u> everything ...
that you've got to point the camera at someone doing
something ... you can't <u>film</u> ideas.

   After a lot of hassling over this point, we
finally came up with a script. It took us about two
weeks, and it was 10 pages long and called for nearly
20 different scenes or shots. I got Danny, a friend
of mine, to help us scout locations. He had a

motorcycle and spent lots of time just riding around the remote areas near where we live. He said he knew of some spots that might pass for another planet. Danny also suggested that we use a church that he knew about as the Martian "town." He had some other ideas about how we could make the country-like area around the church look like the "colony." He was going to fix it all up, he said. He was a real science-fiction freak anyway.

Rick and Dave and I showed the finished script to Mr. Alexander, who was really enthusiastic about it. It was the longest script any student had ever done, he said. After he read it, he gave us a few pointers. Why not have the colonists dressed in some weird way to show that they were on another planet instead of relying on the setting alone? We thought that was a good idea. Rick said he'd ask his girlfriend, Jeanne, who took sewing, to help out with the clothes. Also, Mr. Alexander suggested that we "set the scene" ... begin the film by showing a space ship in flight. We could do this by using a model like kids make and maybe animating it. He called Tim, one of the club members who was into animation, over to talk to us. After Tim heard all about the plot and Mr. A's idea about the establishing shot, he said yes, that it could be done by animating a model. He started to explain to us how to do it, but Mr. Alexander interrupted and asked <u>him</u> to do it for us, since we had enough on our hands just organizing everything. Tim was busy making his own animated film using clay, but he agreed to help us film this one scene. Danny said he could borrow his little brother's model of the Starship Enterprise that he was pretty sure was stuck in some closet at home.

We were getting closer to starting the film: we had the script, the locations, the film, Tim to help us with the opening scene, and plenty of actors. All our friends wanted to be in the film, so that was <u>one</u>

thing that wasn't a problem. Rick had talked to his girlfriend and she suggested that the actors dress alike ... in blue T-shirts and jeans. Then she would make a kind of emblem that she could sew on the shirts. We discussed the idea of the actors' wearing hoods, but decided that it wouldn't be such a good idea not to see their faces.

Finally we were ready to begin. Mr. Alexander loaned us a camera and tripod and assigned the club's best cameraman, Alan, to shoot for us. At first we had a lot of trouble deciding who was going to do what. All three of us (Danny was usually busy fixing up the Martian "town") would be yelling at Alan all at once, telling him what to shoot. He threatened to quit unless we decided first what we wanted and stopped giving him directions all at once.

Finally the problem worked itself out. It turned out that Dave had the best ideas of how to shoot the scene ... so he ended up showing the actors what to do and telling Alan where to place the camera. I became involved in another film, although I still helped on the script whenever there were problems. Rick usually arranged everything; he got all the actors together, made sure the location was ready for them to shoot, borrowed all the stuff they needed, and smoothed over ruffled tempers.

I didn't see them too much during the next couple of months 'cause I was busy on my film, but one day they came up to me and said that they had just shot their last roll of film. It was then nearly four months after they had first gotten the idea to make a film ... still in time to hand in as a semester project (actually it was supposed to have been their <u>quarter</u> project, but Mr. Crow had said that they could make it count as a double project). We had spent about four weeks just getting the script, the locations, the clothes, and all the other stuff we needed; the rest of the time was spent shooting.

When the weather was bad, they shot the indoor scenes. When it was good, they did the outdoor. Many times they'd have to shoot a different scene from the one planned because someone didn't show up. Whenever they finished a roll, they took it to be processed right away. That way, when they got it back the next day and looked at it, they would know if they had to do it over again. Most everything they shot, they liked. They only had to do a few scenes over again ... like the ship model scene.

I was finished with my film by then, so I said I'd help them put the whole thing together. We took all 10 rolls (two had been scrapped) to Mr. Alexander to get his opinion before we did anything. (I'd never really had to edit a film with <u>this</u> many scenes.) Since nothing was in any order, we had to do a lot of explaining to give him an idea of the sequence of shots. He did get the idea, though, and he thought the film looked good ... in fact, he was pretty excited about it. However, he pointed out that some of the scenes were too long and would have to be cut and he also suggested some rearranging of shots. He told us to see Paul about editing.

Paul was president of the Film Club and was on some kind of ego trip. We didn't much like having to ask him for any help. But Rick reminded us that, number one, this film was their WHOLE SEMESTER grade for Social Studies, and number two, we had put a lot of work into it and why not try to make it as good as we possibly could even if it did mean asking Paul for help, and number three, maybe we'd win First Prize in the Film Festival ... an honor that Paul had won two years in a row. We agreed.

First, Paul told us to make an editing box ... take a piece of long thin wood, like lattice , drive as many thin nails into it as possible, and then place the piece of wood with the nails in it in a four-foot high enclosure like a cardboard box. We followed

his instructions, all the time trying to figure out what the devil it was for. When we brought it to him he showed us. The nails were for hanging the strips of film that you cut (you could hang the film by a sprocket hole) and you put a piece of masking tape on each piece of film to describe the scene. The cardboard box was to keep the film as free of dust as possible. Paul told us to buy editing gloves (they were thin white cotton gloves that cost about 50¢).

It all seemed like some sort of trip that Paul was making us go through, but when we started editing, we realized that all the stuff he made us do was worthwhile. Without that box, we would have had film all over the place! We looked at each roll in the viewer (Mr. Alexander set up an editing table for us in his room where we could go every lunch period) and then cut it apart into the separate scenes. We hung the pieces of film on the nails and labeled them, all the time discussing and sometimes arguing about which scenes should be left in and which order they should come in. Oh, yeah! After he showed us how to use the viewer and splicer (we decided to use the cement-splicing method rather than tape, which showed up too much), Paul left us on our own.

Dave ended up making most of the decisions while Rick and I gave our opinions and helped him hang the film and label it. After two weeks of every lunchtime and a few afterschool sessions, we finally had 25 minutes' worth of film. We thought it was <u>great</u>. We decided to show it to Mr. Alexander again to get his opinion (or more truthfully, his <u>praise</u>).

After he saw it, Mr. A. did praise us. He was impressed, we could tell. There was one scene he thought the students wouldn't get. But we argued, saying we didn't care if they got it or not, it was the way <u>we</u> wanted it. He understood. Then he mentioned sound ... what had we planned to do for a sound track. We told him that most of it would be narration, but that we did want some music ... we were going to tape some cuts from some albums we had. He said he thought that was okay, that was what most kids did, but why not think of using some original music. Since we were trying to depict life on Mars, we ought to have some sort of weird music. Go see the music teacher, he told us.

We did. By this time, we were thinking maybe Mr. Alexander was a little weird. But he had been right so far, so we went along with him. We were really surprised to find that Mr. Merrill, the music teacher, was actually interested in our idea and mentioned a couple of students who were playing around with their own compositions. He set up a noon-time session for him and his students to view the film. After they saw it, they got all excited about what kind of "space" music they could create for it. They said they could do it in maybe a week. We thought that was crazy, since it would be only maybe 10 minutes of music altogether. They laughed at us, saying that they had to write it scene by scene ... they couldn't just sit down and compose while they watched. We left the film with them.

While we were waiting for them to do the music, we had to do one more scene--probably the most important one in the film--the credits. We had to ask Mr. Alexander for one more roll of film. He gave it to us and told us that the Film Club had a set of block letters that we could use. I got another friend of mine, Laura, who was good in art, to do some backgrounds for the letters. We did the credits.

We then made the tape recording using the narration and the music that Richard and Jim had written.

The rest is history. We won First Prize in the Film Festival. Rick and Dave got A's in Social Studies. Mr. Alexander showed the film at two noon movies, to the faculty, to a nearby grammar school, and made $100 for the Film Club.

Modern Media
Mr. Alexander

Assignment #1

READ the article, "A Film Is Born," which I've put on ditto (on the table in the front of the room) which Jason so kindly wrote for me regarding the making of "Report From Mars," last year's Film Festival winner.

PLEASE NOTE:

Although an amateur high school production, the film was made exactly the same way a big Hollywood movie is--in these stages: 1. preparation, 2. shooting, 3. editing, 4. distribution and promotion.

ALSO:

Note how the film was made, not in sequence following the story line. The boys looked at the daily RUSHES (see vocabulary sheet for movie terms) just as they do in Hollywood. The music was composed by scene (a very tedious job), not all at once. EDITING is very important, since the scenes can be put together any way the editor thinks is effective. Dave enjoyed the privilege of FINAL CUT, only given an established director. If I had given the film to Paul to edit the way I wanted it, I would have been employing the methods of many Hollywood Studios. Many directors have seen their films ruined by such tactics (Orson Welles' "Magnificent Ambersons" for one; Arthur Penn's "The Chase," for another).

WRITE an idea for a film, not over 250 words. After I look it over, I will make some suggestions for your next step, writing the SCRIPT.

TELEVISION

Television is the youngest child of our age of technology. Its parents—radio and movies. In its early stages, it was radio that furthered its development. RCA (which later formed the NBC network) made the most important innovations, and the Westinghouse and Philco companies also carried on costly experiments. In the 1930s, NBC actually transmitted television broadcasts an hour each night after its last radio broadcast had been made.

During the war, electronic advances, like radar, accelerated television's progress. Soon after the war's end, a clear, steady picture on a 17-inch screen, the sponsorship of advertisers, and the popularity of televised prizefights seen by customers at the local saloon caused everyone to take notice of this electronic child. From 1948 to 1950, TV sets were bought as fast as they could be made. Television became an important element in the entertainment field, threatening the established media, like radio and the motion picture. Many production companies moved to Hollywood and soon lots and studios were given over to producing TV shows.

The '50s saw television's finest hour. Broadcasting was all done live, and the public actually had a theater in its living room. There was live drama, both fictional and real. The public saw plays by the most creative writers in the entertainment field. Viewers became the audience at such real events as the McCarthy hearings and the national political conventions.

By the 1960s, nearly every American home had a TV set and a system was needed to determine whether enough of them were tuning in to assure the sponsor that his money was being well spent. The Nielsen rating system was devised, and the life of a TV show rested on the viewing taste of the 1200 families who make up the system. The dramatic shows were dropped one by one and attempts at realism and relevance met with repeated failure. It was clear that the American public wanted its TV fare bland and easily digestible. Television shows were no longer done live, and laughter came out of the can (added to the TV sound track from recorded laughter).

Television entertainment might comprise a "vast wasteland," but TV still did what it could do best—make what was happening in the world real and immediate. Millions of people attended an assassinated President's funeral, watched one of history's most crucial murders, tuned in to the war abroad and to insurrections at home, and watched mankind's "giant step" on the moon without leaving their homes.

Blamed for many of society's ills, television is a force that is bound to become even more powerful in the next few years. The development of video tape recorders, cable television, and an elaborate communication satellite system forecast changes in our way of life that are sure to be revolutionary. Whether they are for the better or worse remains to be seen.

The Making of a TV Show

It's Friday night, 7:29. In one minute, the first show of a new series, the *Flap Doodle Musical-Variety-Comedy Hour* sponsored by Chromium Motors, will appear on Channel X. The ABS network is counting on this show to knock the rival NBS network's *Eureka!* (top show in this time slot for three years) off the number one position in the Nielsen ratings. Hopes are high that the Flap Doodle Show will get the viewers over to ABS and then keep them there until 11 P.M. out of sheer lethargy (who likes to flip channels on a Friday night!).

The show was taped on Thursday night at the Zenith Auditorium in Hollywood in front of a live audience. Flap, who had learned his trade doing the nightclub circuits, insisted on the live audience-performer rapport. Besides, several other shows which had been using live audiences instead of canned laughter had upped their Nielsen ratings considerably. The rehearsals, which had gone on all week, had run smoothly

. . . with a few exceptions: Flap had been pretty nervous for the camera rehearsal and as a result was not too sure of the camera movements during the taping. Of course, there had been the usual number of last-minute adjustments, like the writers cutting out a comedy bit about backpacking when they realized the possible conflict with the sponsor's interests. There had also been that initial clash when the director decided to give guest Bobby Brash another song. That really annoyed Flap until it was pointed out that they might as well get their money's worth out of Bobby, considering what they had to pay him.

All was patched up after the taping though; Flap and Bobby had played golf and decided to go to Vegas together for the weekend, Flap promising to show up for a script-reading on Monday morning. Some of the crew had gone down to the corner saloon to "unwind." The producer had flown to New York to confer with network brass.

The hour-long show, which is about to start in 30 seconds now, represents a lot of *money*. It cost $250,000 to produce, $25,000 of which went to Flap. Chromium Motors has six one-minute commercial messages, for which they paid ABS $360,000. On top of that, the commercials had cost them $75,000 each to produce. Of course, they expected Flap's audience to buy some of their cars . . . they were especially counting on the 18- to 25-year-olds to go for their new small sports model, the Numbat.

The show involves a lot of *people*, too. Aside from Flap and his guests, Bobby Brash and Lita Lungs, there are 8 bit actors, 12 dancers, a 30-piece studio orchestra, a production and technical crew of 41, and several people at each of the large concerns involved—Chromium Motors, Inc.; Durdston, Dudston, Daffney & Dollnap, the ad agency that handles the account; and, of course, ABS. If all goes as hoped, 35 million people (your Friday night heavy viewers) will also be involved.

So there's a lot riding on this show . . . the hopes of ABS for the lion's share of the Friday night audience and the hopes of Mildred and Harry Johnson, who had turned down the Browns' invitation to join them at the movies just because they didn't think they should miss the Flap Doodle opener.

It's 7:30. Let's look into the homes of some of the people involved and see how they're enjoying the show.

NEW YORK. The producer, David Susnice, is attending a dinner party with Richard Bland, ABS vice president in charge of programming, and Paul Powers, the president of ABS. There are 12 guests in all, including one writer for a smallish, leftwing magazine and two spokeswomen for the women's lib movement. The guests are having their cocktails at Powers' Long Island estate when Bland points to his watch and beckons Susnice. The two men, along with Powers, go into another room to watch the show.

David sips his Scotch-on-the-rocks nervously as he watches the intro . . . Flap walking on while the girl dancers (dressed as shoeshine boys) do their shoeshine number (a kind of folk symbol for Flap whose comedy bit about his days as a shoeshine kid is now famous). David glances over at Bland, who looks bored.

"That number alone cost me 40 thou," he says plaintively.

"It's a nice touch," Bland remarks.

Powers says nothing.

They watch the rest of the show in silence. Only David moves . . . to get another Scotch during a commercial. He pours himself a tall one. At the show's close (Flap getting his shoes shined by the 12 girl dancers), he looks over at Bland.

"Good show," Bland says. "I think it'll knock *Eureka!* off the tube! Don't you think so, Paul?"

"It probably will," Powers mutters as he starts to leave the room to join his other guests, "but to think that out of a thousand and two ideas submitted to ABS, we had to end up with Flap Doodle."

Feeling relieved, David walks over to the portable bar to pour himself another tall Scotch.

Meanwhile, several miles away at the S'Bourbonsville home of J. B. "Skip" Huckster, account executive for D D D & D Skip and his wife and two small children are all sitting in the Hucksters' king-size bed munching Oreo cookies and watching television. As the six o'clock movie ends, Skip sits up expectantly and shushes the kids:

"Well, this is it, kiddoes! If Chromium goes for this show, the Hucksters have got it MADE!" He lights a cigarette even though he's already had his quota of 11 cigarettes for the day.

At the shoeshine number, one of the kids asks why the girls are dressed like tramps, and Skip tells his wife to put the kids to bed. During the rest of the show, Skip doesn't say a word, although his wife makes several favorable comments and laughs twice. He forgets all about the cigarette quota and finishes the pack . . . then he finishes the Oreos.

"I wonder what the Nielsen will be," he murmurs as he drifts off to sleep.

Meanwhile . . . out in Vegas, Flap and Bobby have won a couple of thou between them and are sitting in the cocktail lounge trying to decide which of the several starlets they've noticed around the casino to invite for dinner. They're feeling pretty good and have completely forgotten about the show which is appearing on the set above the bar. The sound is turned off, though, and no one looks up to notice the silent antics of Flap Doodle, favorite of nightclub audiences everywhere . . .

Out in the Hollywood apartment of Fred Fribble, Fred and his roommate, Al, are watching the show. Fred is the technical director for the show; it was his first time out as TD; he'd been floor manager on the Johnny Palaver nighttime talk show for three years. This is his first big break . . . if he makes it as TD, he could go on to direct. In fact, he feels that right now he can already do better than Sturge Sycophant, who was hired to direct the Flap Doodle Show solely on the basis of the Emmy he'd won for directing an adaptation of Shakespeare's *Taming of the Shrew* which people would watch no matter WHO directed it . . . all of which Fred is saying to Al as the show comes on.

"HEAVENS! Why didn't I cut to camera one in that shot . . . Oh, blast! I knew I should have called for a dolly shot in that one . . . cut . . . cut . . .CUT!"

Al, who is stunt man for Earthwide Studios, pops open another beer and ignores his roommate. He is used to Freddie directing every show he watches. However, this is the first time he's gotten THIS involved. "Must be because of his new job . . . whatever it is," Al figures.

"Camera three . . . zoom in on a head shot! Camera two . . . take a cover shot . . . TILT!" Freddie, who sat in the control booth at the studio all day following Sycophant's video direction, feels free now in his own apartment to direct the show as HE would have liked. He gestures animatedly while Al slouches down on the couch watching the show and drinking his seventh beer of the day.

And in White Plains, Nebraska, Mildred and Harry Johnson have just left for the movies . . . the Browns talked them into it after all. The Orpheum is showing the movie made from that book *Quiet on the Set*. Harriet Brown and Mildred had both read the book and assured their husbands that it was "real good." Besides, it had Dee-Dee Clotage in it (in addition to Tory Peck and Barbara Bovine) and Harry and George just HAD to see *her*. They left the TV on, as company for

their dog and also because the Nielsen Rating Service had attached something to their set and they felt kinda obligated to keep it on as much as possible . . .

"Wouldn't YOU like to own a NUMBAT?" a blonde in a bikini is saying on the commercial to the Johnsons' dog, who has fallen asleep. The blonde, a graduate student in forestry at USC, has taken part of the money paid her for the commercial and has purchased two Swiss-made backpacks. She and her boyfriend, a third-year medical student, have gone backpacking for the weekend . . .

A director in action, from the film "The Making of a Live TV Show," Pyramid Films, Santa Monica, CA.

See:

Television Land, a collection of clips from television shows from early TV days to the recent moon walk. Makes the point that television gives equal coverage to the most momentous and the most trivial of human endeavors.

The Making of a Live TV Show, a close-up look at the job of a television director. We watch the intense experience of directing the live 1970 Emmy Award show. This is a rare chance to get into the control booth.

Both films may be rented or purchased from Pyramid Films, Santa Monica, Calif.

Read:

On the history of . . .

Radio . . .
Tune In Tomorrow, Mary Jane Higby, Ace, 1968, $.95.

Movies . . .
The Liveliest Art, Arthur Knight, Mentor, 1957, $.95.
King Cohn, Bob Thomas, Bantam, 1968, $.95.
The Movies, Mr. Griffith & Me, Lillian Gish, Avon, 1969, $1.25.
Hollywood: The Haunted House, Paul Mayersberg, Ballantine, 1967, $.95.

Television . . .
Seven Glorious Days, Seven Fun-Filled Nights, Charles Sopkin, Ace, 1968, $.75.
The Glorious Decade, Tedd Thomey, Ace, 1971, $.95.
Due to Circumstances Beyond Our Control, Fred W. Friendly, Vintage, 1967, $1.95.

Comics . . .
The Steranko History of Comics, James Steranko, Supergraphics, 1970, $3.00.
All in Color for a Dime, edited by Lupoff and Thompson, Ace, 1970, $1.50.

Advertising . . .
Madison Avenue, U.S.A., Martin Mayer, Pocket Books, $.75.

For a behind-the-scenes look at . . .

Movies . . .
People Who Make Movies, Theodore Taylor, Avon, 1967, $.75.
Butch Cassidy and the Sundance Kid, (screenplay) William Goldman, Bantam, 1969, $.75.
The Studio, John Gregory Dunne, Bantam, 1969, $.95.
The Making of Kubrick's 2001, edited by Jerome Agel, Signet, 1970, $1.50.
Picture, Lillian Ross, Avon, 1952, $1.25.

Television . . .
Living Room War, Michael Arlen, Tower, 1967, $.95.
The Making of Star Trek, Stephen E. Whitfield, Ballantine, 1968, $.95.
Inside Laugh-In, James E. Brodhead, Signet, 1969, $.75.
The Other Side of the Rainbow . . . With Judy Garland on the Dawn Patrol, Mel Torme, Bantam, 1970, $1.25.

Advertising . . .
From Those Wonderful Folks Who Gave You Pearl Harbor, Jerry della Femina, Pocket Books, $1.25.
The Hidden Persuaders, Vance Packard, Pocket Books, 1958, $.95.

Disney . . .
The Disney Version, Richard Schickel, Avon, 1968, $1.25.

Magazines . . .
Decline and Fall: The Death Struggle of the Saturday Evening Post, by Otto Friedrich, Ballantine, 1970, $1.25.
Nothing But People: A History of Esquire Magazine, by Arnold Gingrich, Crown, 1971.

Newspapers . . .
A Day in the Life of The New York Times, by Ruth Adler, New York Times Co., 1971.
The Kingdom and the Power: The inside story of the people who run the most powerful newspaper in the world—The New York Times, by Gay Talese, Bantam, 1970, $1.50.

Chapter 3

Making It Pay

As the "Who Else Pays?" column shows (consult page 73), the movie producer and the record company take the greatest financial gamble in producing media for the public. They create a product and hope the public will buy it. They have no source of revenue except *sales* way at the end of the movie/record production line. Especially if artistic talent is thin, they must rely heavily on good "promotion" of their product (that is, "talking it up" as if it were *already* a hit) and on repetition of a hit formula in order to assure themselves profits.

In the recording business, when an artist is very talented and has his own sound or style, such as Santana, Neil Young, James Brown, or Carole King, producers are pretty certain that their records will make money. In many other cases, though, they don't know. So the records need to be promoted, to be "hyped"—a record distributor sometimes goes to unimaginable extremes to get a deejay or program director to listen to the record he is plugging. For he knows that if he can get it played on a popular Top 40 station, he's got it made. Playing a record on such a station almost assures big sales. If it is heard, it is purchased; if it is purchased, it is played more often and therefore heard more often. Round the cycle goes.

The other way to come up with a winner is to imitate a winner. Some record companies analyze a hit and decide upon the formula (the particular combination of ingredients that made it popular) which they repeat in a series of records. When this sure-profit technique is used, the artist is not free to create (or improve) his own style, but is required to fit into the formula. The case of the "Motown Sound" illustrates this point. After the popularity of the Supremes' "Where Did Our Love Go?" and "Baby Love," the Motown producers knew that the formula that they had carefully worked out over a period of years was right. What they did then was to refine the formula and impose it on all the artists that recorded on their label.

What was this formula? First, the drummer hit the snare drum on *every* beat, instead of on every second and fourth beat of the measure. The drums were emphasized and tambourines were added to bring out the beat. There were instrumental and vocal backgrounds that became completely stylized. The melodies were kept simple and the lyrics used repetition. The beat, the sound, the lyrics were kept to a simple, repetitive pattern . . . as background for the lead vocalist, like Diana Ross, who could then use the background either to work with or work against.*

After Frank Sinatra's phenomenal success in the '40s, Columbia records would not allow him to change the slow, sweet way of singing that had made him so popular, even though his records were not going over. He had to break his contract and go to another company, Capitol, to be free to develop the swinging style that he knew was right for the time.

Often, too, people imitate formulas that have made other artists successful. These imitators may enjoy a brief success, but time usually proves that genuine talent lasts and the ones who merely ride the crest of a popular style are quickly forgotten.

———————
*"A Whiter Shade of Black" by Jon Landau, in *The Age of Rock*.

Bing Crosby, Dorothy Lamour, and Bob Hope in "The Road to Bali," a Paramount release.

The Media and $$$

Mass Media	Cost to You	What % of Cost You Pay	Who Else Pays	Who Gets the Profits?
Movie	$5	nearly all	TV rental foreign distribution	Producer (independent or studio) including stockholders Distributor Theater Owners
Record	$10	all		Record Company Distributor Artist (royalties, or percent of profit) Songwriter Record Store
Newspapers	10-15-35¢	20-30%	advertisers	Publisher (individual or chain) Distributor Vendor Newsboy
Magazine	25¢-$1	20-30%	advertisers	Publisher Distributor Vendor Door-to-door salesman
Radio & TV	nothing	none	advertisers	Local station (independent or network affiliate) Network Public TV (non-commercial TV supported by public donations, grants, and gov't.

The process of cashing in on a formula is similar in the movie industry. It sometimes happens that the combined elements of a good script, talented director, and actors will result in a movie that will be just *right* for the time, and people will flock to see it. Such was the case with *The Sound of Music,* which has surpassed *Gone With the Wind* as the greatest money-making movie yet, and *The Graduate,* which was a low budget film featuring unknowns and is among the top five money-making films of all time. *Easy Rider, Bonnie & Clyde,* and *M*A*S*H* had similar successes.* What often happens after such successes is that the same producers, or others, will want to duplicate the success and try to get the same ingredients together in another movie. Too often they find out it doesn't work, and they lose the millions they have invested, despite elaborate promotion. The movie-going public, reading bad reviews or hearing from friends that a movie doesn't make it, sits home and wonders at the rash of big sentimental musicals, or "alienated youth" films, or 1930s criminals-who-became-folk-heroes films.

Sometimes, though, making movies by formula works and *is* successful. Some of the well-known examples are the Fred Astaire—Ginger Rogers musicals of the '30s, the Bing Crosby—Bob Hope "Road to . . ." comedies of the '40s, the Doris Day—Rock Hudson (or reasonable facsimile) "sex comedies," and the "beach party" twist movies of the '60s.

"Gone With the Wind," MGM

———————
*"The Godfather" (1972) became a *colossal* moneymaker.

Generally speaking, though, moviemakers have no sure way of knowing whether or not their movie will be successful. They may know, for example, that the majority of the movie-going public is between the ages of 18 and 25, as it is now in the early '70s, and try to produce films that this age group will like. But beyond that, they're in the dark.

The Supremes

React:

1. What "sound" is currently popular on Top 40 radio? Describe its characteristics in as much detail as possible. *Who* created the sound; in other words, who originated it? Who has imitated it? Which recording artists do you consider to be originators and which, mere formula followers?

2. Think of a hit movie you saw and enjoyed three or four years ago. Were there imitations of it afterwards? Were they good? What were the elements that were imitated?

3. Can you think of an example where a movie company or record company has completely misjudged the youth audience it expected to please?

Dig:

Collect examples of promotional material for a forthcoming movie —from radio, magazines, and TV. What claims, promises, etc. do the producers make? Then go to the movie, check the reviews of it in newspapers and magazines (*Time, Seventeen, The New Yorker,* for instance) and compare what the movie delivered with what it was built up to be.

Since newspapers and magazines have a known readership that the advertiser wants to reach, they are able to sell him space and use the money to pay for most of their production costs. In fact, they *depend* on the advertising dollar to keep them in business. A newspaper nowadays has little fear of losing its advertising revenue for, more often than not, there is no rival newspaper competing for the advertiser's dollar (although it does have competition from other media and the throwaway shopper papers). As long as it keeps its readership (80% of Americans read a daily newspaper), it will have advertisers. Of course, it can always strive to get *more* advertising; the more readers it has, the more advertising it can attract.

Magazines, however, compete with one another and with TV for advertisers. Here are some ads that appeared in *Advertising Age* (the trade journal of the advertising world). They are examples of ads that magazines place to try to get the advertiser's dollar away from TV and other magazines:

- One-third of America's adults seldom—if ever—watch prime-time TV. Twelve million of these very adults read *The Digest* every month. So do 18 million other primary readers. And they spent far more in supermarkets than the viewers of any regular TV show . . . or readers of any other magazine. Think it over.

- If you're a TV advertiser whose brand-recall scores are sinking fast, don't think you're alone. Over the past three years, one major agency tracked television-recall scores for all of its clients' brands—and found an average 27% decrease. TV clutter certainly doesn't help. Yet over the last 10 years ad readership in magazines shows a healthy increase of 45%.

- According to audience figures derived from the 1971 Brand Rating Index report, *LOOK* readers have a higher median household income than the readers of any other major general-interest magazine. Higher than the readers of *LIFE.* Higher than the readers of *Reader's Digest.**

To make such claims to the advertisers, magazines must analyze their readers, find out what age they are, how much income they have, what their education level is, what their interests are. Given these facts, the advertisers will know what products they are most likely to buy. And so, when a magazine says, as *Playboy* does:

What Sort of Man Reads Playboy? He's a young man groomed to zoom. The standout in the corporate crowd, sought out when there's a job to be done. His ability to succeed is the reason. Facts: One out of every three U.S. males 18-34 in professional, managerial or technical occupations reads *Playboy.* It also reaches two out of five U.S. households with incomes $10,000 and over, one out of two with incomes $15,000 and over. Bright men wanted? Recruit them in *Playboy.* It moves men on the move. (Source: 1968 Simmons.)

*This plea for additional advertising apparently did not help *Look's* financial problems. The magazine folded in 1971.

What am I like since the divorce? Well, not exactly starry-eyed but not brimming with tears either. Claude and I didn't turn out to be quite right for each other and it's better that we parted. I'm not taking alimony...after all I have a terrific job, we didn't have children, so why should I be a parasite? I just hope we both find someone else to love very soon. Finding that new person takes time--I was 24 when it happened with Claude-- but thank goodness I have a magazine to keep me cheered, encouraged and advised while I wait! I love that magazine. I guess you could say I'm That COSMOPOLITAN Girl.

If you want to reach me you'll find me reading
COSMOPOLITAN

SIMMONS 1971 MAGAZINE AUDIENCE STUDY (in thousands)

Magazine	Total Adult Audience	Men—By Age			Women—By Age		
		18-34	35-49	50 Plus	18-34	35-49	50 Plus
Cosmopolitan	4,023	427	127	162*	1,629	989	693
Family Weekly	15,606	2,654	2,533	2,849	2,353	2,158	3,063
Fortune	2,071	560	696	286	223	164	144
Glamour	4,223	177**	22**	74**	2,614	762	577
Hot Rod	4,133	2,920	317	267*	319	235*	76**
Life	38,608	9,293	5,679	5,301	6,946	5,823	5,569
Look	31,396	6,929	4,292	4,363	6,570	4,674	4,568
National Geographic	14,861	3,263	2,606	2,431	1,865	2,115	2,584
Parade	30,784	6,377	3,744	4,973	5,343	5,032	5,317
Psychology Today	1,762	538	304	48*	583	202	87*
Reader's Digest	42,046	6,741	5,527	7,404	7,193	6,522	8,660
Seventeen	3,341	67**	39**	86**	1,935	909	308
Sports Illustrated	10,615	5,023	2,301	1,495	808	730	261
Sunset	2,203	232	302	186	430	488	569
Teen	995	28**	53**	38**	413	362	102**
T.V. Guide	33,769	6,965	4,228	4,057	7,921	5,251	5,349

* Projection relatively unstable because of small sample base
**Number of cases too small for reliability

The advertisers of products these men might buy—cosmetics, clothes, stereo equipment, cars—listen and plan their campaign accordingly. And so it pays for a magazine to analyze its readership, not only to convince advertisers, but to keep its own articles "in touch" with its readers' tastes.

The Simmons Study mentioned above in the *Playboy* ad is the standard demographic (people-measuring) study consulted by advertisers. Above is a more recent one.

React:

Using the Simmons Magazine Study, which magazine would you use to advertise a product which is purchased by each of the following groups:

1. men, 18 to 34
2. men, 35 to 49
3. men, over 50
4. women, 18 to 34
5. women, 35 to 49
6. women, over 50

What magazine would you use to appeal to a product for *men only*?
    for women only?
    for men and women, 18 to 34?
    for men and women, over 50?

What magazines would you use for a *mass product,* like toothpaste, that everyone uses?

Since it is no secret that women as a group have more buying power than any other group, many millions of advertising dollars are spent with the woman in mind. In the following selection of ads for women's magazines, notice how each magazine claims that it is the best vehicle for reaching the women with the most money to spend.

Woman's Day delivers The Quality Reader.
The women you need to make sales are reading *Woman's Day*. Of the leading women's service magazines, *Woman's Day* has: The highest concentration of women 25-49, women in Metro-Suburban areas, of women in those big spending families of 3 and over, of women with children under 18 years old, of in-home readers, of women with household income of $8,000.

What are my New Year's resolutions for 1971? Well, I guess it wouldn't be *me* if I weren't vowing to try to be something a little *better* than I was the year before. You know what I mean . . . more willpower . . . fewer temper fits . . . more *courage*. And while we're at it, I wouldn't mind a *bit* finally learning to ski and learning to make decent crêpes (mine always go gummy!). Why this eternal self-improvement? I don't know . . . it just makes me *feel* better, that's all! My favorite magazine says go to it . . . you can have or be anything you want if you'll just hang in there. I love that magazine. I guess you could say I'm That *Cosmopolitan* Girl.

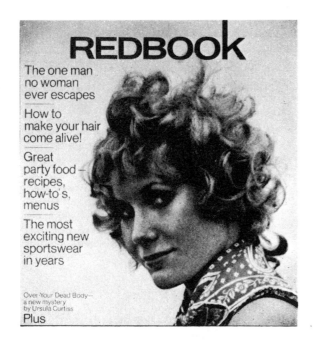

YOUNG MAMAS SPEND MORE THAN BIG DAD–DIES! (And more and more Young Mamas are reading *Redbook* now than a year ago)

And we break our necks each month to write *Redbook* just for women 18-34. No inspirationals about how to enjoy life at 60. No geriatric advice. (For that matter, no ads on denture cleansers.)

gutsy, elegant *NEW WOMAN* magazine . . . *first* magazine for the thinking woman. Who is this woman?

A survey of early *NEW WOMAN* subscribers shows:

- 86.0% consume alcoholic beverages.
- 78.8% select the brand themselves.
- 96.4% use cosmetics.
- 74.2% travel several times a year.
- 33.2% smoke a pack or more a day.
- 99.8% entertain at least once a month.
- 50.2% have personal incomes over $8,000.
- 65.8% spend almost all of it on themselves.

McCALL'S
15,000,000 women take our word for everything. No wonder *McCall's* is the #1 magazine for for women who think.

The Responsible One. Look at her demographically, and she's much like the reader of any woman's magazine. But really get to know her, and you'll find a sense of purpose beyond her years. A commitment to her family, her friends, her community, her environment. And above all, a searching mind. A drive to know everything she can about herself, and her world. In a word, she's responsible. GOOD HOUSEKEEPING.

Mademoiselle doesn't edit for the girls. Not the Gibson Girls or the think-for-me girls or the sensationally single girls. But for the special young women who want a total editorial product for a total human being.

LIBERATION BEGINS AT HOME
To the average American woman, liberation isn't a mass movement, but a very personal movement of her own . . . Her liberation thus begins at home. And a great deal of her freedom is achieved with the help of her women's magazine. For 14 million American women, that helper is the unique *Ladies' Home Journal.*

REACT:

Suppose you were the media buyer of an advertising agency and you had just seen all of these ads for women's magazines in your copy of *Advertising Age*. According to these ads, which magazine would be the best one in which to place an ad for each of the following products:

1. Scotch whiskey
2. denture cleanser
3. boys' jeans
4. perfume
5. luggage
6. cake flour
7. a book club
8. hair spray

Here are some statements from ads for magazines which appeared in **Advertising Age:**

New advertisers who are out to capture a slice of the booming leisure/sportsman's market soon discover *Field & Stream's* magic . . . They're all learning what our leisure/sportsmen advertisers know. The readers of *Field & Stream* are a special breed . . . eight million sportsmen (and 1,600,000 women) with big appetites for living and spending.

The sensational thing about *True Story* isn't our stories, it's our unduplicated audience of six million readers who represent real buying power in this country: they're the wives of the "blue collar workers" or "wage earners."

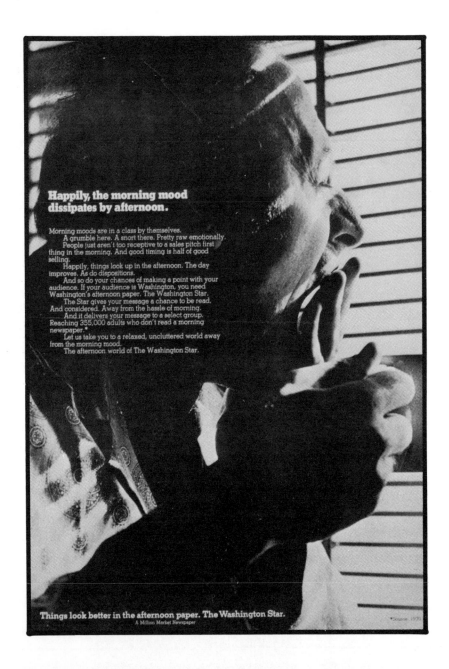

The advertising vitality of *The New Yorker* also continued to be recognized. For, once again, *The New Yorker* carried more pages of advertising than any other consumer magazine. More travel pages, more liquor pages, more retail pages, which reached a uniquely responsive audience. An audience which continues to grow more affluent (their medium income last year was $20,370). And an audience with growing spending requirements.

Tuesday is the only newspaper magazine published for Blacks, by Blacks. *Tuesday's* audience spends 3.2 billion dollars a year for food . . . 250 million for travel . . . 11 million for brandy . . . 103 million for hosiery . . . 75 million for cosmetics . . . and staggering amounts in every product category you can name.

Judging from these statements, the most interesting fact about each magazine's readers is . . . what? The amount of money he has to spend. However, this view of the magazine reader is not the only one. The *editorial* staff of each magazine is undoubtedly concerned only with writing what they think the readers will like and probably couldn't care less about the business side of the magazine. But it is a fact that the advertising revenue is what provides the profits. Many magazine owners are interested in not only what their readers want to *read,* but how they spend their money.

Although some magazines represent sincere efforts to inform, to enlighten, or to inspire, there are some who seem to be calculated business efforts through and through. In these magazines, readers are analyzed, articles and stories are written to suit them, and advertising profits are raked in.

In the magazine *Advertising Age,* in which many magazines advertise, hoping to catch the eye of media buyers at advertising agencies, there appeared this ad for *True Story* magazine:

[The headline contained a sensational sex-related statement.]

I'm Jack Podell, Vice President of Editorial for Macfadden-Bartell, and you've just experienced one of the things that has built *True Story* into a success over the years.

A sensational headline that gets you into a simple story. And the point I'd like to make is that behind the sensational headlines at *True Story* is a serious staff. Some of the most professional and top notch people in the magazine business.

Every flashy headline, every moralistic story, every comma, doesn't just happen, it's planned. Planned to attract a very specific audience of women: the backbone of American consumers, the wife of the "wage earner" or the "blue collar worker." Over the past few years, we've spent nearly one million dollars researching this woman, her emotions, her attitudes, her likes and dislikes . . .

Yet every month six million readers keep coming back to *True Story* to learn about life through the experiences of others . . .

So you could say, while it's sort of a soap opera to our readers, *True Story* is a marketing tool to our advertisers . . .

Our stories are moralistic, where the good girl wins and the bad girl loses. In fact, most of our readers rely on these stories to help them work out their lives . . . We know how to select the right kind of stories for our kind of woman. In fact, if she reads at all, about the only thing she reads is *True Story*.

The people at *True Story* admit:

1. They know (by a million dollars' worth of research) how to select the right kind of story for their readers.
2. They plan the stories to attract the kind of "spender" they want.
3. Their readers rely on these stories (which is the only reading they ever do) to help them work out their lives.

4. The editorial staff recognize the stories as "soap operas" and "fantasies" presenting life in unrealistic terms.

It is not difficult to see that *True Story* (if one believes its ads) takes a completely calculating view of its readers, even to admitting "putting them on" in order to get them to read the magazine. It has even admitted to writing (by formula) unrealistic stories it *knows* its readers go by to work out problems in their own *very real* lives. It has subjugated any claim to responsibility for truth to a completely mercenary attitude.

Fortunately, not all magazines take this attitude, but it is a reminder that magazines, and other mass communications media, are primarily profit-making organizations.

So much for magazines; their attempts to analyze their readership; and their competition, sometimes fierce, for the consumer's coin and the advertiser's dollar.

Since the air waves are public, radio and television broadcasters cannot charge you for listening to or watching a program. However, to support their operation they may sell time (under regulation by the Federal Communications Commission) to advertisers. Thus, an advertiser may purchase time (the cost varies according to the popularity of the program) on a show he thinks his potential customers watch or listen to.

A radio station may charge advertisers for time in direct proportion to the size of its audience—the more listeners it can guarantee, the more it may charge for time (and the more big accounts it can attract). Therefore, it dreads "tuneout." It strives to keep its listeners *tuned in—* by providing the kind of programming format the listener likes. In order to lessen the amount of guesswork, it analyzes the listener audience. In the case of radio, the station's audience is a specialized one. There may be a station that creates its programming for the adult: news, sports, popular music of times past. Another station, perhaps right next to the adult station on the radio band, will be programmed for the teenagers.

Since radio is more popular with young people than with any other segment of the population, there are many more stations with youth-oriented programming designed to keep them *tuned in*. Stations compete for their attention. One of the most successful radio programming formulas was created by Bill Drake—the Top 40 Formula, for which Drake is paid as much as $100,000 by a station wishing to adopt it. This formula consists of a *very* short station jingle (always a variation

Flip Wilson as Geraldine, NBC

of the simple and easily identifiable F-C-G-F-high C motif), such as "The Big Six-Ten, Goldennn"; a time-of-day signal which follows every record; *limited* talk by the disc jockey; and a "tight playlist" (the Top 40 tunes, determined by record store sales, plus a limited number of "hitbounds," not on the sales charts yet).

The formula is simple enough to follow and many stations use it, with varying degrees of success. The main service that Drake provides for the stations that hire him is that he (or one of his assistants) listens to the stations, making sure that the formula is being followed. When he senses a breakdown—the deejay might talk too much or not inject the right kind of "warmth" in the few words he's allowed to say—Drake gets on the "red phone" and smooths out the working of the machinery he has set up. Whereas this formula can insure a tuned-in listening audience for the advertiser, it doesn't allow much room for experimentation in music or announcing.

Dig:

Monitor a Top 40 station for one complete hour.

You might get organized with a group of your friends and do this exercise in such a way that one station gets monitored for an entire day.

Television stations, whose programming appeals to a broader audience than do radio stations, compete with one another for the viewer's attention. In other words, one TV channel is not teen-directed and another middle-aged-directed. All TV stations in one area will be after the same audience at once—although the audience composition changes throughout the day or week: children on Saturday morning, housewives during the day, the large general audience during "prime time" (three of the evening hours between 7 and 11 p.m.). Therefore, an advertiser will want to purchase time or sponsor a show that is watched by more people than the shows on other channels at the same time.

In order to find out how many people *are* watching which shows, the television station owners and ad agencies subscribe to an audience rating system such as the Nielsen Rating service.* This service monitors

---

*An electronic device known as an audimeter films the impulses which indicate which channel is being tuned in and at what times. The family mails the film to the company each week. To get demographic breakdowns (more details *about* the television viewers), Nielsen also arranges for 2200 families to keep a weekly diary (550 families fill one out one week in four) of their television viewing.

approximately 1200 homes, which are supposed to be representative of the entire nation. According to what these families watch, a weekly rating is given each show. These ratings are closely watched by everyone in the business. When a show goes below a 30 share (30% of the viewers) Nielsen rating, it means its death. Even though millions of people may be watching it, more people are watching something else; so the network decides to drop it and find some other show that will draw the viewing audience away from the other channels' shows. Shows which vie for the *large, general* audience are of interest to the advertisers of mass products (those used by most people) such as toothpaste, deodorants, foods, soaps.

However, manufacturers of specialized products like Clearasil, a skin cleanser made to clear up acne, are interested in a specialized audience —teenagers. They want to have their commercial on a show teenagers watch. The advertisers of a specialized product aren't as interested in how many people are watching as in *who* is watching. And so, the Nielsen demographic breakdowns again take on importance, giving the advertiser such facts as: Is this show popular with males? Or females? What age are they? What is their educational level? How much money do they have to spend? What are their interests? What mood are they in at this time of day? (Stomach upset remedies are peddled in the indigestive hours after dinner; the headache remedies at the end of the long hard day.)

Therefore, a popular show may be dropped because it doesn't have the most desirable kind of audience . . . that is, people who will buy the advertiser's product. For example, a show which is liked by the 12-year-olds and the over-50s is considered a "loser" (even though it may have a high Nielsen rating) to the networks and the sponsors.

Dig:

Although consumer groups are usually broken down into potential buying markets in smaller parts than this, consider the general buying markets to be the following:

1—Children (under 12)
2—Teenagers (13-18)
3—Young Adult-Women (18-25)
4—Young Adult-Male (18-25)
5—Women (25-49)

6—Men (25-49)
7—Older Women (50-)
8—Older Men (50-)
9—Mass Audience, cross section of all markets

Suppose you were the media buyer of an advertising agency and you had to find the television show best for advertising each of certain products. First, decide the market (the people who would buy the product) and then the show that delivers the market (the favorite with this group of people).

Dig:

Watch a week's worth of TV shows and jot down the products advertised during each one. What do the commercials tell you about the people who watch the shows (that is, in which of the buying markets listed above do they belong)?

CREATE:

Write a parody of a confessions story. Remember to create an enticing headline, one that promises the reader a "spicy" story.

Here is a sample. This "confessions" story was written following the very strict formula of a confession; that is, the heroine gets into a predicament (usually an immoral one) because of her own wrong decision. Halfway through the story comes the decision-making event, when she has a chance to avoid the predicament by making the right decision. At the end of the story, she realizes her mistake and "repents." The strict formula of the confession story is the reason "insiders" have a nickname for this type of story—"sin, suffer, and repent."

Within the story you will read "plot outlines" that the heroine supposedly read in magazines. Those are actual summaries of stories which appeared in recent magazines. The story "Should I Let My Baby Burn?" is made up, but the other ones the heroine writes are actual stories. Also all the directions that the heroine reads in the *Writer's Handbook* are repeated verbatim as they appear in that book.

Sara reads over the first words of her confession story.

SIN! SUFFER! REPENT!
OR
TIRED OF BEING REJECTED

I COMPROMISED MYSELF! At First It Was the Money . . . Then She Found She COULDN'T QUIT!!

I tore open the envelope eagerly.

"We regret to inform you . . ." I didn't have to read any more. I knew what the rest would say. I had read it often enough. ". . . we have to reject your story. We are not in the market for this type of story at the present time." Another rejection!

I felt the tears surge to my eyes and my lower lip began to quiver. I had so hoped that this story would be accepted, the one I'd poured my heart and soul into. Besides, I needed the money. I had to pay the rent and I had only a few cans of chicken soup left in the cupboard.

Just then the phone rang. I answered it and heard the comforting yet patrician voice of my mother:

"Hello, darling. How are you?"

"Oh, Mother," I sobbed, "I've been rejected again! The *Ladies' Home Journal* sent back my story, and it was the best one and . . ."

I sobbed into the telephone. There was silence at the other end and then my mother's quiet voice:

"Do you want to come home, dear? You know that Dad and I . . ."

"Yes, yes, I know," I interrupted, "you would like me to be home. But when I left Hillsboroughsville after graduating magna cum laude from Smith, I said that I wouldn't come back until I'd sold a story!" My sobs subsided as I felt my determination take over. "I had to leave that solid old New England town where our family has lived for hundreds of years in the same old mansion to see if I could make my own way in New York. Don't you see, Mother?"

Again a few moments of silence. And then:

"Yes, I see. There was a time when I was your age that I . . . but then I met your father and . . . But Sara, surely you could sell a story.

After all, the *Ladies' Home Journal* is not the only magazine . . ."

I could still remember Professor Twead in Advanced Short Story discussing the Slicks and the Pulps and the reverent tone he used to speak of the Slicks, and the utter disgust with which he spoke of the Pulps. Ugh! Just the mere thought of *those* magazines made me shudder.

"But Mother, it's one of the best Slicks, and I have to write for the Slicks. Besides, my story has been rejected by all the *good* magazines, *Redbook, Mademoiselle, Seventeen* . . ." My words choked in my throat and I felt the tears come into my eyes again.

"Have you tried *Vogue*, dear?" my mother asked softly.

"Yes," I cried, "and *Harper's Bazaar, Woman's Day* and . . . even *Family Circle*! They've all rejected me!" I broke into uncontrollable sob-

bing again.

"Well, dear, surely there must be *some* magazine . . ."

Later, after my mother had hung up and I had calmed down, I remembered her soft words, "there must be *some* magazine." I picked up my *Writer's Handbook* and looked through the list. No, there wasn't *one* that I hadn't tried, except for *Boy's Life* and *True*. Perhaps I could rewrite it using a male point of view, I mused. No, I quickly dismissed the thought. Mine was a sensitive love story and could never fit into these magazines. And then I saw the section, "How To Sell a Confession." Automatically I averted my eyes, a little shiver of revulsion running through me. I forced myself to look. One paragraph riveted my attention:

If . . . you can dream up a confused teen-age heroine torn by an emotional problem, have her solve it the wrong way, thereby bringing about some kind of tragedy, go through emotional hell, and see at least a faint light of hope for the future—I can practically guarantee you a letter beginning 'I am happy to inform you . . .' and a beautiful, beautiful check enclosed therein.

"I am happy to inform you," "a beautiful, beautiful check," the words whirled through my brain, sending little shivers of joy through my body. Then I thought of Professor Twead. What would he think of Sara Lawrence, his most promising Creative Writing major, writing a confession? What did he say to her when she said good-bye to him before leaving for New York to start her exciting new life as a writer? "Never prostitute yourself, Sara." His earnest blue eyes had a touch of sadness. He probably was remembering his own lost promise.

A knock on the door interrupted my thoughts. I opened it to see my landlady, a fat woman dressed in a flowered dress, her pasty face wearing its usual defensive expression:

"I came for the rent. I got my bills to pay, too, you know," she whined.

"I can't pay you right now. I . . . I . . . If you could just wait . . ." I stammered. I felt so ashamed I could just die.

"I'll wait two more weeks, and if you don't pay me then, you'll have to move!" She stormed down the hall indignantly, her whining voice trailing behind her.

Move! I felt a sense of defeat overcoming me. I had been lucky to

find this place, as far from ideal as it is. I think it must have been the last place in New York! I slumped down in my desk chair, feeling numb with hopeless defeat. My eyes fell on the open book on the desk, "a beautiful, beautiful check" caught my eye. Suddenly I sat up with quick determination. I'll do it! I'll write a confession! Just one, to pay the rent, then I'll go back to writing for the Slicks. Professor Twead will forgive me just *one*!

Once I'd decided, I pored through the article eagerly. Let's see now, "a teen-age heroine," that's easy. I was a teen-ager only a few years ago. "Torn by an emotional problem." "Have her solve it the wrong way." I wonder why she has to solve it the *wrong* way. I read further into the article.

In the slicks, the heroine always makes the RIGHT decision, but in a confession, she must make the wrong decision. Tragedy follows, then she bumbles her way back through more complications to a logical conclusion with a glimmer of hope at the end.

I didn't understand why she's right in the slicks and wrong in the pulps, but oh, well, if that's the way they want it. I read on.

Emotion in a slick goes deep but it's kept beneath the surface. In a confession it must be kept visible. The reader lacks the refinements of education, which teaches us to look for subtleties . . .

I felt confused but fascinated. This went against everything I had ever been taught. How many times had

Professor Twead said, "Show, don't tell!" Could I ever write this way, even if I wanted to, I wondered.

At first, you may feel very silly when you try to write in this highly emotional style. You'll feel that if anyone should happen to read what you are writing, you'd blush and shrivel with shame. After a while, however, you'll realize that being allowed to write this way is fun. You can be as primitive as you like, say the things you don't dare say aloud in real life . . . Really, confession story writing is a wonderful way to express, via the typewriter, all those instinctive emotions that civilization forces you to control.

Why maybe it'll be easier than I thought. I felt a feeling of confidence swelling within me. How hard I'd tried to *show* how my heroine felt in my *Ladies' Home Journal* story; if I could come right out and *say* it . . . I went back to reading the instructions with a new eagerness.

By the time I'd finished the article, I pretty much knew how to write a confession story. I had to write it as though it was happening to *me* because most of the women who read these stories believe that they are actually true confessions. I had to make myself attractive and strong because, as the article says, "the spineless, jelly-fish, dish-rag" reader doesn't want to read about another woman like *her*; she wants to read about a person she wishes she *were*. I had to come from a lower class background. The only "white collar" characters *allowed* are teachers and doctors. I had to write of the big

purgative emotions that the reader is deprived of and guards against . . . love, anger, and sorrow. As the article said,

Pile the agony high. The more acute the suffering, the more total the degradation of the narrator, the more warmly the readers receive the story . . . If you make the reader cry, you've written a good story. If you make her sob, it's a great story!

I felt challenged. Maybe I could even write a *great* confession! Stop it, you're getting carried away, I admonished myself. You were just going to write *one*, for the rent, remember? You wouldn't want to— I shuddered at the mere thought— *prostitute* yourself, would you? I shook all thoughts of writing a great confession aside and decided that I would go out and buy all the confession magazines I could. I had to read them first before I could write one myself. I hesitated. Maybe I should give up and go back home . . . *NO!* I can't give up! I won't! I went to the cupboard . . . two cans of chicken soup, a half-filled box of Uncle Ben's converted rice, a full bag of baking potatoes. I had some butter and milk in the refrigerator and some lettuce. I'll do it. I can live on this until I finish the story. And then I'll . . . I didn't know what I'd do then. But I won't worry about that *now*. I took my purse and went down to the drugstore at the corner.

At the magazine rack, I was surprised that there were so many "confession" magazines. But then I remembered what the article had said about there being eight million readers. I tried to remember the names of the important ones. I had to spend my last two dollars wisely . . .

"You must be looking for the latest *Vogue,* 'cause you sure don't look like a *Cosmopolitan* Girl!" a teasing voice behind me was saying. I turned around and there was the owner of the voice thumbing through a copy of *Playboy.* He was grinning at me over the foldout, his blue eyes twinkling. He was about the best-looking guy I had ever seen. I could feel the flush come to my cheeks, and the little thrill of excitement I always feel around an attractive man.

"No, actually I'm looking for *True Confessions,*" I blurted out. To cover my embarrassment, I reached down and grabbed a copy of *True Confessions* and three of the other magazines next to it.

"You must like that stuff!" he said in a surprised tone.

Without answering I walked to the counter and paid for the magazines. Was it my imagination, or was the clerk looking at me in a strange way? Embarrassed, I hurried to get out of there as fast as I could. Crash! I bumped right into *him* as he turned into the aisle on his way to pay for his *Playboy.* His strong arms steadied me, his blue eyes, twinkling again, looking straight into mine. I felt the same thrill of excitement, only this time it was greater than any I had ever felt before. He was so attractive!

"My m . . . magazines," I stuttered. They had fallen to the floor.

He picked them up and handed them to me, smiling. "So you like confession stories, do you?" And he walked toward the counter.

Clutching my magazines, I hurried back to my little apartment. I wished I could have explained! If only I could have told him that I was a *writer,* not a *reader* of confessions! Once in the apartment, I soon forgot all about the man with the *Playboy.* Over my bowl of chicken soup, I read my first confession story.

It was the cover story, "My Fiance's Warning: 'Give Up That Black Baby or Me!'" There was a picture of a pretty blonde holding a smiling black baby. The story involved me completely. It was about a nurse whose parents had died and who was very lonely. She decided to adopt a baby. When adoption workers told her they had a baby girl who had had a black father, she didn't care; she'd take her. She had problems right away because her housekeeper who was really great and who loved babies left as soon as she saw the baby was black, leaving a nasty note, accusing the girl of having had the baby herself. The girl had a pretty bad time then because the housekeeper spread this rumor all over town and people wouldn't have anything to do with her, and she couldn't even work because she didn't have a babysitter. Finally she got one, an 18-year-old girl from the orphanage, who turned out to be wonderful.

Then everything was great for a while. She and the town's new druggist fell in love, but he told her that she'd have to give up the baby before he married her. She was torn between her love for him and for the baby, but she couldn't give up the baby. One night the baby became very ill and started to strangle. Since the doctor she worked for was out of town, she called the druggist. He hurried out, saved the baby, and asked the heroine to marry him. He said she could even keep the 18-year-old babysitter too. Although I thought the druggist had changed his mind pretty abruptly, it was a very heart-warming story. I could see what the article meant about pouring on the emotion.

Then I read another story advertised on the cover, "Surprise Party, All My Old Lovers Were Guests." It was about a girl who believed that, when you loved a man, you shouldn't withhold sex, that you shouldn't hold back, as she put it. Her roommate believed that sex belongs to marriage. It turned out that Karen, the heroine, fell in love pretty easily so she was sleeping with one guy after another, while the roommate was having problems with her boyfriend because of her views. Finally Karen found a guy whom she fell in love with and had an affair with, only this time it didn't go "sour" and they got engaged. Meanwhile, Julie's boyfriend broke up with her because she wanted to save sex until marriage.

One day when Karen got home, she got a big surprise. Julie had arranged an engagement party, only she had invited all of Karen's ex-lovers! Karen had a few moments of panic, but it all turned out okay. The old lovers toasted her as a wonderful girl, and Julie's plan to cause her trouble didn't work out at all. It ended with Julie's begging Karen's forgiveness. Karen did forgive her, because she felt so sorry for her, before she left to meet her husband-to-be.

This story certainly had a twist, I thought. It made it seem that having sex before marriage was good and withholding it was bad. All the stories I'd ever read held the opposite view.

I had some more chicken soup and then went on to "The Girl in My Husband's Wallet: Police Say She Was Raped." After that story I was exhausted and fell asleep right on the couch, my *True Story* clutched in my hands. The next morning after a hearty breakfast of buttered rice, I started *Modern Romances.* That evening, while dining on mashed potatoes, I finished the last story in *Love Stories.* (I had finished *True Confessions* at lunch.) My mind was whirling. I was emotionally washed out. I had suffered through prostitution and rape, adultery and incest, endangered lives and marriages; I had enjoyed countless instances of ecstatic love and noble sacrifices. What a day!

I fixed myself some instant coffee, noticing that the jar was almost empty. I must ration myself, I thought. I sat on the couch. Should I go on with my plan to write one of these stories? I thought about all the unhappy women who believed in these stories, who modeled their lives after these phony heroines. Could I contribute to such hypocrisy? But what if I don't? I'll have to go back home to my parents, to admit that I'm a failure.

Just then the phone rang.

"Hello, Sara, how's my favorite writer?" I recognized the familiar baritone voice of Professor Twead.

"Professor Twead, how are you? *Where* are you? How are things at Smith?" The questions poured out. I was so happy to hear his reassuring voice.

"Hold on, there, Sara." He laughed.

"All's well. What I called about is this: You remember my assistant, John Pope? Well, he's quit. Says he's going to write the Great American Novel. So I thought of you. How would you like to come and work with me in the Creative Writing department at Smith?"

Work at Smith, with Professor Twead? *I couldn't think,* it had all hit me too quickly. I'd never even considered such a possibility.

"But, Professor Twead, my writing career. I'd have to give it up. I don't know. I . . ." I cried.

"I know, Sara, you'll have to decide one way or the other. You can't have both. And unfortunately, I have to know right now." His voice was urgent yet understanding.

Decide right *now?* It was a wonderful offer, but it *did* mean admitting that I had failed in my goal—to get a story published in a magazine.

"Professor, it's a wonderful offer, and there's nothing I'd like more than to work with you. You know how I've always admired you, but . . ." I felt myself deciding, feeling *sure,* "I can't, I can't give up. I promised myself that I'd stick it out, even . . . even if it meant *prostituting* myself!"

"Sara, Sara, what do you mean?" Professor Twead asked anxiously.

"It means that I'm going to write a confession story!" As I said it, I felt all the confusion slip away and, taking its place, a new feeling of determination. I pushed away all my doubts, all my hesitation. I *couldn't* go home now, even to accept Professor Twead's wonderful offer.

"A confession? But, Sara, you were my best student in Advanced Short Story. You were meant for the slicks!"

"The slicks rejected me, Professor. And rather than admit I'm a failure, I'll write a confession. I thank you very much, Professor, for the most wonderful offer of my life, but I've made up my mind!"

Professor Twead was shocked, I know, but I think he admired my determination. When he hung up, he assured me that whenever I decided to come home, he would do all that he could to find me a job.

Now that I'd decided, I couldn't wait to get started. I decided to go to bed early. The next morning I awoke refreshed, except I had had the strangest dream. I had dreamed that I had decided to have an affair with Professor Twead in order to save him from raping one of his students after he explained to me that, since his wife had been in a coma for eleven years, he could no longer control himself.

After my breakfast of rice pudding, I started to work. I remembered the advice of the *Writer's Handbook* article, "You've got to put yourself in the lower class mind," "Get your hooks into the reader with the first sentence," "Pile on the agony," "No love—no sale," "SIN, SUFFER, REPENT," "No more than one scream per scene," and sat down to think up a plot.

Through reading, I discovered that there were two kinds of confession stories, the suffering ones and the sexy ones, the ones that made you cry and the ones that made you, well, they *did* appeal to a woman's basic fantasies. Even *I* had often wondered what it would be like to be undressed, to be overcome. I shivered at the thought. What if I wrote a story that combined the two—sin and suffering?

I thought the rest of the morning, abandoning idea after idea until I finally came up with it—I knew it was good the moment that it took shape in my mind. The *great* confession story! If only I could do it! I'd show them, my parents, Professor Twead, and all my friends who had just smiled with amused tolerance when I told them of my ambitions.

I worked out the plot—about a teenaged girl, the mother of a baby, whose husband had been killed in the war, and who is managing the apartment building she'd inherited from her parents who had been killed in an automobile accident. (I decided to use the building I was living in, since I had spent my life in upperclass surroundings.)

My heroine is having an affair with Rick, a tenant in the building, out of loneliness. She feels she is unable to love any other man than her husband. Another man moves into the apartment building, Ron, a widower who feels he can never love another woman. Ron can't afford to keep his two children with him, so they are living with his sister, and he's sad about this. Rick wants my heroine, Debbie, to marry him, but she refuses. Angry at being rejected, he threatens to expose her faulty wiring to the housing inspection authority, for whom he works. She would lose the apartment building. She has no other way to support the baby and she can't afford to pay an electrician. She goes to Ron, who's an electrician, to ask for his help. She says she can't pay him and out of desperation offers to sleep with him as payment. He says he'll fix the wiring but refuses her offer gently.

While they are talking, Rick enters, and in a jealous rage, knocks Ron out and starts to rape Debbie. At this moment a fire breaks out in the apartment building; the baby, who's asleep upstairs, is in danger. Ron regains consciousness; he and Rick run to put out the fire, while Debbie rushes through the flames to save her baby. At the end, the fire is put out; the baby is saved. Rick apologizes and decides to move out. Ron, realizing what a wonderful mother she is, asks Debbie to marry him. Debbie, admiring Ron's nobility, accepts. The story ends with Debbie pointing out that Rick's room would be perfect for his two children.

I sat down at my typewriter and wrote:

"Yes, Rick, you can come over tonight," she sighed. As soon as she hung up the phone, she glanced first at Davey Junior, playing happily in his playpen and then at the picture of Dave in his uniform. Forgive me, Dave, she thought. It's just that I'm so lonely. I don't love him; I could never love any man again. I loved you, and after you were killed in Vietnam, I knew it was all over for me. I would never love any man again. I would just take care of little Davey, take care of the apartments, and cherish your memory.

Then when Rick asked me out for a beer, how excited I'd been at the thought of going out with a man again . . . And then, when he kissed me the first time, I was surprised at how I reacted, how I returned his kisses . . .

I stopped writing. Had I "sunk the hooks into the reader," as the article suggested? I was surprised at how easily the words flowed out. Maybe it would be fun. I'm just doing it for the money, but I might as well enjoy it while I'm at it.

After describing Debbie and the baby and how much Debbie had loved her dead husband Dave, I had Rick arrive. This was it; I had to do a sex scene. In all the other stories I had written, the sex scenes were very beautiful—so subtly stated; but the article said "make the emotions *visible . . .*"

I tried to keep Rick away from me. I didn't really want to go to bed with him. I never wanted to, but I always did. I couldn't help myself. As soon as he touched me, all my good intentions just melted away.

I was doing the dishes, after having put little Davey to bed. Rick was watching TV. Then he came up behind me and put his muscular arms around my waist. I felt the familiar sensations course through my tingling body.

"No, Rick, not tonight," I murmured. But my body was saying, Yes, yes, yes!

He turned me around with savage urgency and pressed his warm lips on mine. Electric sparks seemed to run through every bit of me. Little earthquakes shook my stomach. We seemed to enter together into a surging whirlpool.

I was typing furiously, my breath coming in rapid spurts, my heart pounding in my breast.

I wrote all day, not even stopping to eat. I ended the story as I had planned, the attempted rape, the baby's rescue, the declaration of love.

As I typed, "The End," I noticed that there were tears streaming down my cheeks. Emotionally and physically exhausted, I fell into bed, without even bothering to undress.

I slept soundly, and the next morning I awoke feeling strangely satisfied. Then I remembered . . . the story. I read it over and as I finished, I noticed the same thing had happened again. I was crying. It must be a *good* story, I thought. I spent the day correcting errors and retyping the manuscript. That afternoon I took it over to a confession magazine publisher's office. I didn't even have the money for postage. I left my phone number with the secretary, imploring her to see if my story couldn't be read as soon as possible.

Back home in the apartment, I felt restless. I had ten more days until I had to pay the rent; I had a little food left. I could get back to my serious writing while I waited to hear about my confession. I had a couple of stories plotted out and one that I had already started.

I went to my desk and picked up the story that I had started the day before "Should I Let My Baby Burn?" I had entitled it "Flight of Fantasy"; it was about a teenaged girl who one day met a boy from a motorcycle gang and felt an attraction toward him, although she was of a different "class." She wondered what it would be like to be his girl, then when she saw her own boyfriend that evening, she forgot all about the motorcyclist. It was a *sensitive* story. Reading what I had written, I was disappointed. It was so . . . well, so *dull!* I must have been low that day.

I put paper in the typewriter and began to write. I began to describe the scene where my heroine meets the motorcyclist. It was supposed to be very subtle, very sensitive. I wrote:

There was something different about him.

And then I stopped. I didn't know what to write next. I got up and paced the floor. I had some rice pudding. I had to keep on.

She noticed him right away.

I paced again. I ate again. I felt so nervous, so *strange!* What was *wrong* with me? I sat at the typewriter again:

He had a certain quality.

Then all of a sudden I felt my fingers start to fly. The words just poured out of me. It was as though another force had taken over my body, a force over which I had no control! I just watched the words taking shape on the paper:

I couldn't take my eyes off the guy. He was young, ever so young. His blue eyes were clear, and I could see a bright fire burning, 'way back inside them. His hair glistened in the afternoon sun; and, inside his open shirt, a virile, vibrant body told me that, although young, this guy was all man. He was a bright young stallion who had suddenly galloped into my life.

I wrote feverishly. As I typed, the story took a different turn. Instead of just wondering about the boy, the girl started meeting him at night in the woods. He was a decent guy, who didn't really belong to the rest of the gang, she found out. One day her boyfriend and some of his friends got the motorcycle kid and beat him up trying to force him to tell them where the gang was. He wouldn't tell. The

girl told to save him from more torture. The boyfriend set the place on fire, trying to burn up the gang. Helpless to save the gang, the motorcyclist and the girl made love:

Distraught and filled with guilt, yet unable to release his pent-up feelings, Danny sought consolation and fulfillment from me; and I went up to him willingly, for I knew I loved him enough to do whatever must be done to save him from that fire. As the flames raged below, hot torrents of tenderness swept over us, there on the mountain.

The gang was saved but accused Danny of ratting on them. As they started to drive off without him, he started to cry. The leader of the gang relented, he, too, crying a bit. The girl was glad that the gang took Danny back; she realized that he was a wild stallion, that he had to go.

I ended the story with the girl trying to forget Danny, trying to start anew and to build a fresh future. She can't really forget Danny, though:

But then come the quiet, warm nights, when my windows are open and the sounds of the world drift in to my ears. Then do I wait, then do I breathe softly and strain to hear a sound. It didn't come last month, last week, or last night. But still I wait. And in the still, lonely darkness, my heart cries out, 'Dear God, guide Danny down the long highway. Keep him safe, wherever he is tonight. And please, oh please, let me see him—just once more!'

I typed "The End" and typed in the new title, "Wild Wheels of Love." I was finished! I was emotionally wrung out, but calm. I fell into bed and slept soundly. The next morning I felt wonderful. Then I remembered the story. As I read it over, I felt myself flush with embarrassment. Had *I* written this? It was . . . yes, it was a confession! I had started to write a slick and I had written another confession! What had come over me? Well, I wouldn't let it happen again! I put "Wild Wheels of Love" away and started on one of my serious stories. It was to be about a girl who one summer had baby-sat for a young couple and who had developed a crush on the husband. (I based all my stories on my own experiences.) Nothing much would happen, it would be mostly describing how she *felt*. I was going to send it to *Seventeen*. I was going to call it, "The Summer I Babysat for the Thompsons."

I started to write. Then it . . . it happened again! I couldn't stop myself and I saw the words forming on the paper, words I hadn't intended to write:

And thus the summer ended, the summer of my madness, the summer that had burst upon our town, hot and smoldering. A summer that brought out the longings I used to keep buried inside me, only letting them escape at night in bed when I'd wake from dreams, dreams about love and being with men, men who would send shivers through me with their very glances. And then one torrid afternoon I met Rick Thompson . . .

I wrote about Mr. Thompson (that's what I always called him) walking into the house just after the girl had stepped out of the shower and was admiring her naked body in front of the mirror. (That wasn't how it had *really* happened at all!) I wrote about the affair that developed between the husband and the girl. While the wife went to the doctor, the girl baby-sat. And Rick . . . Mr. Thompson, I mean . . . would come home from the office. Finally, the wife got better and Mr. T. stopped trying to see the girl. The girl threatened to tell the wife and Mr. T. told her off, telling her he had just used her because his wife, whom he really loved, was sick. She saw Mr. T. for what he really was and stopped loving him. Her family left the resort the next day and I ended the story like this:

. . . as the car sped through the woods, I saw the leaves begin to fall, each one a brilliant tear, dropping from the trees above. I sat dry-eyed, looking at them, knowing I would not cry. But I always would remember this summer, this sultry summer I ceased to be a spoiled, unthinking, selfish child; this summer that had seen me become a woman.

The End

I crossed out my original title and changed it to "Thrilled by His Touch and Too Young to Know." My head dropped forward and I fell into a deep, satisfied sleep.

The next morning the same thing happened. I read over the story and felt the hot flames of embarrassment rush to my cheeks. These sex scenes! How could I have written such things?

For a week, the same thing happened every day. I would start to write a story, a story for the slicks, when it would change under my fingers and turn into a confession! Each morning when I read the story, I felt a deep shame that became worse as each terrible day dawned.

One day I was in the middle of a story about a woman who was a wonderful housewife and mother but who would have these black-out periods when she became a prostitute when I heard someone knocking at the door. I opened it to see Mrs. O'Farrell, the landlady, looking at me with open suspicion.

"What's going on in here, anyhow?" she cried, her narrowed eyes searching the room. "You got a man in here or something? You haven't been out of this room for days!"

"Why, no, Mrs. O'Farrell, there's no one here. I've just been . . . writing," I explained. *Why did I feel so guilty?*

"Writing, huh? Well, how come you look so . . . are you *sure* there's no man in here?"

"Come in and look for yourself," I said hotly, and stood aside for her to come in.

She came in and looked around, her eyes taking in the typewriter and the papers piled up on my desk. Then she saw the magazines. She rushed over and grabbed one of them.

"What *is* it, Mrs. O'Farrell?" I was startled.

"Oh, *True Confessions!* I *love* this magazine! I couldn't *live* without it!" she cried, hugging the magazine to her massive bosom. "Are you . . . are you writing your *confession*?"

My confession. What did she mean?

"Well, I'm writing a story about a woman who was a housewife by night and a prostitute by day. You see, she had these blackouts and . . ."

Mrs. O'Farrell's eyes widened and she licked her lips. She sat down in the chair.

"Sit down, dearie, and tell me all about it. Where's your husband now?"

"But you don't understand," I protested, sinking weakly onto the couch. "The story isn't about me!"

"Don't be embarrassed, honey," she patted my hand. "Your secret's safe with me. What'd your husband do when he found out?"

"Well, *the* husband sends the wife to a psychiatrist and he finds out that she had a deep-seated hatred for men and well, she got over her . . . uh, her sickness," I explained warily.

"How come you got the hate for men . . . were you ever . . . *raped*?" she leaned forward, her eager eyes riveted on mine.

"Well, I . . . I mean, *she* wasn't actually raped. Her stepfather had tried to rape her and she'd suppressed the memory of it and . . ."

"Oh, you poor kid!" Mrs. O'Farrell patted my hand again. "Men . . . they're all alike! Did your husband stick with you? Where's he now?"

"I have no husband, Mrs. O'Farrell," I said firmly. I had to make her believe that I was only writing a *story*.

"So . . . he never forgave you, huh," she said understandingly. "Like I said, men . . . they're all alike!"

"But, Mrs. O'Farrell," I protested, "it's just a *story*! I'm making it all up!"

"Sure, sure, kid, I know! That's why they don't put no names in the magazines. They don't wanna embarrass you . . . I don't blame you, honey. After all, it's nobody's business . . . you did get cured and all. Too bad about your husband, though . . . He musta been a bum, huh?"

"Mrs. O'Farrell, really, I . . ."

"Okay, honey, I'm going . . . you finish your confession. It'll make you feel better," she patted my hand again and rose to leave.

"Wait, Mrs. O'Farrell, you must understand . . ."

"Don't worry, I won't tell a soul," she said as she opened the door, "and, listen, don't worry about the rent, honey. A few more weeks'll be okay. Go finish now, get it off your chest."

She'd left. I sat, stunned. She really thought I was writing a *true* confession! How *ridiculous!* But *was* it? The thoughts whirled through my brain. Mrs. O'Farrell's believing that "Heaven and Hell" (that's what I had called the story) was about me, all the stories I'd written, the way I couldn't seem to *help* myself, like I was . . . then it struck me! That's what had happened! I was *hooked!* I was addicted to writing confessions! That explained everything, the way I tried to stop, the way I seemed to get in deeper and deeper, the way I felt ashamed and embarrassed each morning when I read the story I had written while I had been under the power of this drug . . . yes, it was like a drug, this thing that had taken hold of me.

And look at me—I looked down at my sweat shirt and jeans. They were *filthy!* Spots of chicken soup and mashed potatoes had stained my shirt; my jeans were spotted where I had wiped my hands on them. I had been wearing them all week, even sleeping in them, in my drugged frenzy. I went into the bathroom and looked at the mirror. My hair was matted and dirty-looking; my face haggard and drawn. What had become of Sara Lawrence, the most promising short story writer of the Smith graduating class? I thought of Professor Twead, *what would he think of me now?* I remembered his words, "Never prostitute yourself, Sara." That's exactly what I *had* done, I *had* prostituted myself. But luckily, I'd caught myself in time, before sinking to further depths of degradation. Luckily, I hadn't really had a story *printed* yet. Then I re-membered! "Should I Let My Baby Burn?" was at the publisher's office right now! What if they accepted it? What if they printed it without my knowing? I knew this wasn't possible, but I had to get that story back. I had to destroy it, as I had to destroy all the stories I had written while I was under that awful spell.

I took a shower and washed my hair, feeling my old self returning slowly. After I had put on a fresh dress and makeup, I was in full control of myself. I was Sara Lawrence again, young unpublished writer of short stories for the slicks!

At the magazine office, I asked the secretary for my story back. She gave it back to me; it was on her desk right where I had left it. *To think how I had worried!* I hurried out, wanting to get as far away from that place as possible. Down in the lobby of the office building, I walked directly over to the huge trash receptacle that stood near the large glass doors. I tore up the story in little pieces and threw it in. I had brought the other stories with me, too, and the four confession magazines that I had bought, not wanting any reminder left in my apartment of my week of shame and sin. I tore up each story carefully and threw them in the can. Then I threw the magazines in fiercely, heaving a huge sigh of relief. I was *free* again!

"I thought you *liked* that stuff!" a voice behind me said in a teasing tone. I whirled around, startled that anyone had been watching me. It was *him!* The man with the *Playboy,* the man I had bumped into at the drugstore. His blue eyes twinkled down at me.

"No . . . I'm strictly a slick-magazine girl," I smiled up at him.

"Really? I happen to be a slick-magazine editor. My office is just upstairs . . . say, how about having lunch with me? There's a little Italian place I like just down the street," he took my arm, smiling down at me.

"I'd love to," I smiled back, feeling that a whole new life was about to begin.

The End

THE MASS MESSAGE

"All in the Family," CBS

A mass medium is a one-way communication system with you on the receiving end, with mighty few chances to talk back. (Do you ever call in to a radio station? correspond with a columnist? take a celebrity to lunch? bargain with a sales pitchman?)

Let's look at some instances in which you might like to respond to a mass communicator and at the ways you can do so. First of all, have you ever felt that you'd like to talk back to an ad or a commercial you thought was false or misleading or just plain stupid? Often when we feel that way, we do nothing about it because we feel powerless. So we shrug off our annoyance with a resigned sigh: "Oh, well, that's the price we have to pay for all this entertainment." If you look at television entertainment as a gift, which it might seem to be, this attitude is understandable. However, TV entertainment is not a gift. The product manufacturers help defray the cost of advertising by upping the product price. Think of the cost of breakfast cereals, for example, in terms of the common, inexpensive ingredients they contain. Most of the money you pay for cereals goes to pay for the advertising bill. And the annoying ads that interrupt your enjoyment of the Saturday morning cartoons are paying the cost of bringing you the show.

As a paying customer, you have a right to comment on what you are paying for—and furthermore, as a customer, you will be listened to. Advertisers are extremely sensitive to the opinion of the public, so a phone call or a letter can have more effect than you may realize. An instance in which an advertisement was withdrawn owing to readers' complaints is the case of a razor blade company which included a sample blade in its newspaper ad. So many mothers complained that the ad was recalled. However, it isn't always such an obviously dangerous ad campaign that may be changed by consumer response.

Have you ever felt like telling a newspaper or magazine that you didn't like its contents? Trying to change a radio or television station's programming? Telling a record or movie producer that you didn't like the way they did a certain record or movie? Simply not buying a newspaper is one way to express your dislike for it; although in many cities, that will mean doing without a paper. (A more effective answer is to write a letter to the editor.) Not buying or subscribing to a magazine is an expression of opinion that is well understood by the publisher. The same goes for a record or movie producer; when you don't plunk down your money to buy, you have expressed your disapproval with great clarity. However, this answer is only effective when it is made by the mass audience. As an individual, your bypassing a certain magazine or record or movie has little effect. You are merely exercising your freedom of choice.

With television, though, there is actually very little choice in programming. Although the networks compete for your attention, there are only three of them. You either watch a network station, one of your local ones, or tune in to a PBS channel (if there *is* one in your area). If there's nothing you want to watch, you select the *least* offensive program or turn off the set. What sort of control *do* you have over television programming? What *can* you do when the network threatens to drop your favorite show?

There have been instances when viewers have written in to protest the dropping of a favorite show and have failed to change the minds of network officials. However, in one case, fans reversed the network's decision to drop a show. Although relatively few in numbers, "Star Trek" fans proved effective when they protested the cancelling of their favorite show. They succeeded in prolonging the life of the show, but it was subsequently dropped. (Now there is a "Star Trek" fan club, which convenes to share memorabilia.)

Viewer response may be effective when it centers on the ideas, themes, or impressions evident in a show. Ethnic and special interest groups often protest the way they are portrayed on some television programs. For example, an Italian citizens' group protested that the show "The Untouchables" unjustly gave all the gangsters Italian names. "Hogan's Heroes," a long-running comedy program about GIs in a German prison camp, received criticism for its consistent portrayal of Germans as fools, easily tricked by the clever, lovable Americans. Producers are very sensitive to such criticism, mostly out of fear that it will displease the sponsors. Therefore, the producers try to stick to non-controversial subject matter.

"Rowan and Martin's Laugh-In" producers manage to get jokes on taboo subjects past network censors without too much trouble.

The Smothers Brothers show, although very popular, tried the patience of its network producers, who insisted on non-offensive entertainment fare. The Smothers brothers battled the network's attempts at censorship until their show was finally dropped. When "All in the Family" was first aired, the network anxiously awaited to see how the show would be received. Reactions were more favorable than not, so the network officials breathed a sigh of relief and continued the show. (Within a short time, it went to the top of the rating chart as America's favorite show.)

Therefore, despite the fact that the means are few, there *are* ways to answer back at the mass message. Try it. You may be surprised at how effective you can be.

"Laugh-In" hosts with Carol Channing, NBC

However, even if we did "answer back" every time we felt like it, we are still on the receiving end of a constant onslaught of mass messages. We react in ways we aren't even aware of. It is these subtle reactions that we will be talking about in the next chapters.

Chapter 4

The Daily Blat

Here's a test where you're asked to guess the answers . . . and the wilder the better:

1. How many dollars are spent on advertising in the popular arts (like radio and television) in one year?
2. How many selling messages (commercials and advertisements of any "brand-name") is the average American exposed to per day?
3. How many billboards are produced annually in the United States?
4. How much did the political candidates spend on advertising during the 1968 campaign?
5. How many radio and TV sets are there in the United States?
6. What percentage of the American population has at least one TV set?
7. How many hours a day on the average is the TV set turned on?
8. How many Americans read at least one of the daily comics?
9. How many magazines are there in the United States? Daily newspapers? Weekly? Radio stations? Commercial TV stations?
10. How many new magazines were started during the 1960s?
11. Which magazine has the largest circulation of any other?
12. How many people see any given issue of *Life* magazine?
13. How many dollars were spent on purchasing phonograph records and pre-recorded tapes in 1970?
14. How much money did the movie *Easy Rider* take in at the box office?
15. How vast is the TV audience for even the lowest-rated network program?

Answers:

1. *10 billion dollars* are spent on advertising in the popular media in one year.
2. Between the time he picks up his toothpaste tube in the morning until he sees his last commercial on the TV tube, the average American is exposed to *between 300 and 400* selling messages a day.*
3. *Three million billboards* are put up on American highways and in American cities every year.
4. *Three hundred million dollars* were spent in 1968 by political candidates on advertising, with most of the money for radio and TV.
5. There are more radio and TV sets than there are people in the United States—*about 300 million.*
6. *Ninety-five per cent* of the American population has at least one TV set.
7. On the average the TV set is on *5 hours and 45 minutes* each day.

---

*According to a recent survey, women are exposed to 305 advertising messages every day. Men are the targets a little less often. Because they have less opportunity to watch TV they are exposed to a mere 285 advertising messages per day. It breaks down into 35 TV commercials, 38 radio spots, 15 magazine ads, 185 newspaper ads, and 12 outdoor messages. The bill for all this, not counting advertising received through the mail, will be about $20 billion this year—somewhat more than is spent for all public and private education—an expenditure of about $95 for every man, woman, and child in the country.

8. *One hundred million* Americans read at least one comic strip daily.
9. There are 9,000-16,000 magazines in the United States
   - 1,700 daily newspapers
   - 7,500 weekly papers
   - 6,000 radio stations
   - 600 commercial TV stations
10. In the period between 1960 and 1970 a total of *676* new magazines were started. Of that number over 500 are still in existence. In 1968, 100 new magazines were started—all but 21 survived.
11. *Reader's Digest* is the most popular magazine in the United States, with a circulation of over 17 million.
12. *Life* magazine claims that although its circulation is 8.5 million, each issue is seen by *48 million* people, almost a quarter of the American population. (*Life* is now defunct.)
13. *Over a billion and a half* dollars were spent on phonograph records and pre-recorded tapes in 1970.
14. Although *Easy Rider* was made on a comparatively small budget, about $370,000, it will take in an estimated *50 million* dollars at the box office.
15. More people watch even the lowest-rated program than could fill a Broadway theater in 20 years (even if it played to a full house every night).

"Easy Rider," Columbia Pictures

No matter how wild your guesses, you probably underestimated these figures. No wonder. We are living in a time marked by a "communications explosion" when people have more communications media at their disposal than ever before. We are bombarded via sight and sound with colorful and often clever commands to buy everything from pimple cream to Presidents. We have at our fingertips (and this is one time when that advertising cliché is quite accurate) dials and push buttons to tune us into almost any kind of entertainment imaginable. A person can cut one record or make one film on relatively little money and stand to make millions because so many will have purchased the record (which they probably heard first on radio) or have seen the movie.

The nature of this "explosion" is probably best symbolized by the telecast of President Nixon congratulating the astronauts who had just walked on the moon. Approximately one billion people, or one-fourth of the world's population, were watching this event on television *as it happened*. They saw on their screen both President Nixon, telephone in hand, in Washington, D. C., and the spaceship on the moon, 240,000 miles from Earth. (Remember when the expression "man on the moon" stood for the impossible?)

Less than 100 years ago, an inventor, testing a device he had developed to aid the deaf, spoke to his assistant, who was in the next room. This was the first time man's voice was sent any distance. Little by little, through developments like coast-to-coast broadcasting, trans-Atlantic cables, and communications satellites, it has become possible for one person to speak to more and more people farther and farther away. Furthermore, it has become possible not only to send sound but also to send images.

Yet as miraculous as the Nixon-moon telecast seems, experts say that this is only the beginning—that we are on the brink of a communications revolution that will change our entire way of life. They see a day not too far away when everyone will have a portable picture-phone and will be able to dial any number on Earth. They believe that every home will have a communications center in which we can have anything we want in the way of entertainment or information by sight and sound—live or taped TV, stereo music, newspapers, and other printed information—simply by pressing the right button. They claim that the day might come when we won't even have to leave our homes to go to work—that all contact with the world, human and otherwise, will be made electronically.

But before we look into the future, let's look at the communications explosion as it affects us right now. What entertainment and informa-tion are we able to receive *now* in the average home? For one thing, we are making good use of Bell's invention—there is one phone for every two persons in the United States and each one of us uses it an average of over 600 times a year. Almost every home has at least one TV set and many a second one for bedroom or den. There are radios for almost every member of the family and probably one in the car. There might be a stereophonic record player and a tape recorder. There might be an intercom system for transmitting voice or music throughout the house. There is certainly a daily newspaper, a magazine or two, and books—hardbound or paperback. Some of us have home movie outfits, shortwave or ham radios, and some of us may have already purchased a video tape recorder so we can put our favorite television shows on tape. It is even possible to have our own portable television camera! There is no doubt that the average home of today is equipped to receive a vast variety of entertainment and information both in sound and image and, moreover, each individual within that home may have his own private "communications center."

Now let's go back one generation to when your parents were your age—about 1945. What communications and entertainment media were in the home then? Well, there probably was no television set. Most people didn't buy one until 1950. The favorite family entertainment was the radio, which held the centerstage position in the living room (as the TV or the stereo does now). There may have been a smaller radio in another room, but no tiny transistor sets to carry around with you. There might have been a phonograph, but you couldn't take that around with you either—the records, all 78s, were too bulky and, besides, they broke easily. There wasn't a tape recorder; army engineers were trying to perfect the tape recording process they had discovered in Germany during the war. If your parents didn't want to sit around the house listening to Jack Benny or Bob Hope on the radio, they probably went to a double feature down at the local movie theater. *Their* parents didn't have to worry much about the kind of movies they saw— they were all pretty much the same sort of harmless entertainment, such as a Bob Hope-Bing Crosby "Road to . . ." comedy, a John Wayne western, or a Humphrey Bogart-Lauren Bacall detective drama. As you can see, your parents didn't grow up with as much sound around them as surrounds you. Perhaps that is why they cannot understand how you can take as much as you can.

But if your parents had a lot less sound in their homes when they were young, think of your grandparents. Going back two generations, to 1920, we find that radio and movies were still in their infancies. In fact, the movies didn't even have sound yet. Most information was obtained from print, and people went to the vaudeville theater to be entertained. If there was a radio or phonograph in your grandparents' homes, there wasn't a great variety available to them on the air or on record. Maybe they could pick up a concert or special political or sporting event if they lived near one of the few broadcasting stations that were in operation. If they had a phonograph—or Victrola, as it was called then—the music reproduction they enjoyed was a long way from that of today, which comes close to recreating a live performance.

If life in 1920 seems dull without all the entertainment media that we now enjoy, all you need to do is to consider the generation prior to that—the time of your great-grandparents. In 1895, the radio, phonograph and movies had yet to be invented. In fact, Thomas Alva Edison, whom we have to thank for the phonograph and sound-movies, was working on developing them at that very time. He had already helped develop the telegraph, which would be the forerunner of radio. If you wanted to communicate with someone in those days, you either had to see him in person or write him a letter. If you wanted "background" music, you had to make your own. Entertainment was all "live," and the only world people knew was the one surrounding them.

Now, in the 1970s, the world is much smaller and bound to become smaller yet. We can sit in the confines of our own homes and hear sounds being sent to us from hundreds of miles away. We can talk to and be talked at by people we'd never be able to meet in person. We can see events as they are happening anywhere in the world. And we know that there are millions of people seeing and hearing the same things we are. Soon cable television will widen the choice of events we can tune into, and communications satellites will make these events instantaneous for everyone in the world.

If we think of the opportunity for good that an increase in communications might bring, we can welcome these developments. However, we must consider the dangers as well. Instantaneous worldwide communication carries with it the potential for worldwide control. In his book *1984* (written in 1949), George Orwell describes such a state. In the society he describes, everyone is under constant electronic surveillance, and the government, headed by Big Brother, uses the mass media to control the thoughts of the people and even to rewrite history. Our electronic developments are fulfilling Orwell's predictions; the danger is in the possibility that man will *use* these devices as Orwell predicted he would.

As far as entertainment goes, we cannot complain. Future developments will only add to the great variety we have at our disposal now.

When you think about it, you realize that there is a great deal of inexpensive entertainment available to us and a lot more that is "free." It is true that we must pay for a newspaper, a magazine, a book, a record album, or a movie ticket. But when you consider the cost of producing them, you realize that we're getting real bargains. Because there are so many of us, we can pay only $2 to see a movie, for example, that may have cost several millions to make. (And also because there are so many of us, people who produce movies can make enormous profits as well.) Even better bargains are radio and TV. After the initial purchase of the set and the cost of occasional repairs, we then have available to us a great variety of entertainment. At the push of a button or the twist of a dial, we may select the music or the film of our choice.

Just how much of a bargain are we getting, though? How free is "free"? In the words of the cynic, "Nobody ever got anything for nothing." Who pays for all that instant entertainment?

The bills are paid almost entirely by the advertiser—those "words from the sponsor" cost a lot. As we saw in the last chapter, about two-thirds of the cost of publishing a newspaper or a magazine is paid through the advertising. In radio and TV, except for some "public service" broadcasts (like coverage of certain special events) whose cost is absorbed by the networks or local stations, all the costs are paid for out of the sponsor's pocket.

And these costs can get pretty high. One episode of *Bonanza,* for example, costs a quarter of a million dollars. A sponsor may pay as much as a million dollars to place his commercials on a special televised event like a big football game. Superbowl's per-minute asking price—when bought alone—is approximately $200,000 (though major and veteran buyers can get it for closer to $145,000).

"That's a lotta dough!" as they say on the late movie. Yes, it is. But the advertiser is willing to spend it, because it will mean millions of dollars in sales in return. (*That's* where *we* pay.) Despite the fact that viewers (and listeners) often groan when the commercial comes on, advertising is effective. (A recent study showed that the products advertised in the most disliked commercials lead their competitors in sales.)

So, in a way, the cynic who said, "Nobody ever got anything for nothing" is right. We buy the products advertised, giving the sponsor his profits, and proving to him that the money he spent in bringing us our favorite show was well-spent.

"It pays to advertise" is a dictum that is wholeheartedly endorsed by the American businessman. That is why we are exposed to nearly *400 commercial exhortations* a day: Use This, Eat That, Drink This

"Bonanza," NBC

Brand, Smoke These, Buy This One, Drive A —, and Take This for Your Daily Headache.

Think of the barrage this way: Suppose you had a hundred dollars to spend and there were three or four hundred merchants clamoring for you to spend it on their merchandise. Each one will use his own technique to attract you to his particular product. One will shout, one will quietly explain the merits of his merchandise, one will make you laugh, one will flatter you, one will promise you untold delights, one will make you feel vaguely uneasy . . . and each will claim his product is the best.

The communications explosion, then, has brought with it advertising fallout. How do we protect ourselves? Until recently, advertising has been considered a necessary but harmless evil. Although people in the advertising business claimed that it is the very foundation of our economy, no one else took it very seriously. There was a law passed, however, that forbade subliminal advertising (messages that are not exposed long enough for the conscious mind to perceive, but which are "seen" by the subconscious), so there has been at least *some* recognition of advertising's potential power over the mind. Lately that power has been affirmed by certain minority groups as blacks, Mexicans, Indians, and Women's Liberation groups, each of which has protested certain ads that have created or reinforced group stereotypes.

Politicians certainly recognize the power of advertising. It is generally believed that John F. Kennedy won the Presidency in 1960 because of the image he projected via the TV debates with Richard Nixon. Having learned the power of television politics the hard way, Nixon then spent the subsequent eight years trying to build an acceptable image. Today a political candidate must have millions of dollars available to spend on television commercials to advertise himself.

The one thing that man has always fought for, besides his life, has been his freedom. Above all things, man cherishes his free will—his right to choose. Even if he sells his soul to the Devil, at least he has *decided* to do so on his own. To the American, particularly, the most heinous crime of all is that of "brainwashing" or "thought control."

Yet how much "thought control" are we letting ourselves in for in the name of instant, portable entertainment? Just think, by the time you are sixty, if you follow the average pattern, you will have spent nine years of your life watching television (including two and a half of them viewing commercials!).

It's not only the advertising, but the entertainment fare as well that is out to seduce you, that is competing for your attention.

There's a clever little poem about a Martian who comes to Earth and describes its inhabitants, which he mistakenly believes are the cars he sees on the highways. In the last line the Martian asks, "and those soft shapes, shadowy inside the hard bodies, are they the brains or the guts?"* The same question could be asked of the person who punches the buttons or twists the dials. *Is he really at the controls?*

One way to recognize the seducers, to combat "thought control," is to understand the techniques they use. And that's what this book intends to do—to help you to understand the tremendous appeals of modern media, to recognize their influences and effects, and to become the controller rather than the controlled.

Media experts (such as advertising agencies, to whom such information is vital to their business success) have conducted surveys to find out exactly *who* (in terms of age, sex, educational level, economic standing, and so on) is exposed to each medium—how much, how often, what times of the day, and so forth. They have found out the following interesting facts, for example:

- In the average home, the TV is on almost 6 hours a day.

- The older (and the younger) the person, the more TV he watches. In other words, people over 50 and under 15 watch the most TV.

- About two-thirds of the movie audience are people between the ages of 18 and 25. This same age group watches the least TV.

- The hours between 6 and 9 a.m. and 4 and 6 p.m. are the most popular for radio, since most radio listening is done by the working man and woman going to and from work.

- The comics are by far the most popular part of the newspaper and are read by people of all educational levels (not just the least educated, as some people believe).

Do:

How much advertising are you exposed to each day? Keep an advertising "journal" for just one day. You'll be surprised at just how many selling messages are thrown at you!

How much of each TV hour is spent on commercials?
How much of each radio hour is spent on commercial messages?

*"Southbound on the Freeway" by May Swenson.

What percentage of the daily newspaper is comprised of ads? Of any given magazine?

Count the number of billboards you encounter on a typical route, driving from home to school, for example. (Although this would not be the best route to use, since billboards are placed for working men and women to see.)

Here is a number that will surprise you: Count the number of *other* selling messages (not those transmitted by the preceding media) you are exposed to each day. Begin with the labels on your toothpaste and your breakfast food, and continue counting until bedtime. Don't overlook anything—like matchbook covers, for instance. The number should come out to about 300. You don't believe it? Count 'em!

REACT:

For most people, one of the results of their exposure to the Daily Blat is a capacity for completing slogans without even being aware that they know them. Try your powers of slogan retention by mentally filling in the blanks below.

Whaddaya want—good _____ or good _____.
When you've said _____, you've said it all.
It's _____ when you live in the West.
_____ all the gusto you can.
Double your _____, double your _____.
If he kissed you once, will he kiss you again? Be certain with _____.
St-rr-rr-rr-etch-ch your coffee break, chew _____.
She's got the freshest _____ in town.
_____ a piece of the rock.
Fly the _____ skies of United.
You can trust your _____ to the man who wears the _____.
These are the _____ years.
All you add is _____.
GM, mark of _____.
The _____ goes in before the name goes on.
Come to where the _____ is. Come to Marlboro country.

If you've got the _____, we've got the beer.

Aren't you _____ you use Dial? Don't you wish everybody did?

Hallmark . . . when you care enough to _____ the very _____.

When you eat too well, demand _____.

It's the _____ thing. Coke is . . .

_____ has a better idea.

PanAm, the world's most _____ air line.

You can be _____ if it's Westinghouse.

Better living through _____.

grammar	pleasure	fun	send	friendly
Ford	Wonder	love	own	glad
taste	Certs	mouth	grab	best
time	quality	excellence		real
Di-Gel	star	Wrigley's spearmint gum		experienced
car	flavor			sure
chemistry	Bud			Lucky

CREATE:

Working with one or two of the slogans above, put *other* words in the blanks which make the statement true or funny, but not in the expected (ad copy) manner. Example: "When you eat too well, demand . . . *more*."

It might be an interesting experiment to spend some time without modern media to see what it's like. (Of course, if you've gone camping or backpacking, you may already have an idea.) Try spending a week without radio, television, recorded music, and movies. Do you find yourself seeking people out more? Can you imagine life without such things? How would it be different?

CREATE:

● Write a story, or diary, telling of a non-media world. (Feel free to make yourself the main character.)

● Write a conversation between two "over-exposed" (to one or all of the media) people. Use comic strip bubbles. Limit yourself to eight frames.

● Draw a cartoon illustrating "The Daily Blat" you are exposed to.

"Every now and then Roger likes to cut himself off from all media."

Drawing by Joseph G. Farris © 1970 Saturday Review, Inc.

CHAPTER 5

WHAT HAVE THEY DONE TO MY MIND, MA?

> Thanks to television, the next generation will be born with four eyes and no tongue.
>
> *Fred Allen*

Fred Allen's prediction expresses the concern of many—doctors, psychologists, teachers, science fiction writers, young people—who look at our electronically connected environment and wonder: What will be the effect? Will it change the way we perceive our world? Will it influence the way we treat one another? Will it diminish or enhance the quality of our lives? What are some of the observable effects of mass media fall-out? Here are some theories that have been "blowing in the wind" lately:

Our capacity to "contain multitudes" (of media) has expanded.

In 1971, a syndicated news columnist described a ladies' luncheon she attended. One woman mentioned how hard it was to talk to her teenage daughter and be *heard,* because the daughter stared blankly and clicked her fingers in time to some inward melody the whole time. Another mother said her son hummed softly while she reprimanded him. When accused of not listening, he repeated every word she had said, correctly! The columnist herself reported that, even when she got her daughter to turn off the music so they could converse, the daughter still gyrated to the melody that lingered on in her mind.

The media have lulled us into believing that there are magic formulas (ads, teenage romance comics) and simple, quick solutions for even the most complex problems.

- Conflict? Use force, violence. Now!

- Tension? Take a pill, or stomach settler.

- Feeling small, powerless, ineffective? Drink Weltschmerz Scotch! Buy a sports car! Smoke El Longo Cigars ("They look so good you don't even have to light 'em.").

- Parents hard to get along with? Run away from home.

There are no models in the media for the very real "conflict which never resolves," which we must simply live with. Soap operas? Not really. Certainly the conflict is strung out for a long time, but it has little to do with the nature of the conflict. (Mostly, it has to do with getting all those actors to the end of the season and all those viewers right along with them; it strains the scriptwriter's imagination to "keep the conflicts alive.") In fact, soap operas are very often about people who try instant solutions and, by so doing, compound their troubles.

We are becoming "homogenized" by the standardized fare offered us by the mass media:

We are given the same things to think about, the same people to admire or ridicule, the same words and phrases with which to

"Well, she answers the phone during Huntley-Brinkley, and I do the same for her during Julia Child."

Drawing by Henry R. Martin, © 1967 Saturday Review, Inc.

communicate, the same rhythms and sounds to groove with, the same fantasies to escape reality with, and the same goals to strive for.

How, then, is it possible to learn anything from anybody? He's got swimming in his head the same things you've got swimming in yours!

Most obviously, our **living habits have changed.**

* 60% have changed their sleep patterns because of TV;
* 55% have altered their eating schedules;
* 78% have let TV do the baby-sitting.
* Household chores are now crowded into the commercial breaks, causing an overload on water supply systems during those periods.
* In England, when *The Forsyte Saga* was first aired over BBC TV on Sunday nights, Sunday night entertaining ceased "because no one could come!"
* We no longer gather together around the home set; we go our separate ways to our separate apparatuses. Floor plans for houses have changed to accommodate the trend.

We feel we've experienced something when we've only really read it, heard it, or seen it in the media world.

1. "It's only natural" says the ad . . . but it's also a little sad that you can't run through a spring meadow these days without images of . . . Elvira Madigan . . . and Nice & Easy Hair Coloring commercials . . . and the only thing that seems to make *your* running through the meadow different is that you're not in slow motion and you very quickly come to the edge of the meadow. Where you see a brook, a beautiful, fresh, menthol brook! "It happens every Salem."

2. The media take what might have been our greatest wonders and delights, show them to us before we've had a chance to experience them directly . . . so that by the time our very own great moments come we can no longer feel them afresh. We have been told 200 times how we should act and feel.

Among the young, there seems to be a strong resistance to "Linear" presentation: that is, the relating of a thought or a story in an introduction-development-conclusion manner. "One thing at a time, please!" says the linear thinker. "Everything all-at-once, please!" says the media-immersed man.

To communicate an experience, like a rock concert, through print means that it must first be "broken down into parts and then

Attending a rock concert is an "all-at-once" experience.

"Medicine Ball Caravan," Warner Brothers

mediated, eyedropper fashion, one thing at a time, in an abstract, linear, fragmented, sequential way." That, according to Marshall McLuhan, is "the essential structure of print." And he goes on to observe that "once a culture uses such a medium for a few centuries, it begins to perceive the world in a one-thing-at-a-time . . . sequential way. And it shapes its organizations and schools according to the same premises." Books are no longer the dominant medium of our culture, yet the older generation still perceives and presents "linearly."

Do:

Ask someone whom you consider to be book-oriented how he perceives the following (in other words, what pictures come to his mind; how would he "draw" each):

Progress
the Year
Maturing
Schooling
Life
Man's relation to God
Ambition, Drive, Purpose
Communication
Perseverance

Watch the explainer's hand gestures, too. Does he picture these abstract concepts in terms of straight lines? How do *you* picture them?

Create:

Relate an experience linearly, so that someone who is used to reading story-lines would "get it." Then, using a tape recorder, movie camera, and whatever else you want, convey the same experience in an all-at-once manner. Since young people are usually better at this than their parents, have a "showing" of your production and invite "the folks."

Examples of resistance to linear presentation:

A new anthology called *Anti-Story* states, in its introduction, "Structurally the stories are flat, or circular, or cyclic, or mosaic constructions, or . . . incomprehensible in their shape—they are not climactic." A reader of these stories is struck by the lack of events following events; instead, there is simply a "welter of sense impressions" to be gotten through.

"An 18-year-old college freshman or sophomore listening to Janis or Santana or Kristofferson cannot 'hear' an AP news release," says James Goode, the creator of a news service, "Earth News," directed at the "awareness elite." And so his news releases cut through the lineal "President Nixon said today . . ." presentation and somehow engage the new kind of listener on a personal level.

"We don't believe anything we read in *Time* or *Newsweek,* or any of that junk, but we believe what we read in Marvel Comics," a 20-year-old radio station manager told Stan Lee, editor of the comics.

We are losing hold of the uniquely human faculty for expressing our thoughts and feelings verbally and for making fine distinctions.

"I have deep perceptive thoughts, but I can't get them into sentences."

By Robert Censoni © 1969 by Saturday Review, Inc.

We go to newspaper and magazine "reviews" of movies and books to find out how to put our own reactions into words. We eagerly read and listen to news commentaries in order to articulate our opinions on events.

We have a thought; it begins to take an exciting turn, and suddenly it fits into a category we've seen or heard which vaguely seems to "say it" for us and we accept the simplified, media-popularized version instead of allowing our curiosity to take new paths.

We are at a loss with ideas and persons "in the process of becoming."

The media show us *finished, packaged* products and ideas, whereas our daily living surrounds us with things and people and ideas "in the process of becoming." It is "out of style" to have the "courage of our confusions."

In the media, we see commercials that have taken months to put together. We hear a Neil Young recording that is the combination of 50 splicings of the best segments, and a movie that left four times its footage in the waste basket. And then we look at our project for Introductory Art class, lying unconvincingly on our desk, and we hear our younger brother bumbling through Lesson 4 on his guitar, and we have no models from the media to sustain us.

We're caught in a "rising and irresistible tide of expectation" that cannot be met and so leads to a chronic sense of disappointment, discontent, bitterness, and sometimes violence.

The ghetto dweller sees large homes, fast and luxurious cars, a dozen wardrobe changes for the career girl, wax cleaner applied to a 15′ x 30′ kitchen floor by a housewife dressed in heels and silks— all on her tenement television set, which is on almost constantly.

The confused, often ineffective adolescent girl who can't talk to her parents, has just alienated her best friend, and is prone to fits and rages over the colliding pieces of her world, sees a happy "sit com"

> "Unhappiness comes from an uncritical conforming to inaccurate assumptions about what we are and what we need."
> Gail Putney,
> author of *Normal Neurosis.*

family, temporarily upset by a contrived problem, *overcoming* it with grace and laughter and meaningfulness-ever-after—all in 30 minutes.

An adolescent boy, slouched in a chair in the family room, with an "empty" afternoon facing him, has in his mind the media-produced images of "a happening-a-minute" and "grab all the gusto" and "you've got a lot to live." He looks around, and the place, the family, the silence—it all becomes a drag. "Nobody does anything around here." On TV, these "moments between happenings" are never portrayed (unless, of course, they're L&M moments)—those long stretches of time when a person finds himself with no direction, no close-at-hand source for joy or sadness or thrills, no person to talk to or argue with or punch. For many people (now more than ever before, psychologists tell us), these moments are terrifying. Silence, without external stimuli, is one of the few things the media have not prepared us to face. And so most of us, instead of savoring the quiet as a chance for self-discovery or for trying out a talent or for observing the *real* world, immediately involve ourselves in "appropriate" activities (those we have seen done by characters we like).

> "The private self exists only precariously here (America), and there is more need to make a public self . . . The further you are from a sense of who you are, the more emphasis on how you look."
> Kathrin Perutz,
> author of *Beyond the Looking Glass,*
> an analysis of the beauty culture.

> "We can never have enough of that which we really do not want . . . we run fastest and farthest when we run from ourselves."
> Eric Hoffer,
> San Francisco longshoreman and
> philosopher, author of *This I Believe.*

The "flattening out" of our feelings and sensibilities, the uses to which media have put emotion, have blurred the distinction between what people should feel deeply about and those things which engage the feelings only slightly and superficially.

The profound human feelings are identified with anything and everything.

Not all that atypical was the program NBC Nightly News brought us on November 18, 1970. They had a crew covering the devastating typhoon in East Pakistan. The camera had panned over the dead bodies of people and cattle left stranded on the fields by the receding flood.

Then the helicopter-borne lens peered down on a crowd of people, arms outstretched as they begged for food. Now we were on the ground again and the camera focused in on a white-bearded man, openly crying for the relatives he had lost in the floods. As his cries still hung in the air, the camera moved away to watch the setting sun. Then the sky went black and the white moon rose above the horizon to the sound of martial music. Only it wasn't the moon, it was a single tablet of Tums. We had slid straight into the commercial. The Pakistanis were left to the problem of how to get through the next few days alive, while we wrestled with ours: which of five flavors to take for our over-stuffed stomachs.

We take in stride the "permissible lie" and the use of the bizarre and distorted to get our attention.

If only life's problems were so easily solved as the commercials would have us believe. If only we *could* conjure up a boy friend, a sparkling stream and all outdoors just by unwrapping a stick of Wrigley's gum. If only switching our brand of toothpaste *would* make Mr. Wonderful call us for a date. If only we could win adoring looks from our favorite girl simply by applying a "little dab of Brylcream," or "the new dry look" by Gillette. If only we could feel chipper thanks to Haley's M.O.

"Our public is so conditioned to promotion as a way of life, whether in art or politics or products, that elements of exaggeration or distortion are taken for granted."

Marya Mannes, free lance writer
and former magazine editor.

"Of the ten Earthmen I approached, three thought I was promoting a new TV series; two wanted to know what product I was advertising; two started to tell me what their President should do in Vietnam; two told me to get lost—and the last one gave me a quarter."

Drawing by John A. Ruge, © 1969 Saturday Review, Inc.

Our "attention span" has shortened, and with it our patience with people and events that go "on and on" past the point of our enjoying them.

● We listen for a few seconds to a record, a newcomer to school, a mother—and if we don't "dig" it (her) right away, we "tune out."

● A room charged with people in conflict is left, with a shrug of the shoulders and a comment, "Bad vibes."

● The high cost of network time and the need to offer something for everybody produce a discontinuity of programming, a constant

"Don't you understand? This is life, this is what is happening. We can't switch to another channel."

Drawing by Robert Day, © 1970 The New Yorker Magazine, Inc.

shifting from one thing to another, an emphasis on the staccato and motley character of experience.

CREATE:

Take one of the above theories, put it in the mouth of a roving "Man on the Street" interviewer. Then, using magazine pictures to show each man or woman interviewed (young, old, establishment, far out, etc.), give a set of replies which illustrate the different points of view each might have on the theory. Then, if at all possible, go out "on the street" with your camera and tape recorder. Ask the same question and interview the very types of people you have tried to portray. See if the real responses are at all similar to the ones you imagined.

CREATE:

Do a paste-up of the front page of a newspaper with headlines and "leads" about events that prove and disprove some of the theories. These should be actual events; the only thing you're doing to them is placing them on one page and pretending they happened on one day.

DO:

Tape record a conversation between two people in your age group, two people of the older generation, or one young and one older— to see if any of the theories check out. Present the recorded material in class and see if others can guess which theories are being illustrated.

TRY a "generation gap" conversation and see if you can illustrate all the theories at once (assuming, that is, that the older member has not experienced the pleasure of gloriously grooving with the media and that the youngster has not experienced the old-fashioned excitement of "curling up with a good book").

The question remains, "Do the media extend and alter our means of perception and thereby affect our very nature?"

It is the business of art to expand consciousness, while it is the business of mass communications to reduce it.
—Richard Schickel, *The Disney Version,* Avon, 1968, $1.25

CHAPTER 6

OVER-EXPOSURE OF AN IDEA MAKES IT PREY FOR SLOGANEERING

The Price of Popularity

Laugh-In makes a joke about "Look that up in your Funk & Wagnalls!" and the next day sales of the dictionary are up 20 per cent. An author mentions his book on a popular talk show and the following day his book is sold out at the bookstores. A movie gets a spread in *Life* magazine, and box office receipts go way up. Because of the immense audiences and the near-instantaneous nature of the mass media, Instant Popularity is now possible.

For publicity agents, the ability of the mass media to disseminate information so quickly to so many people is very efficient. Thus, it is a very important part of any publicity campaign—for a book, a movie, a Broadway show, even a political candidate—to get exposure on radio and television shows. One of the major factors in a book's becoming a best seller, for example, is the Publicity Appeal of the author. Jacqueline Susann, author of two best sellers, *Valley of the Dolls* and *The Love Machine,* is an unparalleled expert at gaining publicity for her books. There is a film called "Television Land" which consists of quick cuts from twenty years of television. One of the cuts shows Richard Nixon saying "Sock it to me!" It may seem unfit and undignified for a President to be taking part in such high jinks, but then, as a candidate for office, Nixon felt this exposure would help him get elected. The mass media can be *used,* then, as an Instant Popularizer.

The mass media may also be an *inadvertent* Instant Popularizer. That is to say, without benefit of a planned publicity campaign, ideas and attitudes and people may become well known to almost the entire nation simply through exposure in the mass media. For example, it has been said that what happened to Sigmund Freud in forty or fifty years happened to Marshall McLuhan in 18 months. Freud's radical new ideas on psychology were at first highly controversial, so much so that he was rejected by his colleagues. Finally, his ideas were recognized as valid and were accepted as a totally new way of looking at man. He was then considered almost divine and certainly all-knowing. But then Freud lost divinity and was seen in perspective; his ideas were recognized as original and innovative, but were no longer considered the final word on the subject of psychology.

This recognition process—the controversy, the lionization, and the final acceptance with some reservations—began, for Freud, in 1900 and each stage lasted 20 to 30 years. McLuhan's name and his ideas have undergone the same recognition process within a more compressed period of time. McLuhan, a few years ago, was merely a Canadian professor with some interesting new ideas on communication. With the publication of *Understanding Media* in 1964 he came to the public's attention. And he has now passed the saturation point of media exposure. The word "mcluhanisme" is now part of the French vocabulary. You can't read a magazine without coming across a reference to him or to his ideas ("the global village," "hot and cool" media, the "medium is the message," "post-literate man," etc.).

Often, though, Instant Popularization of an idea, instead of bringing more people in contact with meaningful issues and theories, *reduces* those ideas and theories to the point of meaninglessness. For the larger the audience the idea reaches, the more simplified it becomes—until it is bandied about as a word or a slogan or a fresh twist to an old joke. For example, here's a joke taken from a popular magazine:

> Burt, Jr., shares his generation's commendable interest in his environment, but he is unable to persuade his mother that hanging up his clothes would disturb the *ecology* of his room.

What does "ecology" mean in this context?

React:

What IS the definition of *ecology?* Compare your meaning with that of the rest of the class.

Here is the most recent dictionary definition: ecology 1. the branch of biology that deals with the relations between living organisms and their environment 2. *Sociology* the study of the relationship and adjustment of human groups to their geographical environment.—*Webster's New World Dictionary of the American Language,* Second College Edition, 1970

How many people *would* be able to define the word "ecology" accurately? Yet who hasn't heard of it? It is used in jokes, cartoons, comic strips, advertisements. Yet in 1968 it was the name of an obscure science less familiar to the public than entomology.

Let's trace the history of the popularization of the word "ecology" and the idea it refers to: The relationship between man and his physical environment.

1962: Rachel Carson wrote a series of articles for *The New Yorker* magazine in which she warned us of the indiscriminate use of pesticides and how they were killing off fish and wild life. These articles were published as a book, *Silent Spring,* which was received warmly by environmentalists and coldly by businessmen and scientists.

By looking back at the listings in the *Reader's Guide to Periodical Literature,* you can see the development of the idea in the titles of magazine articles:

In 1965-66, under the listing "Ecology," there is this one title: "Ecology of Early Food Production in Mesopotamia," *Science* Magazine.

In 1967-68:
"National Academy of Sciences: Unrest Among the Ecologists," *Science* Magazine.

In 1968-69:
"Have We Reached the Limits of Pollution?" *Reader's Digest,* 1968.
"Myths About Pollution," *Nation's Business,* 1968.
"Do We Really Want Pollution Control?" *Organic Gardening & Farming.*
"Stepping Up Pollution War," *Business Week.*

In 1969-70:
"Can Man Survive?" *Parents' Magazine.*
"Can Man Survive His Environment?" *Senior Scholastic.*
"Can Technology Be Humanized in Time?" *National Parks.*
"Can We Keep Our Planet Habitable?" *UNESCO Courier.*
"Danger: America's Environmental Problem," *Look.*

In May, 1970, there is one full page of listings, including:
"Dirty Dilemma of Oil Spills," *Life.*
"Ecology: the New Religion?" *America.*
"Dawn for the Age of Ecology," *Newsweek.*
"Ecology: a Cause Becomes a Mass Movement," *Life.*
"Fighting to Save the Earth from Man," *Time.*

In August, 1970, "Environment" became a regular column in *Time* magazine, and women's magazines picked up the popularized version of the idea: *Seventeen* featured an environment volunteer directory. "Six Women Who Care" ran in *Good Housekeeping* (in contrast to such traditional approaches as "Six Best Dressed . . ." etc.). "Earth, Love It or Leave It" was a *new* kind of sensationalism for *Redbook.*

In 1971:
"Earth Watch" became a column in *Saturday Review.* EQ, or ecology quotient, became a regular feature in *Senior Scholastic.*

This is only a partial history of an idea's "path to popularity." It does not take into account newspaper, radio, and television coverage. Nor does it take into account all the references—the panel discussions, the comedy skits, the jokes, the casual remarks—made by people in the mass media that help to popularize an idea. If we were to draw a chart to show how an idea or an attitude gets popularized, it might look like this:

```
┌─────────────────────────────────────┐
│  Original idea expressed in a book   │
│  or lecture or small magazine.       │
└─────────────────────────────────────┘

┌──────────────────────┐  ┌──────────────────────┐  ┌──────────────────────┐
│ Idea explained in     │  │ Idea discussed and    │  │ Idea reacted to in    │
│ small magazine,       │  │ visualized in         │  │ small magazine        │
│ book review or on     │  │ a television          │  │ article or in         │
│ news commentary.      │  │ documentary.          │  │ newspaper editorial.  │
└──────────────────────┘  └──────────────────────┘  └──────────────────────┘

┌──────────────────────┐  ┌──────────────────────┐  ┌──────────────────────┐
│ Book reviewed, idea   │  │ Idea discussed on a   │  │ Idea reacted to in    │
│ explained in mass     │  │ television talk show. │  │ television comedy     │
│ magazines like Life,  │  │                       │  │ skits, cartoons,      │
│ Time, Reader's        │  │                       │  │ jokes.                │
│ Digest, Newsweek.     │  │                       │  │                       │
└──────────────────────┘  └──────────────────────┘  └──────────────────────┘

┌──────────────┐  ┌──────────────┐  ┌──────────────┐  ┌──────────────┐
│ Idea referred │  │ Idea referred │  │ Idea referred │  │ Idea exploited │
│ to in women's │  │ to in ads and │  │ to in comic   │  │ in new         │
│ and teen      │  │ TV commercials.│  │ strips.       │  │ products.      │
│ magazines.    │  │               │  │               │  │                │
└──────────────┘  └──────────────┘  └──────────────┘  └──────────────┘
```

And so the complex ideas of Rachel Carson's *Silent Spring* can be diluted and reduced to the size of a laundry detergent box: "E-COLO-G" (a product that, in 1971, was having a hard time making it on the consumer market because it contained skin irritants). The ideas of Betty Friedan in *The Feminine Mystique* and Simone de Beauvoir in *The Second Sex* get simplified to the point of the billboard slogan: "WOMEN'S LIBERATION: Colonel Sander's Kentucky Fried Chicken." And look what happens to "women's lib," "pacifism," Pentagon "red tape," and press conferences in the comic, "Captain America: Hydra Over All":

Captain America, © 1972 Marvel Comics Group

Although the opening scene looks like an authentic meeting of "Hydra, the deadliest of all threats to democracy and world peace," it turns out to be a mock-up composed entirely of LMDs (life model decoys invented by Fury, a good guy) for the pupeses of demonstration and attack techniques for the Pentagon. Those putting on the demonstration are Captain America (the Star Spangled Avenger) and Colonel Fury. The all-woman "Femme Force" helps out at the end. Here are some of the characters' comments:

Capt. America:
"The others are using the new Laser-47's . . . and they're doing some job . . . but weapons aren't for me! Just no way I can fall into that scene. I have to rely on my own special skills . . . fight the battle my way! Though I know it has to be some kind of ego trip I'm on . . . the only way I know to fight is the way of . . . Capt. America."

(A fist fight follows.)

The President, who looks like Richard Nixon, is watching the attack demonstration on a huge screen:
"Excellent, Colonel Fury, you can halt the exercise now, I believe the gentlemen of the Defense Department and myself are sufficiently impressed."

Colonel Fury, answering:
"Keep your Baby Blues glued to the screen another couple 'a seconds . . . we'll show ya some stuff that'll really pop yer eyeballs! I know this wasn't on the program . . . but with the economy in the shape it's in . . . I didn't figure you'd mind gettin' two shows for the price 'a one! Femme Force One . . . Attack!"

Leader of the Femme Force:
"The men haven't left us much to work on . . . but we have to make the most of what there is . . . or forget about gaining equality as agents."

Fury, after the aid of the Femme Force:
"You did pretty fair . . . for a ladies' bridge club, that is!" And then to the President: "Ya wanna let us know what ya think . . . or do we have to sit on our pinkies till yer next press conference?!"

The President:
"Let me make one thing perfectly clear . . . Pentagon, then Cabinet, then Congress, then, maybe you'll get your appropriation."

The President turns it over to technical experts, who say,
"He's a good man, Fury, but he doesn't understand the complexities of running a government. LMDs are considerably more expensive than our human shield operatives. As for the Femme Force . . . well, we should certainly consider more funds for that project."

Fury:
". . . if they could stop spendin' a million bucks a day in Viet Nam and save a dollar or two to save lives here at home!"

A good way to see the process of popularization in action is to keep a record of the occurrence in the various media of some one slang expression or catch phrase. For instance, *Time* magazine reported in its October 5, 1970, issue on the phenomenon of advertising men straining to take over the latest 'in' words for their ad copy.

At one time every product was pictured as the consumer's "bag"; later on, each product promised to help the buyer "do his own thing." Unfortunately for the advertising business, such catchwords soon go out of style. At the time of the article, the current popular phrase was "putting it all together," started by orchestra leaders and football coaches, picked up by the black community and the young, and eventually by the media. Kent cigarettes "got it all together"; the CBS network "got it all together" for the 1971-72 season; Sears, Roebuck "put it all together," and so on. It is interesting to note that, as the catch phrase gets used more and more, people begin punning with it [as in the Coats & Clark thread ad headline, "Put it all together with Dual Duty Plus (thread)]; as if once something or someone becomes your familiar friend you can begin to joke with it.

Do:

Keep track of the tossing around of a catch phrase that is coming into popularity right now. Copy down the date you hear it or see it, the medium on which it appeared, and the way it was used. Clip ads, editorials, articles, headlines. Take pictures. Wherever the phrase lands, *show* it.

The ideas of Malcolm X, as expressed in his *Autobiography of Malcolm X,* are reduced to a slogan, "Black Power." This reduction of an idea to a word or a slogan which may be spread through the mass media may do some good, as in the case of the "Black Is Beautiful" theme. The same process which had reduced the Negro to a stereotype, like Stepin Fetchit and Mammy, was used to instill pride in the black person (even the word "black" superseded "Negro" very quickly through mass media exposure).

In other cases, though, instead of inviting understanding and new awareness, a label or slogan may block them. Take the case of the "hippie." What began as a sincere philosophical movement — which historians saw as a parallel to the early Christian times — was tagged the "hippie" movement. Through publicity, the movement attracted more and more people, some with less than sincere motives. Also, through publicity, the tag "hippie" came to be a catch-all epithet for anyone with unconventional characteristics, like long hair. Therefore, anyone with long hair, from Charles Manson to a "with it" priest, could be called "hippie." Does "hippie" now mean anything more than "person, especially male, with longer than socially acceptable hair"?

React:

Discuss the meanings of these words or phrases:

hippie	escalation
Jesus freak	ecology
women's liberation	the new morality
media	black power
love, peace	the movement
liberal, radical, conservative	hardhat
organic	biodegradable
Vietnamization, pacification	the Establishment

With best Wishes
Ken Maynard

Do:

Make up a list of such words and phrases. Ask people first if they have **heard** of the word or phrase, then ask them to **define** it. You might use a tape recorder, a movie camera, or a video tape recorder if you have one available.

You may discover that people cease to question that which is always with them. It is the child who asks the profound questions.

As ideas become diluted and reduced to simple words, labels, phrases, and slogans in the mass media, so do problems and conflicts become simple black and white issues: the good guys versus the bad guys, for example. Faced with the problem of presenting a conflict and resolving it within 30 minutes (with six or seven minutes reserved for commercials), the writer of a television drama must use short cuts. He will show the audience right away what a character is like by using familiar labels (black clothing, ill-kempt look, snarling face, rough talk indicate the bad guy; the opposite, the hero); present the conflict (the bad guy has or is about to commit an unacceptable act); and resolve it with *no loose ends* left over to plague the audience (the good guy chases the bad guy, catches him and shoots him). Satisfied, the TV viewer is ready for the program in the next time slot.

What would happen to Shakespeare's play, *Hamlet,* if it were adapted as a TV detective drama? The play might present this situation: The head of a large business firm has been killed in an apparent accident. His brother has taken over as head of the firm and is consoling the dead man's widow. The son of the dead man knows that his father would never have had such an accident and suspects his uncle of "arranging" it. Since he can't prove that the "accident" was actually murder, he stages a re-enactment of the accident with himself in the place of his father. He thereby gives his uncle the chance to get rid of him, too, since the uncle realizes that he is trying to prove him a murderer. How would it turn out?

- The nephew would be killed in the accident and the uncle would go undiscovered.

- The nephew would be killed in the accident but the uncle would be discovered in the process.

Stereotypes are a basis for much slapstick comedy.

- The uncle's guilt is revealed, but the nephew is saved (in the nick of time) from being killed in the accident.

The first ending might be done by Alfred Hitchcock, who is fond of the "twist" ending. The second was done by Shakespeare (who didn't like loose ends, either) and is termed a tragedy because the innocent are, wastefully, killed too. The third is the typical TV ending. As you can guess, the uncle would undoubtedly be killed in the accident he had planned for the nephew. That would be fine with the audience, for the uncle was BAD and deserved to die. In Shakespeare's play, though, the uncle isn't all that bad, and you can't help but feel a little sorry for him. Also, Hamlet is not your typical good guy, either. In fact, millions of words have been said and written about the character of Hamlet because Shakespeare made him so human a mixture of strength and weakness.

Experience with program ratings, however, has shown that the TV viewer doesn't want to ponder over a person or a situation, so people and their problems are reduced to their most obvious properties, and solutions are simple and final.

So what?

So, a lot. People may come to see other people in terms of one or two characteristics — by the tags and labels mass media have given them. Also, people may see situations and problems as simpler than they are, and may come to expect simple and final solutions. You don't like what a certain leader stands for? Shoot him. Maybe the problem will go away. Students on campus causing a ruckus? Kick 'em out. You don't like the way the "establishment" does business? Toss a few bombs. We live in an era of the violent act. Is it mere coincidence that this era occurred after 20 years of television, whose favorite fare is violence? The only problem with the violent act in the real world is that it doesn't solve a problem or terminate a situation as it does in television land.

"Love is never having to say you're sorry" is the simple definition made popular by the film, "Love Story."

If violence doesn't work, however, you can always try love or hard work or just being good. Maybe *then* everything will turn out all right. Violence isn't the only simple solution presented by the mass media. How many times have you seen a problem solved by love? "I love you" becomes the magic phrase that can chase away all sorts of demons. No one will deny that loving and being loved are essentials for happiness, but, unfortunately, love does not conquer all, despite the mass media's insistence that it does.

React:

How many movies, TV shows, comic books, short stories, novels, songs do you know that follow one of these basic themes?

- Love conquers all.
- Work hard and you will succeed.
- Virtue is rewarded and evil is punished.
- Faith—in oneself, in another person, or in God—can solve any problem.

How do these precepts stand up in real life? Are they valid? Can a person *suffer* by believing in them? Can you think of instances where these precepts haven't worked out?

Stereotypes, another short-cut created for the sake of simplicity, are spread by the mass media. For example, take the case of the opera. What do you think of when you think of "opera"? What pictures do you see?

- A fat lady with cow horns on her hat?
- Loud, unmelodic singing of inane words?
- An audience of aristocratic dowagers who pretend to like opera because it makes them feel "cultured"?

Many people would answer that they think of opera in terms of pictures like these. Do they like opera? Emphatically, no! Have they ever been to an opera? Well . . . not really. Where did we get these notions of opera, then? From comedy skits, jokes, commercials, scenes from movies, and comic books. One of the standard comedy skits involves a very fat operatic soprano wearing a horned hat, and usually the source of the skit's humor rests on the loudness and silliness of operatic singing. We've seen this scene so often that we have come to accept it as an authentic view of the opera.* If we never see anything to contradict this view, how can we know that it is false?

Ethnic stereotypes are spread in this same manner. For example, what does "Mexican" make you envision? A man with a sombrero over his face, sitting in the street, taking his siesta? A bandit? A woman in

---

*See the clip in the film "Television Land." A perfect example.

"Love Story," Paramount Pictures Corp.

a bar, who dances suggestively for the norteamericano? These are the ways Mexicans have been pictured in the mass media, until finally objections were made. The Frito Bandito symbol, which was used by the Frito-Lay Corporation to sell corn chips, was dropped after objections were made by the Mexican-American Anti-Defamation League. Bill Dana decided to drop his José Jimenez character as a comedy routine. Veteran actor Ricardo Montalban has formed an organization called "Nosotros" to improve the film-TV image of the Mexican. It may take a while, however, to erase the stereotype. Meanwhile, Mexican-American kids have to get used to being called "banditos" by their classmates. (In her book, *Daybreak,* Joan Baez discusses the discrimination she encountered as a child of Mexican ancestry.)

Do:

What are some other ethnic stereotypes fostered by the mass media? For the following, jot down the first thoughts that come to mind:

> African
> British
> Chinese
> French
> German
> American Indian
> Irish
> Italian
> Japanese
> Russian

Compare your thoughts with those of others in the class. See if you can discover the source of the stereotypes. Compare the stereotypes with one person you know well from each of these ethnic groups.

CREATE:

A contrast page in which you show an ethnic stereotype from comics, cartoons, or a TV character; opposite it, place the picture (photo) of a real person who happens to be of that particular ethnic group. Try to show at least six different sets.

The ultimate condensation of an idea or attitude is a button, or bumper sticker, or poster. Mass-produced and very mobile, they can move around the country faster than gossip. Some examples of each are given below. Discuss their effect. (Do any of them make you feel as though you're being shouted at? Lectured? Nagged? Do any of them tease your thoughts, or do they try to direct them? Do any of them encourage exploration of a complex issue, or do some try to make up your mind for you and *block* exploration? Which of them perfectly echo your own thoughts?)

BUMPER STICKERS

America: Love it or leave it.
If you don't like police, the next time you need help call a hippie.
Warning: Your local police are armed and dangerous.
Have a nice day.
Make Love Not War.
Chicken Little was right.
What if they gave a war and nobody came.
If you love Jesus, honk twice.
When they outlaw guns, only outlaws will have guns.

Buttons

Clean air smells funny.
Pollution stinks.
When you've seen one atomic war, you've seen them all.
War is unhealthy for children and all living things.
Where is Oswald, now that we need him?
Warning: Military Service May Be Hazardous to Your
   Health.

POSTERS

Make a commitment today.
Everyone's gone to the moon.
War is good business. Invest your son.
Love is a four-letter word.
You have not converted a man because
   you have silenced him.
Love is real.
Old soldiers never die.

REACT:

Why do you think people wear buttons, put bumper stickers on their cars, and hang posters in their rooms? Do they want you to think about the *message*? Or about *them*? Why do *you* display them (if you do)?

CREATE:

Create your own buttons, bumper stickers, and posters (the kind you would display).

CHAPTER 7

Human Needs and Media – Sponsored Attitudes

Man's basic needs are five. First, he must have *food,* enough to sustain life and health. Second, he needs *shelter* and *safety,* protection from the elements (wind, rain, wild beasts, etc.) by means of a roof overhead. Third, he needs *love,* closeness to others and to life. Fourth, he must have a feeling of *self-esteem,* a sense of importance and worth as a human being. Fifth, he seeks *self-actualization,* to find his uniqueness and then to "let it shine forth."

These needs can be filled easily and simply. The oft-quoted lines of the Persian poet equate paradise with a "jug of wine, a loaf of bread, and thou . . . beneath the bough." Think of how many needs are being satisfied for the poem's speaker in the situation he describes. We often find ourselves the happiest in the simplest of situations.

Advertising, however, takes the simplicity out of the basic needs and makes it more difficult to satisfy them. "Create a need and fill it" is the slogan of the advertiser-manufacturer team, and we find ourselves suddenly dependent upon a product that we had done without for years.

Man's basic needs, then, when translated by advertising, become something else again. In the advertising world, food satisfies needs much more complex than simple sustenance. Food provides comfort (eat Toastems for the after-school slump; drink tea as a pick-me-up). Food also is a way to reveal the cook's personality (easy-going vs. attentive to detail; up-on-the-latest vs. traditional; full of fun vs. full of common sense and practicality).

The need for shelter and safety cannot be met by a mere roof over the head, according to the ads. Shelter means the best house, the cleanest, biggest, most gadget-filled, color-coordinated, easy-care, efficiently running showcase on the block. How many people believe that happiness will automatically follow their installation into the just-right home?

What happens to the need for love, that most sought-after and elusive feeling of all, when translated into advertising terms? Love is what happens when you give her diamonds, flowers, a new clothes dryer, a car, or whatever. Love is what you get if you use the right toiletries and set the right atmosphere with stereos, have the right decorative furnishings, and serve the right food and drink for the occasion. No wonder we are so confused in our search to satisfy the need for love.

Where the need for love is often difficult to satisfy (if you operate according to advertising), the need for self-esteem is fairly easy to fulfill. You may simply buy it. Self-esteem is what you feel, say the ads, when you dress right, drive the best car, and in general surround yourself with prestige material possessions. You have self-esteem when you cause others to feel envious of, or inferior to, you.

When have you found yourself, certain of your specialness, in the world of advertising-generated needs? Self-actualization is what you have reached when you add up the images you have bought and have discovered that the total is a currently fashionable personality profile.

Could it be owing to Madison Avenue's interpretations of man's basic needs that he has such a difficult time satisfying them?

Needs

If it is true — as the psychologists claim — that man's Basic Needs are these five, then a "happy life" should consist of, simply, filling these needs, right? Only five things to do each day and to help *others* do. It sounds easy. So how come so few people are happy? There are many, many reasons how come. The ones we want you to dig up are those that are perpetuated by the advertising media:

Magazine Ads, TV Commercials
- Do they "play on" basic human needs, but offer you ineffective ways of fulfilling them?
- Do they "create" needs and so cut you off from finding your own ways of meeting the basic ones?

Do:

Collect examples from magazines and TV commercials, and answer four questions about each one:
1. What need is being "played on" or created here?
2. Can it be traced back to a basic need? Which one(s)?
3. Can the product satisfy that need? For what kind of person?
4. What is another more effective way of answering this need, for *you*?

Collect five ads, each of which appeals to a different basic need.

CREATE:

Do a collage to illustrate the "wants" and the "needs" mentioned in this quote:

> "Who are, one cannot help but ask, the writers who manage to combine the sales of products with the selling-out of human dreams and dignity? Who know . . . so much about *presumed wants* and so little about *crying needs?*"
>
> —Marya Mannes

ADVERTISING

Before we leave the world of advertising and its manipulation of human needs, let's take a close look at "image" advertising of one particular product—cigarettes. One of the "permissible lies" we have come to accept is that, when we buy a cigarette, we reveal our taste in "life styles." We buy (or borrow for a moment) an "image" of ourselves. How did this incredible equation of cigarettes with life style get started? In an affluent society, not only are some products that are advertised unnecessary, but often different brands of any one product have no real differences between them. Consequently, advertisers must either dream up differences (how many ways can you talk about a tobacco leaf? or a filter?) or they must sell an *image* rather than the product.

"Over-choice" is a new phenomenon. Philip Morris sold a single major brand of cigarettes for 21 years. Since 1954, by contrast, it has introduced six new brands with so many options as to size, filter, and menthol that the smoker now has a choice among 16 different variations. We, the consumers, love to feel we are choosing among alternatives; *and* we love to be offered *flattering and clearly defined images of ourselves.*

REACT:

Here are some examples of cigarette advertising—the actual copy and a description of the accompanying picture. Put into your own words the "image" each advertiser is trying to sell.

Camel Filters. They're not for everybody. (But then, they don't try to be.)
(Picture: Handsome man, corduroy jacket over shoulder, alone and pleased.)

Philip Morris Multifilter. Full Kentucky flavor in a low-tar cigarette.
(Picture: Man and woman, dressed in expensive country

tweeds, standing in the shade of sycamores. A thorough-bred horse trots over the Kentucky turf behind them, but they are engrossed in their cigarettes.)

Old Gold Filters. "I want to taste the tobacco in my cigarette. I get what I want. I smoke Old Gold Filters."

(Picture: Handsome, rugged young man, Levi jacket, rough hiking shoes, lying back on one elbow on a granite rock, weeds all around. A look on his face like "Nobody talks me into anything!")

L & M. The week was a grind with phone calls and late nights and skipping lunches but now the job is done and . . . This . . . is the L & M moment. Light up, lean back and just plain don't do a thing but relax. With the easy-going richness of your L & M. It's time well spent.

(Picture: Medium-attractive executive with tie loosened, shirt cuffs rolled up, "finished" papers stacked to his left, the desk pen — still warm — laid to rest in its holder, the plastic spirals of the telephone cord just catch the light. It is late at night. He is leaning back.)

Salem Super King. The long, long Springtime. That's what you get with the extra length of Salem Super Kings. And the Springtime taste of Natural Menthol, not the artificial kind, is yours in every extra puff.

(Picture: One big man whose handsomeness is almost hidden underneath his rumpled fishing hat. He's stream fishing, and he's caught one! It's big, too. He's up to his knees in the cold, clear stream. And he's alone.)

Winston's Down Home Taste. Real and rich and good, like a cigarette should.

(Picture: Attractive, natural-look girl in sharp jeans, ribbed sweater, soft, cuffed jacket, laughing and chatting with an older man—in sweatshirt and baseball cap—and young man in work clothes; buses and cars in the background; a gas pump and a heavy-duty pulley can be glimpsed. The young ones are smoking.)

Eve. The first truly feminine cigarette—it's almost as pretty as you are . . . pretty filter tip . . . pretty pack. Rich, yet gentle flavor.

"I want to taste the tobacco in my cigarette. I get what I want. I smoke Old Gold Filters."

Old Gold Filters. The cigarette for independent people.

19 mg. "tar," 1.2 mg. nicotine av. per cigarette, FTC Report Nov. '70.

KING SIZE
OLD GOLD
FILTER
5 Gift Stars

This ad provides an image for the cigarette smoker.

(Picture: Delicate pink fingernails on the woman's hand holding the pack of Eden-innocent cigarettes. The lady on the pack is so pure she doesn't smoke!)

Virginia Slims: You've come a long way, baby.
(Picture: Old brown photographs of what it used to be like: a woman churning butter, pumping water, and shoveling coal into the stove—her hair seems to be falling down from all the activity. Full-color picture below the old-time ones: the sequined, dazzling, provocative Virginia Slims lady. Her hair is also curling down in her eyes, but she wants it that way . . . she's a woman with style and with rights!)

Viceroy Longs: Her clothes? She's always wanted an original. Today's the day. The designer? Herself. She knows what she wants. Her cigarette? Nothing short of Viceroy Longs. She won't settle for less.
(Picture: Another dazzling young lady, standing, cigarette in tapered fingers, in front of the dressmaker's mirror. She's very pleased. So is the dressmaker, who's at her feet, hemming the "original.")

Marlboro: Come to where the flavor is. Come to Marlboro Country.
(Picture: Could anyone *not* know the Marlboro man? Rugged, but clean, cowboy . . . always outside . . . silent.)

CREATE:

Write a verbal exchange between any two of the "people" you met above. Put them in any setting you want, but keep their remarks true to character. Make it cartoon style. Cut out pictures from magazines and put their words in balloons.

DO:

Collect examples of at least five other "sell-an-image" ads, other than cigarette ads. Be prepared to describe how the picture reinforces the words of the ad (notice details).

NEEDS: HOW DO THE OTHER MEDIA ANSWER THEM?

We have seen how magazine ads and commercials attempt to fill human needs—if not the most basic ones, then at least the most vulnerable ones. Other media—newspapers, comics, radio, records, and television—although they are not as aggressive about *activating* our needs, certainly must answer many of them, or why would we subscribe, pay for, or turn the dial for them? In the following discussion, the need for "food" and "shelter" will no longer be limited to *bodily* survival. Rather, think of "food" as food for the imagination or spirit, that which each age *craves* for survival in the face of events; and think of "shelter" as anything which protects a person from real and threatening outside influences.

Newspapers

"Take my cat away, take my games away, even my jelly, but leave me my newspaper," humorist Will Rogers once said, and in one short sentence suggested how a newspaper could take the place of companionship, fun and games, and food.

To a newspaper-buff, this attachment to one's newspaper is completely understandable. Marshall McLuhan said, more recently, "People don't read newspapers, they step into them like a warm bath." The reading session is eagerly anticipated for its opportunity for "immersion" into a familiar reading and reacting routine.

Picture the aging business executive at the end of a trying day ("trying," that is, to adjust to all the new and everything-at-once ways of doing things and feeling his wisdom has become obsolete). He sits down and takes the newspaper into his lap. The familiar ritual begins: scanning headlines with alternating alarm and relief (that many of the troubles are not his own); checking in with favorite columnists who reaffirm with charm and clarity his view of life; the catch-in-his-breath attention to the obituaries; the escape and light-hearted release of the comic section; the measuring of himself and his knowledge as he zeroes in on the financial page; and the penny-wise scrutiny of the ads and classifieds. This daily "happening"—which is not just the man and not only the newspaper, but really the meeting ground between them—is something to be savored daily.

He has been given "food for thought," information, and food for the sagging spirit (even the *bad* news induces a certain euphoria of "survivor emotion"). If he has been selective in his reading, he has probably been able to shelter himself from "what's out there" with "but-I-don't-want-to-know-about-it." If he has not found self-actualization with a letter to the editor, he has been able to experience it vicariously through others (those articulate columnists and critics he agrees with). If the newspaper is a good one, reporting on a variety of local events and personalities, then this man will feel a sense of his own worth as he sees pictures and news which give exposure and importance to his line of work or his way of life. And what about love? closeness? belonging? If that paper has lessened his sense of alienation and put him in touch with a community of people, then it has indeed proved itself a valued friend.

COMICS

The types of comic books are many and the motives for reading them undoubtedly numerous. For the purposes of this discussion, we will take one, *The Incredible Hulk,* from the Marvel Comics Group, and see if and how it answers basic human needs.

The cover — with three flaming torches lighting the scene of an enormous green "brute-man" battling an ominous, armored, and caped machine-man in front of a castle and under a purple and pink sky—right away separates the fan from the non-fan. A person doesn't casually pick up such a magazine, unaware of the contents. It *announces* its fantasy world at the outset.

Inside the front cover is an ad for a "novelty" mail order house (everything from a bald-headed rubber mask to a spy "pen" radio so you can "listen in secret" anywhere). And now . . . the story!

Opening picture shows the Hulk (the big green one with blue hair) smashing through a brick wall and a lamp post as he goes after the enemy. A note from the editor, as we go to turn the page, assures us

The Hulk, © 1972 Marvel Comics Group

that we haven't missed an issue due to daylight saving time. The story unfolds . . . for two pages, anyway, and then is interrupted by an ad for a correspondence school (the pictures accompanying it show a boy realizing he needs a high school diploma in order to "be somebody," getting it, and ending up in suit and tie behind a desk with a secretary asking for his signature and approval on a business form).

On with the Hulk. He is getting into more trouble, smashing things. "What Hulk doesn't like, he destroys," he says. And later, "Friends? Hulk has no friends. Some have *said* they were Hulk's friends . . . but then they always tried to trick Hulk—*hurt* him." Two more ads—for Marvel posters and for prizes if you sell lots of Christmas cards. And now back to Hulk, knocked unconscious and returned to his normal self—a helpless, weak, harmless man named Bruce Banner. Ad for muscle building equipment follows. A woman intervenes and the Hulk reactivates himself and charges through more brick walls to get revenge on his tormentor, Victor von Doom. More ads (they're coming every other page now). Hulk has the machine-man, von Doom, by the throat. "You tried to use Hulk . . . then made fun of him. Now we'll see who's laughing at the end of the battle." Hulk stops without killing. "Bah! Hulk has beaten you—and Hulk knows it! Thus—Hulk will fight no more!" Hulk becomes sad, as he is reminded of his past and his love for a girl. He leaves (by leaping over canyons with a single bound), saying, "Hulk doesn't care about this fight . . . or *any* fight. All Hulk wants . . . is to be far away . . . and all alone!"

The comic ends with news from the Bullpen, Marvel Comics headquarters, consisting of chatty items about the writers, illustrators, the editor, and even the office girl! Then, letters from the fans, answered by the Bullpen men.

An excellent format—a ritual of reassurance for a certain kind of reader who finds the demands of his life in the real world, well . . . fantastic, unreal. If the ads are an accurate reflection of this reader, he relates to gimmicks, disguises, and anything that transforms him, gets him out of his own skin.

And then there is the main character, Hulk, the big, all-powerful, yet merciful and sad monster with vague stirrings of a better life, somewhere, with love in it. Simply told, graphically illustrated, the story has fed the imagination amply, sheltered the reader from evil (in the character of Victor von Doom), and hinted that love is possible even to brute-men.

Through asides to the reader, chatty personal revelations from the Bullpen, and answers to letters, the editors have helped assure him of

his worth and *actual* identity: "We know you exist, out there," they seem to be saying, "and we understand." Could one wish for a more complete circle of friends?

React:

Explain the special needs radio answers.

Media: How They Mirror Prevailing Attitudes

Do:

Attitudes Toward Age

Conduct the following survey. Ask 10 people, men and women, of each age group.
   Age (circle one): 14-18, 19-25, 26-35, 36-50, over 50.
   Male or Female.
   What age would you like to be? _____
   Which is the *best* age to be? _____
   Which age do *most* people think is the best age to be? _____
   At what age is a woman "old"? _____ A man? _____
   (according to you)
   At what age is a woman "old"? _____ A man? _____
   (according to society)

Results: How many people think the age they are is best? _____
   Of those who think another age is best, is that age younger
      or older than they are now? _____
   What age does society think is best? _____
   Do individuals in that age group agree? _____
   Do people in older age groups agree? _____

REACT:

Although your survey may produce different results, let's assume that the survey shows that most people feel that their *own age* is best but that "society" feels that age 19 to 25 is best. If *individuals* don't feel that this age is best and "society" does, what *is* society, if it isn't a lot of people? Where does this idea come from, that age 19 to 25 is the best age to be?

Many of our attitudes, whether we get them directly or indirectly, come from the mass media. For example, let's look at these statements from ads and other mass media sources about one aspect of being "old":

- "People took me for forty, before I lost 68 pounds. . . . It was then I knew I'd better come down off my 202-pound peak, if I wanted to lose those ten unwanted years."

- Never let your beauty fade.

- Those horrid age spots . . . weathered brown spots on the surface of your hands and face tell the world you're getting old—perhaps before you really are.

- Rinses yellow away and adds silver highlights to gray hair . . . "My hair never looked better," says Sarah, "and it makes me feel younger." Would you believe she has daughters in their twenties? (Silk & Silver ad.)

- "I looked years younger . . . in only 2 Short Months!! Yes! This is my unbelievable story of how 'I,' a 50 year old woman . . . transformed herself into a radiant woman who looked years younger!"

- The Youth Kick. And how to kick back. (A philosophy for every woman over 25: Part 2.)
  It would be funny, if it weren't so sad. Just when a woman reaches the age where she's discovered who she is—and all of the marvelous, interesting, compassionate, gorgeous things she's grown to be—this youthful world starts telling her she's really for the attic. Or, at best, on the way. You're passing 25? You're over 30? Prepare, they say, to die. A little more each year. (Ad for Clairol's "Loving Care," Hair Color Lotion, Washes Away Only the Gray.)

"*Isn't this the eighteenth day of your twenty-one-day beauty plan?*"

Drawing by Leo Garel, © 1969 Saturday Review, Inc.

- "I sipped the beer and watched Ellen move around the kitchen. She was still a good-looking woman, even if she was thirty-five." (Line from a story in *True Story* magazine.)

- Wanted: Secretary, personable, attractive. Under 35.

According to these statements, when does a woman become old? 25? 30? 35? 40?

How can an "old" woman be beautiful? _____

How do women feel about getting old? _____

Manufacturers sell products—diet aids, hair dyes and bleaches, skin creams—by appealing to a woman's desire to look younger and, therefore, attractive. A woman feels that she must look young to be attractive. But how much of this feeling is created by the ads that are appealing to it? Have you ever seen it stated that an older woman (or man) is attractive (without looking younger)? Or is it a fact of life that only younger people are able to be good-looking?

How do ads depict the various stages of life?

Do:

Select an age group: Childhood (under 14), young (15 to 25 or thereabouts—the age before the wrinkles begin), and "older" (with wrinkles). In watching the TV commercials for a week, note each time that age group is shown. Are the people shown as smiling (happy) or frowning (distressed)? What has made them happy? What has made them distressed?

Collect magazine ads which portray the age group you have selected. Look at them as you have the commercials. What has made the people happy or sad?

Compare results in class and draw some conclusions. According to advertising, what things make each age group happy or distressed? Make a particular note of those things that bring happiness to older persons—anything besides *relief* that they no longer look and feel old?

Compare the things that are shown to make a younger person happy with those that are shown to make an older person happy. Is it possible for an older person to be made happy by the same things as the younger? Why aren't older people shown as lovers enjoying a quiet moment with a cigarette, for example?

> The historians and archaeologists will one day discover that the ads of our times are the richest and most faithful daily reflections that any society ever made of its entire range of activities.
>
> —Marshall McLuhan

Jennifer O'Neill is the current ideal of feminine beauty.

Do:

Attitudes Toward Marriage

- Collect magazine advertisements and watch TV commercials which portray the married woman. When a married woman is shown as happy (smiling), what is shown as making her happy? When she is shown as displeased (frowning), what is causing her displeasure? Draw some conclusions. *Make a list* of the things that you have found in the advertisements that may make this woman happy. According to this list, what are the goals of a married woman—pleasing her husband, keeping her house and the laundry clean — what? Are these valid goals? Are they the goals *you* have for yourself, or for your wife-to-be?

- Many ads on TV and radio attempt a "humorous" look at marriage by depicting it *realistically*. In these ads, what is the wife usually like? What about the husband? Notice the names that the wife and husband are given. Are there any names that are common with advertising couples? Why were these names selected? Is marriage shown as a happy state?

Attitudes Toward "Beauty/Handsomeness"

Do you like the way you look?
Fill out this questionnaire yourself and give blank ones to a few of your friends to fill out.
Are you a boy? _____ A girl? _____ What is your age? _____

Describe your . . .	Are you happy with this characteristic?	How would you want to change?
Hair		
Eyes		
Nose		
Mouth		

Ryan O'Neal has the sort of looks people now admire.

Gilbert Roland, one of the handsome actors of movie silents.

Skin_____ _____ _____

Figure/
Physique_____ _____ _____

Height_____ _____ _____

Using this same questionnaire, describe your boyfriend or girlfriend (either the one you've got or the one you'd like to have).

If you had to, name one person from each of the following groups of people you'd like to look like or that you'd like your boyfriend/girlfriend to look like:

	You	Your boyfriend/girlfriend
Movie Star	_____	_____
TV Star	_____	_____
Musician/Singer	_____	_____
Ad Model	_____	_____

Compare your results with your classmates' results. Who got the most votes?

Do:

Notice TV commercials and collect magazine ads which show male or female models who are supposed to be good-looking. Do you notice any similarities among the models? Is there any *one* kind of looks that seems to predominate in ads? Of all the ads you checked out, describe the typical good-looking male and female model:

	Male	Female
What age?	_____	_____
What color hair?	_____	_____
What color eyes?	_____	_____

Gloria Swanson, one of the most beautiful early movie actresses.

What kind of figure?   _____   _____

What kind of mouth?   _____   _____

What kind of "image"?   _____   _____

Do you know anyone who looks like an ad model? _____

Would *you* want to look like an ad model? _____

So far, we have looked only at ads and commercials to see the attitudes they reinforce—attitudes towards getting old, being married, and being handsome/beautiful.

Next, let's look at the TV programs themselves—do they show any other widely accepted attitudes?

TELEVISION

DOES IT HOLD UP A MIRROR?

The question is often debated, but never really answered: Do the popular TV shows reflect what most of us value? Or do they actually educate us in what we *should* value?
If the popularity of quiz and game shows is any indication, Wow!

Do:

Watch any quiz and game show on television. Make a list of the prizes. Also make a list of those objects which are considered the "booby prizes." Some shows, for example, have the prizes concealed from the contestant. Notice, if you happen to watch such a show, what her reaction is when she sees the prize she has won. What is the audience's reaction? By their reactions, you can judge what it is these people value. Supposing one lady won a stereo console and another won a cow. What would the audience's reaction be? Would your reaction be the same as the winner's? Do you find the same things valuable as the people on these shows? To whom do these shows appeal? If you get a chance, watch *Sesame Street* for the take-off it does on such shows; called "Pick Your Pet," it shows the contestant perfectly delighted with a prize the audience considered ugly.

Password, ABC

React:

Do you think that people who watch these shows steadily, especially children, could acquire a distorted sense of values?

Family Life

Many of the situation comedies revolve around a family. Choose one of these and move in for a month. Take notes on the following:

What is their *standard of living?*
  What is their home like? What kind of house in what neighborhood in your area would it be comparable to? What would it cost? How is it decorated? Is it ever messy? Is there a TV set in the house (and do the family members ever watch it)? What is the neighborhood like? How does the family get along with the neighbors?
  What is the father's job? Is he a blue or white-collar worker, a skilled worker, a professional man, an executive, or what? Would you say he has an average income, or above average? Does he like his job? Does he want to advance? Does the mother work?

React:

Would you say the family's standard of living is average, below average, or above average? Do most family shows on TV seem to have an above average standard? (Compare your observations with those of your classmates.)

What are their personal relationships like?
  How do the mother and father treat each other? Do they ever display affection? Under what circumstances? Do they ever argue? About what? How do the parents treat the children, and vice versa? How do the parents punish the children?

What are the family's interests outside the family?
  What are their recreations? What do they do as individuals? What are their political beliefs? What are their cultural interests? Do you see them attending musical events, going to movies or plays, traveling, reading?

The Brady Bunch, ABC

The Partridge Family, ABC

What are their problems?

Are they individual or family problems? Are they personal? Do they have any problems outside the family? How do they solve them—through love, faith, virtue, hard work, scheming, or luck?

What do they believe in?

What does the family consider to be good behavior? What do they consider *bad* behavior? Do they have a religion? What would be the five qualities the family considers most important? How do nighttime families differ from the daytime ones?

React:

Which of the following statements (made by Joan Barthel in *Life* Magazine, September 10, 1971) do you consider true after having watched a TV family in action for a month? What would you add to these statements?

TV children can be myriad, like the Bradys, or musical, like the Partridges, but they can never malfunction.

It is a butterscotch world where nobody suffers, nobody gets shrill, nobody gets spanked on screen.

Maybe . . . someday . . . my daughter will be able to see TV families living pretty much the way we live: gladly, grumpily, mostly happy, reasonably insecure. . . . Papa would be neither a sap nor a Solomon; Mama would have neither a prison record nor an over-waxed floor. It wouldn't have to be realistic, just true.

> Although they are usually composed of stupid husbands, smug wives, and ill-mannered children, there is one thing you have to admire about the families in the TV serials—they don't waste their time watching TV.
>
> —*The Modern Handbook of Humor*
> Denver Post

Bright Promise, NBC

Another World, NBC

Views of Unmarried Family Life

Look at shows which feature unmarried men or women. Choose one and eavesdrop for a month.

React:

Are the single parents with children widowed? Or divorced? (In real life, there is a much larger percentage of American people who have been divorced than who have been widowed.) In the show you watch, what are the major problems of the single parent? What does the single parent admire in the opposite sex? What does he *like* someone for? *Reject* someone for? What is his attitude toward sex—if there *is* an attitude? Is sex, in any of its ramifications, ever mentioned? What are the single person's goals? Are the man's goals different from the woman's?

What do we think is funny?

Flip Wilson, NBC

In a recent controversy over whether "canned" laughter should be retained as a "laughter trigger" in comedy shows, several letters from TV viewers stated that they "needed help in knowing when they should laugh." A few shows decided to brave it without a laugh track, confident that their writers and performers could make people laugh without any outside help.

React:

Watch several comedy shows, or a comedian on a variety show. Note the topics and situations the laugh-getter thinks are comedy material. What does the subject of the humor (or *how* the laughs are gotten) tell you about the people who watch the show? Could you tell if the laughter was canned or live? If you found yourself *not* laughing when everyone else was, how do you account for the different reactions?

Dean Martin, NBC

Do:

What kind of know-how do we admire?

Watch some "law and order" shows and some "inside the world of . . . professionals" shows and see what kind of know-how or power wins the day (or decides the plot) for the hero. Is it technical skill and gadgetry? Official power? Power of being in the right and having the ability to *expose* people in the wrong? Muscle power? Persuasive power? Personal magnitude? Power in numbers?

Johnny Carson, NBC

Adam-12, NBC

Do:

What people do we consider interesting?

Watch the talk shows for a week. Make a list of the questions asked by the host and the guests' answers you found most interesting. Note the costumes and gestures of the guests. How did your reactions compare with the studio audience's?

REACT:

Do you know people in real life who possess the same kind of know-how as the TV heroes? Do they "win out" in real-life situations? Do you know someone with a kind of know-how you admire which is never portrayed on a TV show?

Some of the media—the ads, commercials, TV programs we have looked at in this chapter—are doing a pretty good job of fixing our attention on certain attitudes. Repetition makes it even harder to separate these attitudes from the ones we are forming through our real life experiences with real people. How do we find out what our attitudes are? What we value and what we don't value? Maybe that's the most important question we can ask ourselves in the midst of media fallout. One way to find out is to "try on" the environments the media are constantly surrounding us with. "It isn't me," we might say when we try out a new outfit or a new hairdo and it doesn't seem right. So it goes with the suits of values preferred by the media. Listen to your head. Try to distinguish your specialness as separate from the "mass mind."

CREATE:

Write a general plot summary for a "pilot" show (one to be tested on a TV audience first, before it is developed into a series) in which the people and things *you* value win out. Suggest actors and actresses for the various roles. Select a specific setting and a dramatic conflict.

In retrospect, I am amazed the series ever got on the air in the first place. I am also convinced that anyone who wants to produce a television series, particularly one as complex as *Star Trek,* has to be (1) an absolute genius and (2) completely out of his mind.
—Stephen E. Whitfield, *The Making of Star Trek,* Ballantine, 1968, $.95

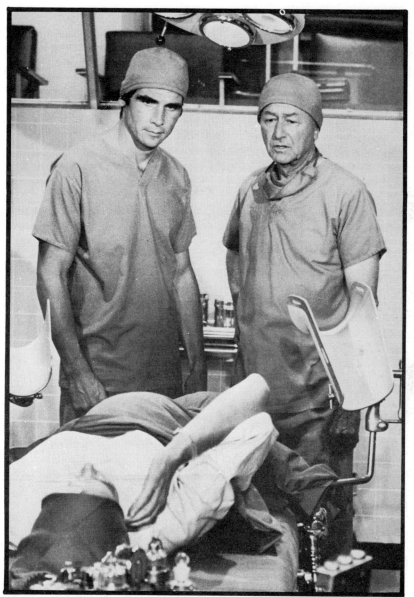

Marcus Welby, ABC

Chapter 8

Best Sellers and Magazines: Do They Tell Us What We Are?

Magazines: How They Tell Women What They Are

Women's magazines are worth close study because they so obviously illustrate the two-way function of most of the popular media—namely, the recording of current tastes, but also the directing of them to a great extent; the mirroring of prevailing attitudes and the forming—or at least solidifying—of them as well; the answering of basic needs, and the creating of pseudo-needs and consumer appetites.

There are hundreds of magazines directed at the American woman, from those devoted to the "house and garden" to the ones which "reveal" the secrets of ordinary or celebrated people (the confession and fan magazines). One reason for the abundance is that the woman is the big spender in our economy; she spends billions of dollars a year on cosmetics and other "beauty" products for herself, and billions more on food and other household items (including clothes) for herself and her family. Advertisers are able to support the many magazines whose market is women.

Magazines appeal to a woman's need for fantasy. In our male-oriented society, the man is freer to pursue his interests. Even the entertainment that a man and woman seek together—the movies and television—are written predominantly from the male viewpoint. (For example, the annual list of the 10 top money-makers at the box office is dominated by men. A few women, like Elizabeth Taylor or Doris Day, are the only actresses to appear on the list with the men.)† So the woman is left to live her fantasy life in the afternoons when the family is away or through the privacy of a magazine read at the beauty parlor or late at night when everyone's gone to bed.

Comparable to the sweetness of the L & M Moment and the MJB Moment, then, is the Magazine Moment. And what does she get from the magazine? A lot more than recipes and decorating hints. She gets recipes for living and hints on how to decorate herself. Once she's found the magazine for her, she's told *who* she is.

The Slicks*—How They Tell Women How to Look

How do fashions get started? *Women's Wear Daily,* the "bible" of the fashion world, may come out with a new "look" for women—a change in the hem lines or a new hair style. It will be picked up and enlarged upon—with a fashion spread featuring one of the top models—in *Vogue* or *Harper's Bazaar,* the fashion authorities among the slicks.

---

†In the 1971 list, Ali McGraw was the only female star.

*The traditional name for "quality" magazines, so-called because of the type of paper they're printed on, as opposed to the "pulps," magazines printed on the cheaper type of newsprint and with a more sensational content.

The new look is then spread by other magazines, each catering to its own special readership, until finally it will even appear in the Sears, Roebuck catalogue, several months after *Vogue* introduced it.

Sometimes fashions fail to be accepted by the American woman. For example, after pushing it vigorously in its pages, WWD finally had to declare "The Maxi is Dead!" After showing their legs by wearing the mini-skirt, women refused to cover them up with the maxi. This rebellion, however, is one of the rare times that women didn't follow the dictates of the fashion world, whose word is spread by the women's slicks.

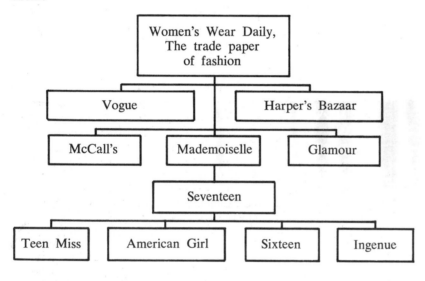

Advertising helps create a "look," too, particularly in make-up and in hair style. Cosmetics and hair products are the two most advertised items in women's magazines. The ads make the women feel they *need* the product—the skin cream or the hair coloring—to become beautiful. So they buy it, spending billions of dollars a year on hope—hope that the promise made by the ad will come true. Since nearly 80% of Revlon's budget goes to advertising, a product that costs $3 could conceivably be sold for 60¢. (If it were offered for 60¢, however, women wouldn't buy it. Cosmetic manufacturers have found that the higher the price of a cosmetic, the more women will buy it. The greater the amount of money spent on the promise, women feel, the greater the chance of its coming true.)

Promise Her Anything . . .

What are some of the promises made by cosmetic and hair product ads?
- In the time it takes to dry your hair, you can see it looking stronger and healthier, fuller and thicker.

- Just spray on Sun-In under the sun, and see what happens. To your hair, maybe even to your life. . . . Just spray on Sun-In. You may never have to wonder where all the boys go in summer.

- Once her only problems were skin problems. 'Til she discovered Bonne Bell Ten-O-Six Lotion. . . . Now she's got boy problems.

- Coppertone. Beautiful tan today. Young looking skin tomorrow.

- Absolutely the fastest, smoothest, easiest, most accurate way to draw well-shaped, big, beautiful eyes.

- Turn on a tan, baby. And you'll turn on a hero.

- And as you tan, not only will your teeth look whiter (Basic Law of Contrasts) but you'll have a lot more to smile about. (Basic Law of Guy Meets Chick or vice versa.)

Even if you have thin hair, blemished skin, smallish eyes, and no tan, you too can be beautiful and popular, promise the ads—just buy the *right* products (*that's* the secret) and your hair will become fuller, your eyes big and beautiful, your skin clear and "young looking," and then if you get a tan (using the proper tanning lotion) you'll have to chase the boys away.

> The beauty culture provides a modern quest for youth and love, the hope of seeming what one has not become, and a chance to disappear into the fabled America of wealth and liberty.
>
> —by Kathrin Perutz, *Beyond The Looking Glass*

Do:

Make a collection of ads for beauty products. What are the

promises made? Are they *realistic* ones, or do they promise more than the product can give? (A shampoo will *clean* the hair, but it won't make a girl popular.) It might be interesting to write to the manufacturer of a certain product that makes wild promises and challenge its advertising. One group of students did just that and the company sent a real live model to discuss the product and its promises with the class!

Magazines—How They Tell You Who You Are. A Static Image?

A magazine is more than a collection of ads (though with some that may be hard to believe, there's so much advertising). A magazine, especially those written for women (of all ages), creates through its articles and features an *image* of its reader—the "you" it keeps referring to. If you like the image and read the magazine, that particular image is constantly dangled before you, and you are given instructions on how to mold yourself into the man or woman that is the magazine's ideal.

For example, if a woman feels she is "The Responsible One," then *Good Housekeeping* is the magazine for her. Or, if she feels that "Liberation Begins at Home," then there's the *Ladies' Home Journal*. Here's how *Woman's Day* magazine advertises itself:

> "When *Woman's Day* talks about kids . . . I can see myself. . . . Because the activities for my children and myself in *Woman's Day* are ones I can see myself doing . . . the ideas are ones I can actually use, even the instructions and details are ones I can follow and pertain to me—but *Woman's Day* is that way about everything."
>
> We think we have a special relationship with our reader. Because of the way we try to help her. As a friend—and as equals. We talk to her woman-to-woman. We don't try to shock her. We never talk down. We simply share ideas with her; and try to complete every idea we give—in detail. In return, our friends have made *Woman's Day* first in single copy sales of all woman's magazines. We think it's because she sees herself in *Woman's Day*. And maybe that's why we have the highest ad readership of any woman's magazine. She sees herself in *Woman's Day*.
>
> —from an ad

The main point of this ad can be carried further to "A woman sees herself in her magazine." At least, the magazine *acts* as though she does.

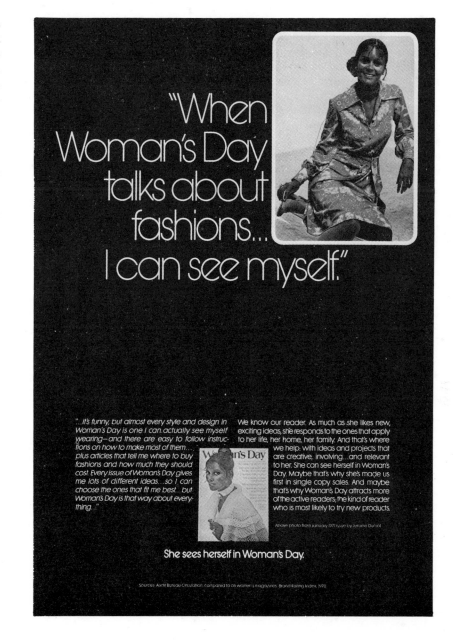

What if a woman does not see herself in any of the magazines written for her? Then she reads *Playboy! Playboy* claims to have a higher readership among women than any woman's magazine. Perhaps the women who read *Playboy* find women's magazines too limited; they may have interests *beyond* fashion, food, and furniture.

Whether as a deliberate attempt to get the female readership away from *Playboy,* or simply as a recognition of the new openness regarding female sexuality, there are two women's magazines which are trying to do what Hugh Hefner successfully did with *Playboy*—that is, to make sex acceptable to the middle-class female.

One is an old magazine that has changed its image and one is brand new. The new one, *New Woman,* is still struggling for acceptance. But the old one, *Cosmopolitan,* is a success story. Cosmopolitan was on shaky ground in the early 60's. Then it got a new editor, the author of the best-selling books, *Sex and the Single Girl* and *Sex and the Office.* "Women like to talk about sex and read about it," Helen Gurley Brown stated to a newspaper interviewer in 1965; the phenomenal comeback of *Cosmopolitan* proved she was right. Since Mrs. Brown took over the editorship of this once-traditional woman's magazine, it has placed an unremitting emphasis on sex. The cover usually rivals *Playboy* in revealing poses, and just reading the table of contents would make many people blush.

Is *Cosmopolitan* the female *Playboy?* Editor Helen Gurley Brown says it is not. In her regular column, "Step Into My Parlor," she declared in the August, 1971, issue:

> People often ask if COSMOPOLITAN is a female *Playboy.* (More often they *tell* us it is!) Actually we are *not. Playboy,* by its own definition, is a magazine of entertainment for men. . . . The *Playboy* man is depicted as handsome, affluent, successful, discriminating (he likes his girls nubile, his cars sleek, his wines mellow, his yachts leather-lavished), and he hasn't an emotional hangup to his name. COSMO, on the other hand, is for a girl who does *not* necessarily "have it made" . . . who wants a great deal more out of life than she is now getting. Monthly . . . *hourly* we pour into her loving advice and, hopefully, inspiration on how to find someone to love, keeping him once she's found him, coping with parents, bosses, jealousy, rage, envy, insecurity . . . *all* the goblins.

The "loving advice and inspiration" offered by COSMO is pretty similar to the *Playboy* philosophy.

> A person who exists only on the level of physical attraction is the Image as presented most spectacularly by *Playboy* . . . and *Cosmopolitan* . . . both of which stand on the premise that members of our own sex are real people, while members of the other are playthings. The prospect of living with a cosmopolitan girl or playboy is as hospitable as moving into a Hollywood set.
>
> —Kathrin Perutz, *Beyond the Looking Glass*

Do:

Get copies of magazines written for teens: *Teen, American Girl, Sixteen, Ingenue, Seventeen, Boys' Life, Co-Ed* and whatever others of this sort are available. Compare them as to the subject matter of the articles and features, the models they use, the products they advertise, the main characters in the short stories, the people they write about, the letters to the editor. And then figure out, "What is the Image each magazine projects?" Describe the reader the magazine is addressing itself to. Is he or she like you? Or like anyone you know?

Write the name of your favorite teen magazine on a piece of paper (you don't have to sign your own name) and submit it as your vote for the best teen magazine award. Count the votes from all the members of the class and see if there are any favorites.

Interview a person outside your age group about his favorite magazine. Discuss with this person the magazine's *image.* Does the person identify with this image? Or is he just fascinated with it because it's so unlike him? Does he seek advice from the magazine? Diversion? Escape? Know-how? Information? Does the magazine make him feel dissatisfied with himself in any way?

Read the front-cover headlines of some fan magazines. Guess what each story's contents will be. Are the promises of sensational disclosures fulfilled in the articles?

Even if such magazines are not purchased and not read, isn't it possible that an "after-image" is carried around in the mind of the casual passer-by, a false perspective on the persons involved (aren't the cover photos which accompany the provocative headlines *always* "caught-in-the-act" startled exposé types)?

READ:

Wolfe, Tom. "King of the Status Drop-Outs" in *Pump House Gang*. An article on Hugh Hefner, describing his revolving bed and his electronic bedside equipment.

Iverson, William. *Venus U.S.A.* An examination of the content of women's magazines as a clue to the needs of the American female.

Perutz, Kathrin. *Beyond the Looking Glass*. About "Life in the Beauty Culture," Chapter 1 discusses the effect of the magazine in promoting the quest for "beauty."

> "What makes a best seller? This is the sixty-four dollar question. It can be answered, though largely by guess and surmise, and never satisfactorily to the inquirer, who always wants a formula. There is no formula which may be depended upon to produce a best seller."
> —Frank Luther Mott, *Golden Multitudes*, 1947, R. R. Bowker & Co.

> "People don't buy a best seller to *read* it. They buy it to *have* it. A best seller is a magical object, a wishing stone. People believe that just having it will make them rich or healthy or thin or sexy or successful or happy. A best seller is a mass dream."
> —Lyle Stuart, publisher of the fastest-selling paperback in history, *The Sensuous Woman* by "J," which sold over six million copies in less than 3 months.

BEST SELLERS: DO THEY TELL US WHAT WE ARE?

A look at best sellers of times past reveals the changing psychological needs of a nation's people. Each era, in its response to events and circumstances, whether they be wars, Prohibition, economic depression, or affluence, craves something different in its pop reading—an outlet, perhaps, for whatever hope or right is currently being frustrated. Best-seller reading has often been equated with "naughty" reading—a book becomes popular because it dares to say what has been suppressed. It needn't say it well; it needn't even represent the common, everyday truth of things. In fact, more and more the content of best sellers borrows from the abnormal and the bizarre in its attempt to capture the attention of its audience. It hasn't always been so.

World War I

Although the United States had proclaimed its neutrality in 1914, by 1917 the U.S. was embroiled in World War I. The following year, in 1918, Germany surrendered and the armistice was signed. During the war the best-selling novel was *Mr. Britling Sees It Through,* by H. G. Wells, which tells of the effects of war on Mr. Britling, a famous British writer. At the novel's end, one of Mr. Britling's sons, as well as a young German friend, has been killed. Britling, however, has reconciled himself to their deaths because he feels they have died in order to make "a better world."

Among the best-selling non-fiction books were three books of poetry, all with war-time appeal: *Rhymes of a Red Cross Man* by Robert W. Service, *Treasury of War Poetry* by G. H. Clark, and the *Poems of Alan Seeger* (1917). The Seeger book was a best seller mainly because of one poem, "I Have a Rendezvous with Death."

REACT:

Compare the sentiments of this popular poem of World War I

with some of the sentiments toward the Vietnam crisis: MAKE LOVE, NOT WAR, for example. Is it the underlying reason for each war that has created the difference in attitude, or have a young man's priorities changed? Do you think a person's first obligation is to his country or to his loved ones?

After "the war to end all wars," the country celebrated. It was a ten-year party, now called "The Roaring Twenties." The 18th Amendment (1919) had prohibited the sale of alcohol and the 19th (1920) had given women the right to vote. Prohibition inspired people to drink, and the right to vote caused women to feel somewhat liberated from Victorian repression. They cut their hair, shortened their skirts, and joined the men to drink illegally in the "speakeasies." They danced the Charleston and the Big Apple to jazz bands, and followed the activities of Al Capone, Legs Diamond, and other notorious gangsters who were making millions from the sale of illegal booze. They joined the nation in admiration for Charles Lindbergh, who had flown from New York to Paris (in 1927) in an heroic solo flight, and were horrified over the kidnapping and death of his baby (1932).

Enough women bought and read E. M. Hull's novel, *The Sheik,* for it to be the best-selling novel of both 1921 and 1922. Called "poisonously salacious" by the *Literary Review,* it told of Diana Mayo, the beautiful and haughty daughter of a British aristocrat, who, while touring Egypt, was carried off into the desert by an Arab chieftain. The story tells of how she is brought to yield to the "sheik's" masterful love-making. The novel was made into a silent movie starring Rudolph Valentino, who became synonymous with the "sheik" character. His movie, *The Son of the Sheik,* was playing to packed theaters when Valentino was stricken suddenly and died, to the shock of the nation. (See Chapter 9, page 191.) The word "sheik" became part of the language, meaning "lover."*

Other best sellers of the 1920s were *The Plastic Age* by Percy Marks, *Gentlemen Prefer Blondes* by Anita Loos, *Bad Girl* by Vina Delmar,

---

*sheik n. 1 A handsome male lover, esp. if given somewhat to melancholia; a male sweetheart; a ladies' man. 1921: *The Sheik,* a book by Edith M. Hull. First popularized by Edith Hull's widely read novel; further popularized by Rudolph Valentino's portrayal of the book's hero in the very popular movie of the same name. Very common c1921-c1927. Presented publicly as a dark, dashing, moody person, Valentino was identified as the typical sheik and was called "The Sheik," which may have restricted the usage from further popularity.

—*Dictionary of American Slang*

Scarlet Sister Mary by Julia Peterkin, *The Beautiful and the Damned* by F. Scott Fitzgerald, and *Flaming Youth* by Warner Fabian.

REACT:

Judging by the titles alone, what were the concerns of the 1920s? What did people want to read about?

Here is the jacket copy from the 1925 Pocket Book edition of Anita Loos' best-selling novel *Gentlemen Prefer Blondes*:

She was a GIVE AND TAKE GIRL. Lorelei Lee was a cute number with lots of sex appeal and the ability to make it pay off. With her chorus girl friend, Dorothy, she embarked on a tour of England and the Continent. And none of the men who crossed their path was ever the same again.

When one of Lorelei's admirers sent her a diary she decided to write about her adventures. They began with Gus Eisman, the Button King, who wanted to improve her "mind" and reached a climax in her society debut party—a three-day circus that rocked Broadway to its foundations.

A hilarious field study of the American chorus girl in action set down in her own inimitable style!

In 1925, the life of a Broadway chorus girl was thought to be "adventurous." What occupations for women today are comparable? If you were to write a comic novel about a young woman's adventures, what occupation would you give her? Compare the realities and the myths about certain occupations.

For example, is an airline stewardess as great as it seems to be? List the *most* and *least* desirable jobs. Interview people who actually hold these jobs to see if the imagined notions about them are true.

The Party's Over . . .

On Black Friday, October 29, 1929, the roar of the 1920s was silenced. The country was thrown into a depression which reached its low point in the years 1932 and 1933. The St. Valentine's Day massacre, in 1929, marked the peak of the gangster wars and foreshadowed the end of the gangster's heyday. In 1933, newly-elected Franklin Delano Roosevelt introduced his "New Deal" with a bank holiday to lessen the severe economic crisis. Prohibition was repealed; a drought hit the Great Plains, and three years later (in 1936) the once-fertile area was termed the "Dust Bowl." It was as though the country was paying for the excesses of the previous decade.

At the severest time of the Great Depression, the big best seller was the 1,224-page *Anthony Adverse* by Hervey Allen (best seller in 1933 and 1934). The story tells of the many adventures and romances of its handsome hero, Anthony, who is named for what he must constantly face—adversity. He does, however, overcome all his trials and survives all his misfortunes. In fact, he is hardly affected by the tragic events of his life. No matter what terrible event occurs, it is followed soon after by something good. (For example, Anthony loses his wife and child in a fire, but within two chapters he is remarried and begetting a larger family than before.) With each troublesome event in his life, Anthony grows stronger. At one point, the author states about Anthony: "More important, however, was a discovery about himself. In situations of great danger he did not grow weak and tremble; he became strong from anger. . . . He felt suddenly sure of himself. He could bend those about him to his own ends."

If the strength and victory of the hero appealed to the reader, mired in the unhappy state of economic depression, so did the setting of the long novel. The story took the reader out of his world and into the romantic one of the late eighteenth and early nineteenth centuries in such exotic places as Africa, Paris, New Orleans, the American West, and Mexico. In his eventful life, Anthony becomes involved in the African slave trade, fathers a son with one of Napoleon's mistresses, and is captured by a tribe of Indians, just to name a few of his many adventures.

Is it any wonder that *Anthony Adverse* was such a big seller? It provided more than a thousand pages of pure escape.

REACT:

What were some of the other "escapes" of the depression years? (For example, the top box office star of the years 1935 through 1938 was Shirley Temple.) Interview a person who recalls the

Vivien Leigh as Scarlett O'Hara in GWTW

depression years. Ask him to give you the names of the popular songs, movies, and to tell you of the diversions of the times—the popular dances and the other activities of the young.

Read:

They Shoot Horses, Don't They? by Horace McCoy, Avon, 1966. This paperback contains both the 1935 novel by Horace McCoy and the screenplay by Robert E. Thompson. The story is set against the background of the dance marathon, one of the "entertainments" of the '30s.

A few years later, in 1936, a book was published which is still unrivaled as a best seller. *Gone With the Wind* by Margaret Mitchell sold one million (hardbound) copies in six months. Booksellers couldn't supply the demand for this long historical romance. The story of the beautiful, willful Scarlett O'Hara who used every means at her disposal to regain Tara, the family plantation which was endangered by events during the Civil War, was a favorite topic of conversation. Readers begged the author to answer the question, "Did Rhett Butler go back to Scarlett?" Miss Mitchell never did.

This still-popular novel is the only one Margaret Mitchell wrote. The motion picture, filmed in a new process called Technicolor in 1939, is one of the most popular of all time. Until *The Sound of Music,* it headed the list of all-time moneymakers. (In 1968, the owners of the film had it "modernized." It was transferred, through a complicated process, into Cinemascope with stereophonic sound.) It still plays to packed houses, just as the novel is still read with great interest.

The other two best-selling novels of the '30s were also about a family's struggle for survival and its relationship with the land. *The Good Earth* by Pearl S. Buck (1931) was set in China. It told the story of a peasant farmer and his bond with "the good earth."

The other best seller was considered "sensational" at the time of its publication in 1939 because of the frankness of some of its passages. (In the 1970s the book is used in school literature courses.) *The Grapes of Wrath* by John Steinbeck is the story of the Joad family, one of the "Okie" families who lost their land during the drought, who were lured to California with promises of high-paying jobs as fruitpickers.

Best-selling books often have a certain topical interest that accounts for their popularity, but sometimes a best seller also appeals to the *literati*: that is, if it is finely written and speaks truths that outlast its particular time. Both *The Good Earth* and *The Grapes of Wrath* fall into this category. Both authors are among the six Americans who have won the Nobel Prize for Literature.

React:

Each of these four best-selling novels of the '30s has as its main character a strong, indomitable person who remains undefeated throughout the severest trials. Do you think the circumstances of the times contributed to the appeal of these characters and to the popularity of the books? What kind of character do you find in popular novels today?

In the non-fiction category, a best-selling book of the '30s and, incidentally, one of the all-time best sellers, was *How to Win Friends and Influence People* by Dale Carnegie. The book sets forth several simple rules for becoming successful, for example:

1. Try to figure out the other man's good points. Give him honest, sincere appreciation for them and he will cherish your words years after you have forgotten them.

2. You can make more friends in two months by becoming interested in other people than you can in two years by trying to get other people interested in you.

3. One of the simplest, most obvious, and most important ways of gaining good will and making people feel important is by remembering names. Remember that a man's name is to him the sweetest and most important sound in the English language.

React:

What do you think of these rules? Do you think they could help a person become successful?

Do:

Compare advice books. A recent best seller is *Psycho-Cybernetics* (although the book was written in 1960, the paperback edition in 1969 gave it a surge of popularity). How does the advice in it compare to that of *How to Win Friends and Influence People* and/or *Peace of Mind,* two very popular books of their time? Interview some men who have bought "advice" books like *Psycho-Cybernetics.* Ask them if the book actually benefitted them, if they are putting the book's advice into practice.

Black Friday had plunged the United States into the Great Depression. Another infamous day was to mark the beginning of another tragic era in American history—December 7, 1941, the day the Japanese attacked Pearl Harbor, which precipitated the United States' entry into World War II. U.S. soldiers fought in Asia and Europe for four years. In 1945, the dropping of atomic bombs on the Japanese cities of Hiroshima and Nagasaki put an abrupt end to the fighting. In August, 1945, Japan surrendered, and the war was over.

During the war years, the best-selling book with a war theme was *See Here, Private Hargrove* by Marion Hargrove, a collection of amusing anecdotes about the trials of a raw recruit at boot camp. *One World,* a collection of speeches by industrialist Wendell L. Wilkie (who ran for President against Franklin Roosevelt in 1940) explained his theory of international government and was a big seller both in this country and in Europe. A third big seller was Ernie Pyle's *Here Is Your War,* a collection of the reporter's letters about the Tunisian campaign of 1942. Another book about the war by Ernie Pyle, *Brave Men,* led all books in sales in 1945. The other popular book of the World War II years was Bob Hope's *I Never Left Home,* an account of the comedian's experiences entertaining the troops—full of jokes, high spirits, and stories about "our boys."

Here are the last few paragraphs of *See Here, Private Hargrove.* Hargrove is describing the recruits leaving boot camp; it is just after war has been declared:

They board the train and they sit waiting for it to take them to their permanent Army post and their part in the war.

As a special favor and for old times' sake, the band swings slowly into the song that is the voice of their nostalgia, "The Sidewalks of New York." Yankee or Rebel, Minnesotan or Nevadan, they love that song.

You can see their faces tightening a little, and a gently melancholy look comes into their eyes as the trombone wails beneath the current of the music. Their melancholy is melancholy with a shrug now. Home and whatever else was dearest to them a few months ago are still dear, but a soldier has to push them into the background when there's a war to be fought. . . .

An old sergeant, kept in the Replacement Center to train the men whose fathers fought with him a generation ago, stands off to the side and watches them with a firm, proud look.

"Give 'em hell, boys," he shouts behind them. "Give 'em hell!"

React:

This excerpt from *See Here, Private Hargrove* is typical of the attitude taken toward the United States' involvement in World War II in popular culture—in books, popular songs, and movies. Americans were seen as heroic "saviors" sent to save the innocent part of the world from the barbaric villainy of Japan, Germany, and Italy. Was this attitude created by propaganda or was it a reflection of the way things were? Is it possible that this attitude has carried over to the Korean and Vietnam conflicts (in the minds of those people who were exposed to World War II popular culture) and might account in part for the difference in attitude between the older and the younger generations?

Do:

Collect other reflections of the popular attitude toward World War II from the mass media (popular songs, comic books, cartoons, movies, books, magazine short stories). Compare that attitude with that toward the other military conflicts the U.S. has been involved in.

Do:

Interview a veteran of World War II. Ask him how he and his

"The Robe," 20th Century-Fox

comrades felt about their involvement in the war. Did they feel as though they were "saving" their country?

Do:

Collect examples from popular culture which reflect the attitude toward Vietnam. How much *humorous* material is there? How much *sentimental* material exists? Account for the difference in the amount of humor and sentiment in the material about World War II and that about Vietnam.

Read:

Chapter 8, "Pleasures, Pastimes, Fads and Follies," of *Don't You Know There's a War On?* by Richard R. Lingeman, Paperback Library, 1971. $1.50.

Religious and Inspirational Books

The author who has had more best-selling novels than any other is Lloyd C. Douglas, a Protestant minister who began writing at the age of 40. When he began writing, he said he was not resigning from the ministry but simply enlarging his congregation. Although he told good stories, he moralized in his books: Be virtuous and ye shall be rewarded in this world and in the next. His best-selling books were *The Magnificent Obsession* (1929), *Green Light* (1935), *The Robe* (1943), *The Big Fisherman* (1948), and *The Robe* (a special movie edition, which was the best seller of 1953).

The Robe is the story of Marcellus, a Roman soldier who had been in charge of the crucifixion of Christ and who comes to embrace Christianity. At the book's end, he is put on trial by the Romans. He is told that he will be condemned to death unless he renounces his allegiance to Christ. He replies:

"Your Majesty, if the Empire desires peace and justice and good will among all men, my King (Christ) will be on the side of the Empire and her Emperor. If the Empire and the Emperor desire to pursue the slavery and slaughter that have brought agony and despair to the world"—Marcellus' voice had risen to a clarion tone—"if there is then nothing further for men to hope for but chains and hunger at the hands of our Empire—my King will march forward to right this wrong! Not tomorrow, sire! Your Majesty may not be so fortunate as to witness the establishment of this Kingdom—but it is coming!"

Marcellus is condemned to death. His wife Diana demands to be executed with him. The final words of the book describe their procession to death:

Hand in hand, Diana and Marcellus kept step with the Guards. They were both pale—but smiling. With measured tread the procession marched briskly the length of the corridor, and down the marble steps into the congested plaza. The massed multitude, not knowing what was afoot, but assuming that this was the first contingent of the notables who would join the gaudy parade to the Temple of Jupiter, raised a mighty shout. . . .

Old Marcipor strode forward from the edge of the crowd, tears streaming down his face. Marcellus whispered something into Diana's ear. She smiled—and nodded.

Slipping between two of the guards, she tossed the Robe into the old man's arms.

"For the Big Fisherman!" she said.

The great success of *The Robe* was not simply the appeal of the book itself. It was also due to the need of the people at that time to believe in a higher good and in self-sacrifice. Between 1941 and 1953, the first or second best-selling book on the fiction list was a novel with a religious theme:

1941 *The Keys of the Kingdom,* by A. J. Cronin
1942 *The Song of Bernadette,* by Franz Werfel
1943 *The Robe,* Lloyd C. Douglas
1944 *The Robe* (#2)
1945 *The Robe* (#2)
1946 This year was an exception. The best seller was *The King's General,* by Daphne du Maurier
1947 *The Miracle of the Bells,* Russell Janney
1948 *The Big Fisherman,* Lloyd C. Douglas
1949 *The Big Fisherman* (#2)
1950 *The Cardinal,* Henry Morton Robinson

1951 Another exception. The best seller was *From Here to Eternity* by James Jones
1952 *The Silver Chalice,* Thomas B. Costain
1953 *The Robe*

Further evidence of the popular attraction toward inspiration and optimism can be seen in non-fiction books which led the best-seller lists of the '40s and '50s. *Peace of Mind,* by Joshua L. Liebman, was the best seller in 1947 and 1948. Those which followed were *How to Stop Worrying and Start Living* by Dale Carnegie (#2, 1948), *A Guide to Confident Living* by Norman Vincent Peale (#9, 1948), *Peace of Soul* by Fulton J. Sheen, *The Power of Positive Thinking* by Norman Vincent Peale (#2, 1953), and *Life Is Worth Living* by Fulton J. Sheen (#5, 1953).

The best-seller list for 1953, for example, reveals the foremost concerns of the American people. The top two fiction books were *The Robe* and *The Silver Chalice,* both optimistic affirmations of Christianity. Seven of the best-selling non-fiction books held this same theme. They were: *The Holy Bible Revised Standard Version, The Power of Positive Thinking, Angel Unaware* by Dale Evans Rogers, *Life Is Worth Living, A Man Called Peter* by Catherine Marshall, *This I Believe,* edited by Edward P. Morgan, and *The Greatest Faith Ever Known* by Oursler and Armstrong.

What was happening in the U.S. during this time, when people wanted to read books about faith?

Between 1941 and 1953, the United States was engaged in war: World War II lasted from 1941 to 1945. Then came its aftermath—the continued occupancy of U.S. soldiers in Europe, the reconstruction of the war-torn countries of Europe and Asia, the Cold War with Russia, and the determination of guilt and responsibility toward the awesome events of the war: the wholesale slaughter of millions of Jews and the use of atomic bombs. Then, between 1950 and 1953, the United States was engaged in the Korean conflict, for which there were no clear-cut motivations as there had been in the previous wars America had fought.

React:

Do you think these events account for the American people's interest in books which expressed optimism and avowed faith in Christianity? If not, how *do* you account for this interest?

"The Man in the Gray Flannel Suit," 20th Century-Fox

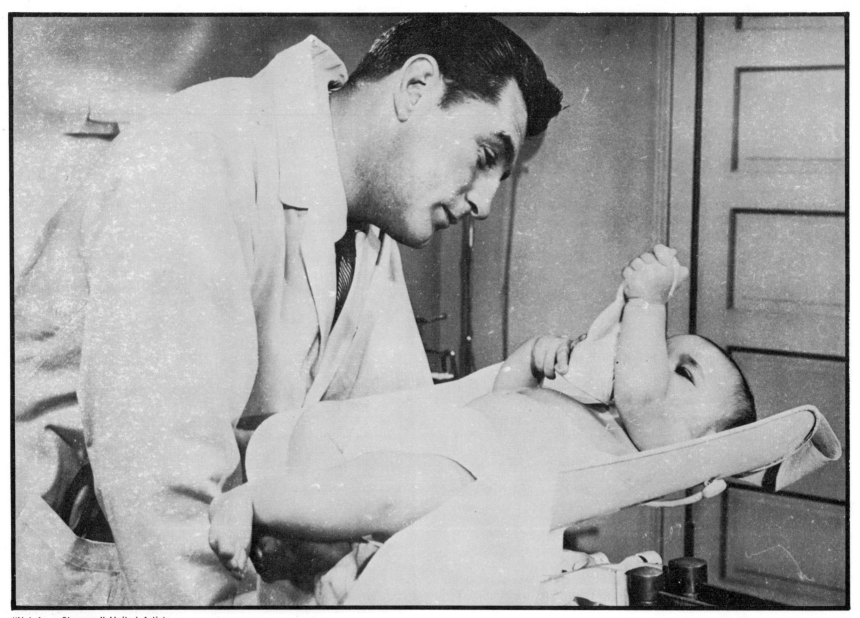

"Not As a Stranger," United Artists

The Eisenhower years (1952-1960) were "uneventful"; young people were considered "apathetic." Major events were the launching (in 1957) of the Soviet satellite "Sputnik," which marked the beginning of the space race between the U.S. and Russia, and the McCarthy hearings (1953) during which the Wisconsin Senator accused the administration of subversion and Communist infiltration. These years were also the first decade when there was a television set in America's living room.

What were the best-selling books during these "dull" years?

In 1954, the best seller was *Not As a Stranger* by Morton Thompson. The story begins when Lucas is a child, even then expressing his strong desire to become a doctor. It goes on to describe Lucas' struggle through medical school (he marries a girl who is in love with him so that she can pay his way through school) and then of his later struggle as a doctor to retain his idealism toward practicing medicine while other doctors, whose primary concern is making money, are achieving great financial success. Lucas has an affair with a woman but, in a moment of personal danger, he realizes that he really does love his faithful wife, Kris. The book ends with Lucas and Kris, who is pregnant, fighting a meningitis epidemic:

He stood up. He walked into the reception room.
She was waiting.
Capped and caped, Kristina held the door open for him.
The sick were waiting. The maimed and the dying, the stupid and the brilliant, the lucky and the blind and the world in which they lived in the shadow of their doom.
Ahead was the future.
Ahead was all a man can be.
He picked up his bag and went out in the world and began the practice of medicine.

In 1955, one of the best-selling books was *The Man in the Gray Flannel Suit* by Sloan Wilson. It is about disenchantment with the American Dream: get a good job in the city, buy a beautiful home in the suburbs for the family, and live happily ever after. The book's theme reflected a common concern. The expression "man in a gray flannel suit" entered the vocabulary as "Babbitt" (from the 1922 novel of the same name by

Sinclair Lewis) had earlier been coined to describe the American businessman. The book opens with this paragraph:

By the time they had lived seven years in the little house on Greentree Avenue in Westport, Connecticut, they both detested it. There were many reasons, none of them logical, but all of them compelling. For one thing, the house had a kind of evil genius for displaying proof of their weaknesses and wiping out all traces of their strengths. The ragged lawn and weed-filled garden proclaimed to passers-by and the neighbors that Thomas R. Rath and his family disliked "working around the place" and couldn't afford to pay someone else to do it.

Tom had a chance at a better paying job (as a public relations man) and his wife sees it as a chance to "get out of this house." Tom goes to apply for the job:

The next morning, Tom put on his best suit, a freshly cleaned and pressed gray flannel. On his way to work he stopped in Grand Central Station to buy a clean white handkerchief and to have his shoes shined. During his luncheon hour he set out to visit the United Broadcasting Corporation (to apply for the job). As he walked across Rockefeller Plaza, he thought wryly of the days when he and Betsy had assured each other that money didn't matter. . . . The hell with that, he thought. The real trouble is that up to now we've been kidding ourselves. We might as well admit that what we want is a big house and a new car and trips to Florida in the winter, and plenty of life insurance. When you come right down to it, a man with three children has no damn right to say that money doesn't matter.

He gets the job but finds that it only makes his life worse, because of all the tensions of the job and because he has so little time with his family. His encounter with an army friend brings into his life the fact of an illegitimate baby he had fathered in a love affair with an Italian girl during the war. He decides that he has got himself into a trap:

. . . I really don't know what I was looking for when I got back from the war, but it seemed as though all I could see was a lot of bright young men in gray flannel suits rushing around New York in a frantic parade to nowhere. They seemed to me to be pursuing a routine. For a long while I thought I was on the side lines watching that parade, and it was quite a shock to glance down and see that I too was wearing a gray flannel suit.

Tom and his wife decide to send $100 a month to the Italian mother for Tom's baby. Tom refuses to accept a high-powered executive job that would encroach upon his family life and is given the directorship of a mental health project. The book ends on a happy note, with a declaration of love between Tom and his wife.

People read what they want to believe. Judging by these two books (*Not As a Stranger* and *The Man in the Gray Flannel Suit*), we can see that in the mid-'50s people wanted to believe in the strength of married love—that it should come before all other matters—and that they wanted to believe that a man is motivated by principles higher than mercenary ones. They wanted their people to be good and they wanted happy endings.

In the 1960s, though, it was a different matter: the media discovered sex. Like a child testing his mother to see how far he can go without punishment, the media tried to see what they could get away with in presenting what had heretofore been considered taboo. Words that were seen only on bathroom walls or in books that were banned began to appear in books and then in magazines. (In a series of test cases the courts upheld defense lawyers who argued for freedom of artistic expression.) Sexual activities, which once were described either indirectly or symbolically, came to be described as graphically as they are in hard-core pornography. The movies, which once were not allowed (by the Hays Office) to show even a married couple in the same bed, went a little further with each "shocker" until nudity and sex scenes became almost *de rigueur,* even in the Westerns. Words once considered taboo were said with regularity, even by the sweetest of heroines (in *Love Story,* for example). Nudes were used in magazine advertisements, and TV commercials used sexy slogans to sell products ("Take it off. Take it all off."). Pornography was sold openly in book stores and on magazine stands. People accepted the fact that they could watch, look at, and read about sex without feeling "low class," and took advantage of the new attitudes with the lusty enthusiasm of a shipload of sailors in a foreign port.

Needless to say, books appearing on best-selling lists were much different from what they were in the '50s. Where heroes in best sellers of the 1950s were motivated by high principles and had discovered meaning in life by doing noble work and through the love of one's wife, in the '60s the best sellers were about people and their sex lives. Where

once everyone was reading *The Power of Positive Thinking,* in the '60s it was *Everything You've Always Wanted to Know About Sex and Were Afraid to Ask,* which title pretty well sums up the prevailing attitude. Instead of being concerned about success and/or the lack of it, people were concerned about *feelings* and/or the lack of them. People were reading *The Sensuous Woman, The Sensuous Man, Please Touch, Body Language, Any Woman Can*—all concerned with physical feelings and the individual's ability to develop them. In the years of the apathetic '50s, people wanted to read about men who were deeply committed; in the years of alienation (which is the way social scientists have described the '60s), people were concerned with communication and feeling.

Do:

Take a look at the best-seller list of today (*Time* magazine provides one in each issue). Judging only by titles, can you determine what topics people seem to be concerned about?

REACT:

The "Shocking" Novel. In nearly every decade, there has been a novel that has become *the* book to read. It's a favorite topic of conversation for a while, making people who haven't read it feel left out. Often, it's a fantasy trip for women and, therefore, it has to be a bit "shocking." (Incidentally, the author of each of the following books is a woman.) It allows women to enjoy a brief escape into an exciting and naughty life, a life far removed from housewifely chores. In 1921, it was *The Sheik* (by Edith Hull) which told of an aristocratic girl who succumbed to the masculine charms of an Arabian lover. In 1936, it was *Gone With the Wind* (by Margaret Mitchell) which told of the handsome, ruthless Rhett Butler's unrequited love for Scarlett O'Hara. In 1945, it was *Forever Amber* (by Kathleen Winsor) which told of the amorous adventures of a beautiful girl in 17th century England. In 1956 it was *Peyton Place* (by Grace Metalious) which told of the sexual shenanigans of people in small town suburbia. (A nighttime soap opera for television was based upon this novel.) In 1966, it was *Valley of the Dolls* (by Jacqueline Susann) which took the reader on a fantasy trip into show biz and also provided much conjecture as to whom the novel was really about. (Was Neely O'Hara *really* Judy Garland?* Was Helen Dawson *really* Ethel Merman?) Make a list of those books read by at least one person in the class.

REACT:

Compare the heroines of these books. Near the beginning of each book the heroine with whom the reader is supposed to identify will be described. She will have the qualities that the reader would like to have. What are they? How do the heroines differ from one another? Compare the descriptions of a heroine from a best-selling novel of another time to one of today. (For example, compare Scarlett O'Hara to a heroine of a current novel.)

REACT:

Compare heroes. What are the men like? Just as the leading woman character will possess all those traits that the feminine reader would like to have, so will the men of the book be idealistic projections of the "dream man." What does he look like? How does he get his *power*—from money, position, brawn, intellect? (For example, the hero of *The Sheik* is an Arab chieftain, and in *Valley of the Dolls* he's a show business lawyer and agent.)

REACT:

Compare the "worlds" of the novels. These are the worlds that women find fascinating, ones that they would like to live in, at least in fantasy. How do these "worlds" reflect the times in which the books were popular? Is there any similarity among the worlds of today's popular novels?

---

*Read: *The Other Side of the Rainbow* by Mel Torme, which *is* about Judy Garland.

DO:

- Try casting a popular novel. What actors and actresses would you like to see playing the various parts when the book is made into a movie?

- Interview a salesman in a book store, asking him about trends in the kinds of books that are popular.

- Make a movie or video-tape. You can act out a scene from a popular novel, or create your own detective or spy movie.

READ:

The Writing of One Novel, by Irving Wallace.

Fairy Tales for Men and Women . . .

What happens when you get too old for Superman and Cinderella? Simple: you read James Bond and Jacqueline Susann: These books are nothing more than fairy tales with sex. Think of it, what is a male's most basic fantasy? To be the strongest man in the world. And what is the female's? To be the most desirable woman in the world. Comic books and fairy tales appeal to these basic desires. When boys and girls get too old for comic books and fairy tales, they seek more elaborate stories, ones that are closer to adult life. For a man, there are Western or detective novels and for a woman, the romantic novel. In the permissive era of today, these books contain plenty of sex and violence, which seem to be important parts of the adult fantasy world.

Sean Connery as James Bond in "Dr. No," United Artists

Superman Plus . . .

Beyond a certain age, it becomes increasingly difficult for a male to identify with Superman. Superman's outfit is rather outlandish, the way he bounds over tall buildings is conspicuously far-fetched, and his life is fairly limited to combatting evil forces. Furthermore, Superman (or his cover identity, Clark Kent) never relaxes. He does not indulge in any of the male pleasures; he doesn't even like girls. As a fantasy hero, Superman is strictly kid stuff.

James Bond, on the other hand, is a man's superman. He is tall, dark, and handsome. He is frequently described (by the women who are attracted to him) as looking "cruel." He is expert, and he is tough. Whatever he may do—from playing cards to driving a car—he does better than anyone else. No matter what predicament Bond finds himself in (and Ian Fleming thought up some wild ones), he extricates himself (along with the beautiful girl that he has met along the way) through his resourcefulness, courage, and physical toughness.

Although Bond is tough, he is not uncouth. He is at home in the finest society, and is a connoisseur of fine food and drink. He is tremendously attractive to women and, although he likes women and never hesitates to take up with a beautiful girl who flirts with him, he never lets a woman deter him from completing his assignment. He is, naturally, a wonderful lover. What man wouldn't want to be like James Bond? What woman wouldn't want a man like him?

Apparently, millions of men and women are attracted to James Bond. Eleven Bond books by Ian Fleming were big sellers, and the series of movies that were made from the books were big box office hits. In fact, one of the films, *Thunderball,* is among the top ten grossers of all time.

Let's take a closer look at one of the Bond books, *Goldfinger,* Fleming's sixth Bond book, written in 1959.

Bond, who is agent 007 for the British Secret Service, is assigned to recover the gold that the Soviet SMERSH agent, Auric Goldfinger, is somehow smuggling out of the country.

Bond first meets Goldfinger when he is hired by a wealthy Miami businessman to discover how Goldfinger is cheating him at canasta. Bond cleverly deduces that Goldfinger is having the descriptions of his opponent's cards radioed to him by an assistant stationed up in his hotel room. The assistant, Bond discovers, is a beautiful blonde dressed only in her underwear. Bond is about to foil Goldfinger's scheme, when the girl begs him not to:

"If only you'd leave him alone, I'd do—" the words came out in a rush—"I'd do *anything.*"

Bond smiled. He took the girl's hand off his arm and squeezed it. "Sorry, I'm being paid to do this job and I must do it. . . ."

In his next encounter with Goldfinger, Bond beats him at golf despite Goldfinger's clever cheating. Ultimately, Bond (and another beautiful girl he has met, Jill Masterson's sister, who is seeking to kill Goldfinger in revenge for Jill's murder) comes under the power of the arch-villain, who has devised an awesome plan for robbing Fort Knox.

Goldfinger's scheme seems foolproof. It's up to Bond to prevent the annihilation of 60,000 citizens and the theft of the gold from Fort Knox. He is under constant surveillance by Oddjob, the murderous Korean karate expert, yet he shrewdly manages to send a message to a friend at the Pinkerton Detective Agency.

In an anti-climactic chapter, Bond is again under Goldfinger's control—on a plane bound for Moscow and SMERSH headquarters. Again Bond conceives an ingenious plan of escape. He knocks a hole in the window, causing Oddjob to be sucked out of the plane, and causing enough chaos among the crooks for him to take over. He strangles Goldfinger and brings the plane down. He has, meanwhile, attracted a woman gangster who has deserted Goldfinger and declared her allegiance to Bond.

She said, "I never met a man before. . . ."

Bond smiled down into the pale, beautiful face. He said, "All you need is a course of T.L.C. . . . ."

. . . and Tender Loving Care from Bond is certain to set her straight.

> James Bond movies belong to the 1960s, especially the early '60s, when the adventures of 007 reflected a public fascination with modern technology, Playboy sexuality and the kind of elegant style embodied in the short reign of John F. Kennedy.
>
> Paul Zimmerman Newsweek 1971

> New model heroes are receptacles into which we pour our own purposelessness.
>
> *The Popular Arts,* Hall & Whanell.

Success, Cinderella Style

Remember the story of Cinderella? A beautiful and sweet girl, Cinderella is living with her stepmother and her daughters, who force her into doing all the drudgery of the household chores while they pursue their social-climbing activities. A fairy godmother appears and magically equips Cinderella with what she needs to attend the king's ball. At the ball, she is acclaimed as the most beautiful girl there. Naturally, the handsome prince dances with her and falls immediately in love with this perfect girl. She leaves mysteriously in order to keep her promise to be home by midnight. Later, the prince tries to find the mysterious beauty by trying—on all the girls in town—the slipper she had left behind. When he finally discovers that the beautiful girl is none other than the drudge employed by the social-climbing lady with the two ugly daughters, he declares his love for her, disregarding her poor circumstances. A Cinderella story, then, is one in which all the good things come to a girl because of her natural beauty and goodness.

In *Valley of the Dolls,* Cinderella is Anne Welles. Anne has come to New York from the "solid, orderly life of Lawrenceville. The same orderly life her mother had lived. And her mother's mother. In the same orderly kind of a house. A house that a good New England family had lived in generation after generation, its inhabitants smothered with orderly, unused emotions, emotions stifled beneath the creaky iron armor called 'manners.'" She had gone to Radcliffe but was not accepted by the other girls. She had a rich boyfriend, whom she didn't enjoy kissing. (Although they had gone together for four years, she had only kissed him "a few times.")

In the first few pages of the book, we have learned that Anne comes from an aristocratic background, is intelligent, and is pure. But what does she *look* like? She is described by Henry Bellamy, the theatrical attorney to whom she is sent to interview for a job:

Henry Bellamy couldn't believe his eyes. She couldn't be for real. In her way, maybe she was one of the most beautiful girls he had ever seen, and he was accustomed to beautiful girls. And instead of wearing the outrageous pompadour and platform shoes that had come into style, this one just let her hair hang lose, natural, and it was that light blonde color that looked real. But it was her eyes that really rattled him. They were really blue, sky blue—but glacial.

Anne is indeed Cinderella, the undiscovered perfect girl, and she has

just met her fairy godmother. Henry hires Anne and becomes her friend and protector. Through her job, she is able to enter the exciting world of show business. She meets a handsome prince in the form of Allen Cooper, whom she thinks is a shy, struggling insurance salesman. After going out with him for six weeks (during which time he hasn't so much as held her hand), she discovers that he is actually a millionaire playboy. (Just treat the frog kindly; he may turn into a prince.) He insists that she become engaged to him, over her protestations that she doesn't love him. Allen, however, is not the *real* handsome prince. The *real* one is Lyon Burke:

She was still unprepared for anyone as striking as Lyon Burke. . . . Henry Bellamy was a tall man, but Lyon Burke towered over him by a good three inches. His hair was Indian black and his skin seemed burned into a permanent tan.

Lyon comes to work at the theatrical attorney's office. Later, while at the opening of a musical in New Haven (the "ball"), the handsome prince declares his interest in Cinderella:

"And what are you fighting for, Lyon?"
"You."
Their eyes met. "You don't have to fight," she said quietly.

Cinderella, however, not only intrigues the handsome prince, she is also the belle of the ball. Anne goes to a celebration for her movie star friend, Jennifer North, at "21"—a New York nightclub. One of the men there is Kevin Gillmore, owner of Gillian Cosmetics, who takes one look at Anne and asks her to become "The Gillian Girl," exclusive model for Gillian Cosmetic ads:

"She's beautiful, but not too sexy. The All-American Girl."

Yes, in the fantasy world of fiction, Anne Welles *is* the All-American Girl. She's our own Cinderella. It's an *adult* fairy tale, however, so there has to be some unhappiness to give a semblance of reality. The book ends on this note:

She brushed her hair and freshened her makeup. She looked fine. She had Lyon, the beautiful apartment, the beautiful child, the nice career of her own, New York—everything she had ever wanted. And from now on, she could never be hurt badly. She could always keep busy during the day, and at night—the lonely ones—there were always the beautiful dolls [pills] for company. She'd take two of them tonight. Why not? After all, it was New Year's Eve!

"Valley of the Dolls," 20th Century-Fox

So it's not so great to be Cinderella! The reader sighs with relief, feeling a little better about being her not-so-perfect self.

REACT:

The movie version of *Valley of the Dolls* ends with Anne deciding to return to New England, representing her escape from the sin and artificiality (and the *dolls*—drugs) of the "exciting" world of show business. Presumably, if a movie is to be successful and rake in big profits, it should have a happy ending. Apparently novel-readers can take a tragic ending.

Have you ever read a book and then seen the movie version? Were there changes in the movie version? Were the changes for better or worse?

Because of the phenomenal success of *Valley of the Dolls,* many writers have tried to follow Jacqueline Susann's success formula: take three girls of varying backgrounds, looks, and character and follow what happens to them in a kind of world the reader finds exciting and glamorous.

For example, in one such book, *The Beauty Trap* by Jeanne Rejaunier, the reader is introduced to the three girls in the first few pages:

> Eve Petroangeli, a Catholic high school girl, who lives with her grocer father and her mother in Floral Park, Long Island.
> Carrie Richards, a Quaker graduate from Sarah Lawrence College, with an "old family" background in Virginia, who wants to write.
> Dolores Haynes, aggressively ambitious, who'd been in a few movies in bit parts, who wants more than anything to be a star, and who uses men to get the expensive things she can't afford.

The reader then can choose a character with whom to identify. Or she can identify with all three, finding in each a trait she can relate to herself.

REACT:

Which one is the "Cinderella"? What kind of reader will identify with each of these girls?

_____ stood in full view, her well-proportioned body framed in the doorway. Her expressive, softly molded face was set off by a long, silky mane of honey and amber; hazel eyes flecked with jade reflected a high degree of intelligence. So accustomed had Charlene (the owner of the model agency) become to the hundreds of New York models who all looked as if they had been manufactured from one mold she'd almost forgotten the effect singularity such as _____'s natural beauty caused.

A second later _____ appeared. Rex knew immediately the agency could make money with her. She had the ingredients: tall, with dark hair, she knew how to dress, she moved well, she had style, poise, and assurance. . . . Rex appraised the slender body, the carefully done face with its small mouth painted into a glossy, pearlized, and unmistakably avaricious *moue* and the well madeup deep-set eyes bordered by a fringe of dark, thick, fake lashes.

_____ is here, luv, and she's a great type. . . . Sensual and primary. Innocent, earthy.

REACT:

Which description goes with each girl? The first one describes Carrie, the perfect girl—a character like Anne Welles of *Valley of the Dolls.* The second is Dolores, the *ambitious* girl— the opposite of Carrie, who is "natural" and has pure quality. The third is Eve, the *innocent* one.

When the book ends, this is the state of mind of each girl:

> She knew! At last she really knew. Yes, she had found that core of herself, that essence of realness where the truth of her

own being lay. In speaking spontaneously, she was discovering a person she had never dreamed existed, a person of strength and honesty and depth, one who stood on her own two feet and had faith and self-respect. No longer was she Bruce Forman's ding-a-ling, or anybody's trinket, she was a person in her own right.

You remember Peter Talbott—the doctor. He's back from Vietnam. Well, seeing him again, hearing about what he'd been doing for the Friends in Quan Ngai, it made me aware of a whole world out there that could use help from people who care enough. This business has a way of making you get involved with yourself, so that it's easy to forget that. All of a sudden, seeing Peter again, I was ashamed, ashamed at the triviality of my life. I wanted to change, to do something that counts.

How wonderful it was going to be, very soon now, with all her goals finally at the point of materialization. Could she ever want more than what was soon to be hers? A film career, a lovely house in Mayfair; rich, worldly, important friends, chic European clothes, admiration, adulation. Yes, at last the horizon was coming to her. She could feel it in her pores, the close reality of it. She would start right in entertaining, and all London would be vying for invitations to her parties. In short order she would be established as a luminary.

React:

One girl gained self-knowledge; one gained selflessness; one gained money and fame. Which one gained the most? Can you tell which girl is thinking in the above passages? (You are right if you said Eve, Carrie, and Dolores.)

The Big Money Novel Hoax

Although some experts claim that there is no sure-fire formula for producing a best seller, a group of writers did get together and plan out a book designed to break into the big money bracket. They were inspired by the success of *Valley of the Dolls* and *The Adventurers* by Harold Robbins, the two big selling books of 1966. They analyzed these two and other books of the type (what they call the BM book—for "big money") to arrive at a formula.

The formula they found was consistent with all the BM books that have appeared since 1966:

There will be an unremitting emphasis on sex and violence. Also, true excellence in writing will be quickly blue-penciled into oblivion.

Mike McGrady, then a reporter for *Newsday,* masterminded the plot, partly to parody Jacqueline Susann, whose two books, *Valley of the Dolls* and *The Love Machine,* were big money makers. He assigned a chapter to each of his writing colleagues who agreed to go in on the scheme. The final result was the combined efforts of 24 different writers. In addition to the above formula, McGrady decided upon minimal requirements for each chapter:

In the editing, he followed certain rules for cutting—taking out, for example, words of more than one syllable, all symbolism, all interesting character descriptions, almost all nature description, and all qualifying words (i.e., "slightly," "rather," "somewhat").

What was left was the simply told adventures of Gillian Blake, the wife of the team of Billy & Gilly who star in a morning radio show which offers advice on how to make a marriage work. After discovering Billy has been having an affair, Gilly sets out to destroy the happy marriages of her suburban neighbors.

In creating the character of Gillian Blake, McGrady followed the advice of Bernard Geis, successful publisher of big money books:

The element that very few writers are aware of is identification between the reader and the heroine. One of the secrets is to remember that a lot of women do not have a satisfactory life in the real world and therefore dwell in an imaginary world. And they dream of things and there's a lot of wish-fulfillment and so on. Now, in reading a book about a female protagonist, or heroine, they respond more affirmatively if they can identify with that heroine. And the secret . . . is not to begin at the top, but with the woman or the girl in relatively humble circumstances so that the shop girl at Woolworth's or the humble housewife can say "Gee, there's a lot about this girl that's like me." And then, once you've made this identification at the beginning of the book, you can carry her up into the clouds—because she's been there before in her own mind. And she can imagine herself becoming a famous motion picture actress like the heroine of the book, and marrying the most handsome man and the most over-sexed man who ever drew a breath and all the rest of it. Then it fulfills its mission.

Even though McGrady had given all of his authors a week to do his or her chapter (there were four female writers), it was two years before the book was published. Then came the most important part about creating a best seller: the promotion. Since radio interviews and TV talk shows are vitally important in promoting a best seller, the authors had to find someone interesting enough to intrigue the audience. After interviewing many women, they decided upon Mike McGrady's sister-in-law, a 38-year-old mother of six who had written a couple of unpublished novels. After training her a little, they sent her out into the talk show circuit, where she was accepted as Penelope Ashe, the "demure suburban housewife" who had written this dirty book.

Sales were good, and the book was almost at best-seller level when the news leaked out that the whole thing was a hoax, that "Penelope Ashe" was merely a front for the 24 people who had actually written the book. Whether this news helped sales or not is a matter of conjecture, but the book did actually become a best seller. It was a successful hoax. However, Mike McGrady and the other writers have mixed feelings about their triumph. As McGrady says in the closing paragraph of his book, *Stranger Than Naked, or How to Write Dirty Books for Fun & Profit* (Peter H. Wyden, Inc., 1970):

> Later, as it all came to pass, there were always counter-emotions, unexpected misgivings that took the edge off elation. It was too easy; it all went too smoothly. America, you sit there, you plump beauty, still buying neckties from sidewalk sharpies, still guessing which walnut shell contains the pea, still praying along with Elmer Gantry. America, sometimes I worry about you.

The Detective Novel

Ever since 1841, when *Graham's,* the first mass-circulation magazine, published Edgar Allan Poe's "The Murders in the Rue Morgue," detective or mystery fiction has been extremely popular. In fact, this genre

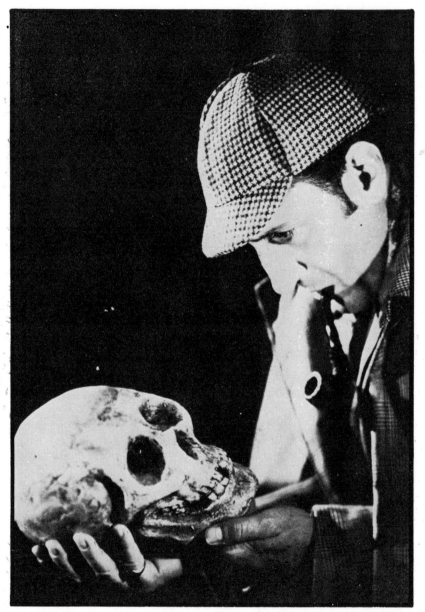

Basil Rathbone as Sherlock Holmes

comprises America's most popular fiction reading. The overall list of best-selling books is dominated by detective stories. Most writers of this type of fiction are prolific writers, some with many books to their credit, sometimes writing about more than one detective and using another name to claim authorship. So, in order to talk about this type of best-selling book, we will talk not of individual titles but of each detective who has been made popular by the series of books written about him.

Sherlock Holmes, The detective created by Arthur Conan Doyle is tall, aristocratic, with cap, and wears a tweed cape, and seldom without a pipe. The British detective solves the crime *intellectually,* by figuring it out through the clues he very cleverly finds. "Elementary, my dear Watson!" became a popular phrase and a "sherlock" is another name for detective.

Ellery Queen, created by the writing team of two cousins, Frederic Dannay and Manfred B. Lee, solves crimes *logically* in the tradition of Sherlock Holmes. Intricate plots, relieved with touches of humor, help to make Ellery Queen novels extremely popular.

Perry Mason, by Erle Stanley Gardner, is a smart, fast-moving lawyer, who, with his faithful secretary, Della Street, befriends some underdog who seems very guilty of some crime or other. Perry becomes involved, and in the middle of his client's trial uncovers the real murderer.

Mike Hammer, by Mickey Spillane, is a 6-foot, 190-pound New York detective, the toughest, most sadistic in the annals of murder fiction. The stories in which Mike figures involve the same formula: a friend of his gets killed and Mike avenges his death by savagely killing the murderer. Along the way, through New York's sleazier side, every girl he meets goes crazy over him. The seven books featuring Mike Hammer are the top-selling seven books of all detective novels.

James Bond, by Ian Fleming, is an agent for British Intelligence. Agent 007 is tall, handsome, tough, and sophisticated. He orders the finest foods, wines, and liquors, but can match the toughest thug in physical prowess and endurance. Beautiful women throw themselves at him, attracted to his "cold, cruel eyes;" he usually accepts, although he's soon back at the assignment.

REACT:

Compare detectives and/or spies. Do you prefer the intellectual approach to solving crimes (the Sherlock Holmes method) or the tough-guy approach (the Mike Hammer approach)? Interview a detective novel buff (many people in high-powered jobs read mystery fiction for relaxation).

CREATE:

Do a collage for an era. On it show the popular pastimes of the age: the current dance-step, claims for attention (flag-pole sitting? goldfish swallowing?), fashions in clothing, movie idols, best seller titles, magazine ads, popular song lyrics, etc. Use anything that contributes to a sense of "the times." Experiment with materials—for instance, sequins and tassels for the '20s. Include newspaper headlines to connect the popular emotional outlets with actual events. If you can't get photos from the past, make up a friend to look like an old movie idol, then take his picture.

Just as the pop music of the Forties seems more redolent of that age's anxieties and attitudes than its rather self-conscious literature, so phenomena like SF film may one day be seen to represent more completely than any other art form the *angst* of this decade.

—John Baxter, *Science Fiction in the Cinema,* Paperback, 1970. $1.25

Chapter 9

HEROES: DO THEY TELL US WHAT WE WANT TO BE?

THE HISTORY OF THE SUPERHERO

Wouldn't it be great if, when confronted with a tough situation, one that's hard to face for one reason or another, you could merely step into a phone booth, rip off your clothes, and emerge as the Super-You —perfectly outfitted, perfectly formed, perfectly equipped to handle the situation, no matter what it is? How marvelous to be not only perfect, but *invulnerable*—unsusceptible to all the fears, doubts, anxieties, hurts, and suspicions that we endure. It is an appealing thought.

It is to this common desire—to be perfect and invulnerable under our normal-looking exterior—that the comic strip *Superman* makes its appeal. Ever since it first appeared in *Action Comics* in 1938, Superman has been the most popular of the superheroes. (*Captain Marvel,* started soon after *Superman,* was a close rival, but the publishers of *Superman* sued *Captain Marvel's* publishers for copying. Captain Marvel was subsequently dropped. He was successfully revived, though, in 1961 by Stan Lee of Marvel Comics and is still thrilling young readers today with his cry of "Shazam!")

One of the reasons for Superman's popularity is that he is a *genuine* superhero. He really *is* Superman; he only *pretends* to be Clark Kent, the inept, mild-mannered reporter who is in love with the rejecting Lois Lane. Other superheroes are human first and need to be transformed into their heroic alter-egos. In addition, Superman is a *self-sufficient* superhero; he doesn't *need* anything. Think of all the gear, for example, Bruce Wayne needs to become Batman. Especially important is the Batmobile. Superman, however, provides his own transportation, "leaping over high buildings with a single bound," and so on. He is so completely independent that he has no need for girls. Like all true heroes in our entertainment media, he couldn't care less about women, even though they are wild over him.

Is it any wonder that Superman is so appealing to children? After all, children are little people in a world of big people who tell them what to do. How marvelous for a child (or even an adult) to imagine himself with all the powers of Superman.

Even though Hitler and Mussolini were favorite villains for comic book superheroes and crime fighters before the United States entered the war against Germany, Italy, and Japan in 1941, the years of World War II became the so-called "Golden Age" of comics. After the war, the popularity of comic books declined. There was a minor boom during the Korean War, and again a decline in interest when that fighting ended. In the mid-1960s, with the fighting in Vietnam, comic book sales went up again. A coincidence? Hardly. Wars mean good business for comic books. It is probably because war provides easy plot material and the enemy, a real villain. Young readers can then identify with the

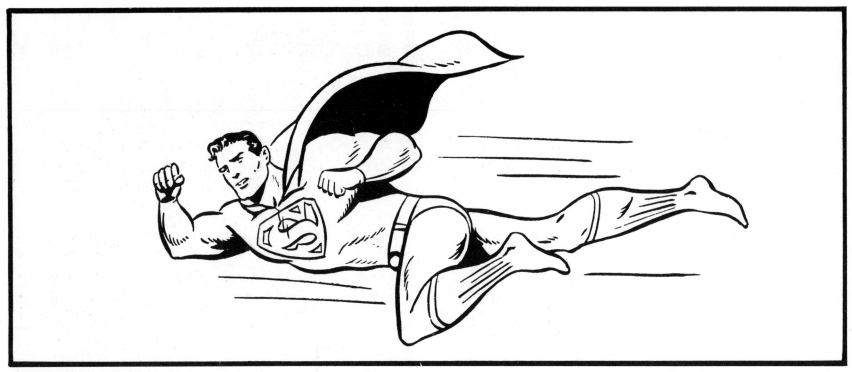

Superman, © National Periodical Publications 1972

heroes and vicariously join the war effort to help overcome the forces of evil.

During the "Golden Age," hundreds of superheroes were introduced; some caught on with the comic book fans and some didn't. Along with Superman and Captain Marvel, there were Batman, the Human Torch, the Flash, the Green Lantern, the Spectre, Hawkman, Wonder Woman, Sub Mariner, and Captain America. Each hero had his own colorful costume; many had "boy companions"; and all were "super." That is, they had powers that were beyond those of human beings.

The true superhero, though, has always been the one under the Clark Kent outfit.

The superheroes are not confined to the comics. In the 1930s, after the tremendous popularity of Superman and the other comic book heroes was ensured, enterprising movie producers sought to cash in on

this popularity. They bought the rights to the stories, and hundreds of films based on the comic heroes were churned out. These films were the basis of the Saturday afternoon serials, the 13-week series that each week left its youthful audiences dangling in suspense, hardly able to wait until next Saturday's episode when they would learn the fate of their favorite hero or heroine.

It was probably the immediate thrills of the fast-paced adventure that they enjoyed, for the serials were so quickly filmed and so haphazardly put together that oftentimes the predicament that the hero was left in was completely ignored in the "next episode." These films, following as they did the comic book genre, were probably the most action-oriented films ever made. That is to say, the characters were not allowed any movements of any kind that were not done at break-neck speed—the actors jumped out of cars, bounded through doors, and ran from place to place. The dialogue was often dubbed in to accompany the action and to provide logic to the hastily contrived plot.

In viewing these serials now, one is hard put to imagine that they provided the excitement that they once did. First, remember that their audience was children, probably from ages 7 through 14 or so, for whom this was the treat of the week. Not having television, they didn't have the ready, constant escape fare we have today. There was radio, of course, with the afternoon serials (often the same heroes would appear in all three media: the comics, radio, and the movies). There were the comics, too. But only film can provide an experience so close to reality. It more or less combined radio and comics—the sounds plus the visual—and it tried to provide the best of both media.

The most famous of all the movie serial heroines was Pauline Smith of *The Perils of Pauline*. Week after week, Pauline was left in some precarious position, such as being tied to railroad tracks on which a train was rapidly approaching. (Pauline did her own stunts, of course. That's why she got the job.)

The most famous serial actor was Buster Crabbe, who played the hero of seven different serials. His most famous role, and the "classic" of the Saturday afternoon serials, was *Flash Gordon*. This series was also one of the first science fiction thrillers, as well. Most of Flash's adventures were on the planet Mongo where the Emperor Ming oversaw such sophisticated devices as television (remember, this series was made in 1936, two years before the first experimental television broadcast), interplanetary communication (not to mention travel by rocket ship), and other not so scientific phenomena like winged men who could fly with ease and other such animal-human creatures. As amateurish as this series seems to the modern audience, it was by far, in its attempt at believability, the best movie serial made.

Buster Crabbe played other roles such as Buck Rogers and Tarzan, and was busily employed until the demise of the serials in the '50s, when the availability of the new medium, television, made serials obsolete. He remains to this day the symbol of the afternoon serial at its best.

Television supplanted not only the movie serial but radio programs as well. The comic book, though, has continued to survive. Perhaps this is because reading is a private act, and privacy provides a better fantasy trip.

The Superhero will survive so long as there are children who need a fantasy outlet.

Buster Crabbe as Flash Gordon

Pearl White, "Days of Thrills and Laughter," 20th Century-Fox

THE WESTERN HERO, THE CRIME-FIGHTER, AND THE REBEL

Through the history of American popular culture, three hero-types have been perennial favorites: The Western hero, the crime-fighter, and the rebel. Each has appeared in every entertainment media, beginning in the "dime novel," then in the movies, on radio, in comics, and finally on television. Each reflects certain traits that are particularly American.

The Western Hero

The Western is said to be one of America's two great contributions to world culture (the other being jazz). When, during the 1880s, men were "conquering" the West, they were in a situation in which the battle lines—the forces of good and the forces of evil—were relatively clear-cut. The land was there for man to "civilize" and to "tame." The western pioneer, then, in his efforts to "create a new world," was Good and anything which stood in his way—whether it be a natural or a human obstacle—was Evil. Further simplified, this basic situation evolved into a form of entertainment known as The Western, which, although offering only a few basic plots, is consistently popular no matter what form it takes.

The Western first appeared in what were known as "dime novels" (the original paperback books) which became popular in the late 1880s, just as the expansion to the West was ending. Then, when movies began in the early 1900s, the Western was adopted wholeheartedly by this infant industry. It had all the elements to make a good movie— plenty of action, an obvious conflict, a hero and a villain. Just to make sure the audience knew which was which, the directors dressed the hero in white, from his hat to his horse, and the villain in black. (This has become a Western tradition. Even the youngest child watching a Western on TV can tell the "good guys" from the "bad guys" by the way they *look*.)

The first actor specializing in Westerns was William S. Hart, who tried to be realistically heroic. There was Ken Maynard, who did his own fabulous trick riding while being heroic. Then there were the

Roy Rogers and his faithful dog.

Clint Eastwood in "A Fistful of Dollars," United Artists

Singing Cowboys, Gene Autry and Roy Rogers, who *sang* while they were being heroic.

Since the 1930s, after sound had been developed and the movies were in their heyday, certain movie actors have been synonymous with the Western movie. They have been more than actors merely playing a part well. They seemed to embody the characteristics that have made the Western hero a particular favorite among Americans. Although many popular American actors have tried their hands at the Western, and many have tried more than once—Randolph Scott, Joel McCrea, Henry Fonda, James Stewart, Gregory Peck, Robert Mitchum, Kirk Douglas, William Holden, and even Dean Martin and Frank Sinatra—the two actors who seem to fit the role best are Gary Cooper and John Wayne.* (In 1971, Wayne led the list of box office draws. In the past 22 years, he has seldom been off the list.)

First of all, in physical appearance, they fit the requirements of the Western hero: tall, lean, and handsome. They have something more than these traits, however. There are other popular actors who are tall, lean, and handsome—Cary Grant and Rex Harrison, for example—who still do not have the *look* of a Western hero. Grant and Harrison have too much *humor* in their faces, as though they like to flirt with women. And although they are lean, they have the filled-in appearance of a well-fed man. These actors are definitely of the city. But Gary Cooper and John Wayne (in his younger and leaner days) have the *look* of the West. Their faces are fairly impassive, almost sad, as though they were so used to a hardened existence that they could no longer smile. Furthermore, their faces are lined with the loneliness of men on whom much responsibility falls. For the Western hero is a man who is tall and strong and capable. He can outride, outfight, and outshoot other men. But his strongest characteristic is his sense of responsibility. When he sees that his strength is needed, he cannot refuse to offer himself, even in the face of death. This is what makes him a hero, and this is what makes him sad.

Two of the most famous of all Western films, *High Noon* and *Shane,* illustrate this heroic quality very well.

In *High Noon,* the town marshal, played by Gary Cooper, learns on his wedding day that the "bad guys" are coming in to town, seeking revenge for having been sent to jail (by the marshal, who is credited with having "cleaned up" the town). The marshal receives no support whatsoever from anyone: in fact, his bride threatens to leave him; his deputy

---

*And more recently, Clint Eastwood.

Gary Cooper in "High Noon," United Artists

Alan Ladd in "Shane," Paramount Pictures

beats him up over his ex-girlfriend; and his mentor, the town's previous marshal, advises him to leave town with his new bride and let the townspeople face their own problems. Realizing that he is the only one who can really stop the "forces of evil," the gunmen, from destroying the "forces of good," the town's budding civilization, the marshal, risking all, remains to face the men.

In *Shane,* the hero, played by Alan Ladd, is a fast gun, who, tired of killing, hires on with a homesteading family whom he comes to love and admire. The family and the other homesteaders are threatened by evil ranchers. Although he realizes that in doing so he'll have to give up what he cares about most, his new life with the family and his respite from violence, Shane offers his strength and skill to save the homesteaders.

In each film, the hero "does what he has to do," saving the "good" people by destroying the "bad," and then leaves town. His leaving seems to emphasize that he does what he has to out of pure principle. It's not even *his* town that he saves.

These films illustrate another characteristic of the Western, the one that is probably the reason for its continuing popularity: *the hero always wins.* Or, to look at it more generally, *good triumphs over evil.* It's an ending more satisfying to the ego (of each boy and man in the audience who identifies with the hero, and of each girl and woman who admires him) and to one's general outlook on life. Consider that most people go to the movies (or read a book, or watch a TV show) for an uplift. They don't want to see the hero defeated, and they don't want to see what seems to them the right way of living giving way to the wrong.

Since the Western is based on a specific era of American history, the settings and costuming are always the same. Since there are still some areas of the country that are "untouched by civilization," a Western film may use real scenery as a backdrop to the action. In a Western, therefore, whether it be in the movies or on television, the audience knows exactly what to expect. It will see a familiar setting, whether it be the plains, the mountains, or the town; it will see familiar people in familiar outfits (the "bad guys" are always unshaven and dark; the "good" woman will be fair and dressed in light clothing). It will be a familiar plot: the town, the ranch, the wagon train, the herd (whatever it is, it always represents the forging of civilization in the wild West) will be threatened by those who would wish to thwart, to rob, or to destroy it. The hero comes to the rescue, oftentimes going over the head of the law (which is often portrayed as weak and ineffectual, if

The homesteaders in "Shane"

not downright crooked), and through violent means (by fist or by gun) destroys the threatening element.

When you read about Greek drama, you read that the Greeks often went to see different enactments of the same story, like that of Oedipus the King, enjoying the *process* of the unfolding of the familiar plot— enjoying *how it was done* more than how it all turned out. Perhaps it is the same with us and the Western. We enjoy seeing the scenery and the *way* the plot is worked out. We never need to worry about whether or not the good guy will win, just as the Greeks never doubted that what fate had predicted would indeed come about. Perhaps two or three thousand years from now, another people, perhaps even on another planet, will look back on American civilization in the 20th Century as we now look back on Greek civilization in the 5th Century B.C., and wonder what we believed in. If they look at the Western (from the earliest "dime novel" through the popular television shows of *Gunsmoke* and *Bonanza* and including *The Lone Ranger* of comic book and radio fame), they will discover that we believed in the following:

- The introduction of civilization in the untamed country was a noble task; man and his needs were more important than the planet's (trees were cut for lumber, for example).

- Men who acquired vast fortunes in land or cattle through hard work were admirable.

- To protect one's property (that which one had worked for) any means was permissible, including murder.

- When the law proved ineffectual, an individual could take the law into his own gun-toting hands.

If they look at the heroes of our Westerns, they will find that we admired:

- Men who in stature were tall and slender and whose faces were lined with the tensions and burdens of a hard and dangerous life.

- Men who did not display emotions, either their joys or their fears.

- Men who were wanted by women, but who did not really have a place for women in their lives and who, therefore, ignored them.

- Men whose sole existence was to protect the weak and helpless from those who would harm them.

John Wayne

When a person goes to a Western movie or watches a Western on television or reads a Western novel, he is often doing more than spending his leisure time pleasantly. Often he is seeking to have his basic beliefs confirmed. If these beliefs exist solely in the fictional world of the Western, they would comprise a *mythology*. If they also operate in the world of reality, then they represent a *value system*. Some people believe the beliefs expressed in Westerns to be myths, and some to be true values. This is one example of the disparity of beliefs that is prevalent in modern society. This disparity may be called a "generation gap" or a "cultural gap" or whatever, but when one person tells another that the beliefs he's based his life on are all make-believe, it's the equivalent of a threat to his life. And a person reacts to a threat on his life in his own way and according to his own value system. He may just believe in a shoot-out.

Take the movie *Easy Rider,* for example. You could make a case for the film as a negation of the values of a Western. The heroes make a fortune, not through hard work, but through a "deal." They ride on motorcycles, the modern-day equivalent of the horse. They travel eastward, reversing the westward movement, you might say.

Along the way, the heroes come across evidence of the failure of the Western value system: the farmer who had started West but who got stuck along the way and who was vague about where Los Angeles was (This episode contained some obvious symbolism. While the young men were fixing a flat tire on their motorcycle, the farmer was shoeing his horse); the young people of the commune who were trying to live off "the fat of the land," only the land wasn't fat; the alcoholic lawyer who couldn't take the narrow-mindedness and the limited life in the small Western town. The shocking ending was a direct comment on one of the principal beliefs of the Western: when a man threatens your way of life, shoot him! The long-haired hippies on motorcycles were as threatening to the rednecks as the Apaches might be to the homesteaders in some Western movie.

Compare the hero, Peter Fonda, with a Western hero like John Wayne, for example. Rather than being strong and stoical, he is vulnerable and sensitive. He doesn't exist merely to combat evil but to find some meaning in life *for himself.* He believes in letting everyone "do his thing"; he accepts his own weaknesses.

When a father admires and identifies with the Western hero and his son admires and identifies with the motorcycle hero, you have not only a "generation gap" but a "cultural gap." Each despises what is admired by the other. Most of us, though, can handle such differences in our

Peter Fonda

Humphrey Bogart in "The Maltese Falcon"

stride. We manage to keep our fantasy life separate from our real one. When people begin to confuse fantasy with reality, then trouble starts. (See essay at end of chapter.)

We soon learn that wearing the same kind of clothes or wearing our hair the same way or using the same expressions doesn't magically transform us into the person we admire. We learn that we must *act* like him. Then we may "try on" a trait here and a characteristic there to see how they work out. This is how we develop our personalities. But we usually take the traits and characteristics from more than one person, not just from one fantasy hero. We take them from our parents and other members of our family, our friends and peer group, and finally from people we read about or see in movies or on TV. Young people just out of the complacent, self-centered world of childhood are apt to do this constantly, and yet it is a process that continues in one form or another throughout our lives. The more a person "tries on" other ways of acting, the more he grows. And the more sources he has for imitation, the more chance he has of growing the most.

It is unlikely, therefore, that a man will model himself completely after a John Wayne or a Peter Fonda. He is more likely to have more than one hero. That is why there is room for more than just the Western hero in our world of popular culture.

Another popular American hero—one with traits similar to the Western hero—is the detective. If the Western hero protects civilization in its vulnerable early stages, the detective tries to rid it of the corrupt elements which are a part of its advanced, "modern" stage. His milieu, where he operates, is the big city. The forces of evil he combats are crooks, gangsters, and the politically unscrupulous—those people who would take from the innocent what they value most, their money or their freedom to make money. His weapons are his fists and his gun. Like the Western hero, he often works outside the law which, as in the early Western days, is often depicted as ineffectual. Very seldom, however, is the law shown as crooked. It is more often portrayed as handicapped by an obligation to do things "by the book," a handicap the detective is not burdened with. The hero may be a dedicated policeman, a lawyer, an international spy, a "private eye," or simply a private citizen who may be called upon to come to the aid of the victimized.

Like the Western, the detective type of story has been popular in the various popular entertainment forms—in books by Dashiell Hammett, Raymond Chandler, Mickey Spillane, and Ian Fleming. In the comics, Dick Tracy has been one of the most popular strips since its inception in 1931, and was also a movie serial. Then on TV, there are many such detective heroes—perhaps the most enduring being Perry Mason and Joe Friday of *Dragnet.* Perhaps the most romantic detective hero is found in the movies, which aren't as rooted in reality as television is. (People can be larger than life on the big screen.)

The actor who best personified the detective hero was undoubtedly Humphrey Bogart, who seemed to have some of the same personality traits as the character he often portrayed. In the late '30s and '40s, he played the same character in a series of movies which are considered the best of the form. In *The Maltese Falcon,* for example (based on the Dashiell Hammett novel), he played Sam Spade, a shady private detective. Through a woman with whom he falls in love, he becomes involved in a plot to recover a statuette of a falcon which is supposedly made of solid gold. He is drugged, beaten up, accused of murder by the police, but at the end he turns the woman over to the police, following a creed which involves seeing that his partner's murderer is brought to justice, even though it be the woman he's in love with. Like the Western hero, the detective follows an heroic creed which transcends such mundane matters as personal relationships.

In another "classic" of its type, *Casablanca,* Bogart plays an American who has divorced himself from all commitment to society and has created his own little world in the form of "Rick's," a nightclub in the city of Casablanca. His world is invaded, however, in the person of a woman he had been in love with and her husband, who is the leader of an underground political movement. Although Rick could act selfishly, taking the woman for himself and turning her husband over to the political leaders who wish to murder him, he does not. He helps to save the husband for the greater cause of freedom from political oppression—not for himself, but for the helpless others who don't have his strength.

Like the Western hero, the detective hero will risk his own life and happiness to save the innocent from the forces of evil. As the Western hero is able to meet the "bad guy" on his terms—in the shoot-out on main street, the Western hero will win because he's "faster"—so does the detective hero meet the city's "bad guys" on *their* terms. He's tough, able with his fists and his gun, but more important, he's *aware.* Nobody can "con" him because he's seen it all. He's aware of all the corruption the city can offer, but through it all, he's retained his honor and his sense of what's right. His awareness is what gives him his advantage over the police and the other citizens. He can use all the tricks of the trade, but it's okay because he's doing it on the side of Good. What is so appealing about the detective hero is that he answers to no one. He

Paul Newman in "Harper," in the Bogart tradition, Warner Bros.

is completely self-sufficient, even to creating his own morality.

Is it any wonder that the detective hero is such an attractive figure to men and women alike? To men, he is what they'd like to be—the toughest guy of all, afraid of no one and answerable only to himself. To women, he's what they want—the ultimate of protectors. Life being what it is, however, he's also pretty far from real.

As a reaction to this kind of romantic heroism, there emerged in popular culture a kind of hero that came to be known as an anti-hero. He is not strong or powerful or superior; in fact, his main appeal lies in his role as the underdog. He is heroic only in his refusal to knuckle under to the powerful forces that try to control him. This type of hero, popular in the '50s, was best exemplified by Marlon Brando, who played several roles of this sort when he first went into the movies.* (James Dean also played an anti-hero in *Rebel Without a Cause,* for example. At his death—in an auto accident—a cult was formed, its basis being the anti-heroism of the actor.)

The Wild One is a good example of a film with an anti-hero. In this film, Brando plays the leader of a motorcycle gang that descends upon a small California town. There's another gang in town, and its leader (played by Lee Marvin) and Brando are rivals. Subsequently, the cyclists (in the '50s a motorcycle was not accepted by society's mainstream; it was a symbol of rebellion and outlawism) terrorize the town in drunken revelry and Brando saves a girl from a probable gang rape. He thus makes a human connection with the girl and her father, the town sheriff, who has treated Brando decently. When Brando leaves, he gives the girl a trophy he has stolen from the motorcycle races—the symbol of his anti-social behavior and of his need for bravado.

These three types of heroes—the Westerner, the detective, and the rebel—will undoubtedly continue to be popular in the various forms of mass culture unless, of course, our values undergo a radical change. There is some evidence that they might. Television has seen the development of a new kind of hero—the *group* hero. In an effort to provide more characters for people to identify with, shows are providing heroic teams, as on such popular shows as *Mission: Impossible, Star Trek* (now in re-run), and *Mod Squad.*

In the shows involving doctors and policemen, there is often a representative of each age group—one under 30, one about 40 who is

*In the '60s, Paul Newman took up the mantle of the anti-hero, playing him in such movies as *The Hustler, Hud, Cool-Hand Luke,* and most recently *Sometimes a Great Notion.*

Marlon Brando in "The Wild Ones"

"The Mod Squad" heroes, ABC

usually the nominal leader, and one in his 50s. Although the purpose of having these teams is obvious, to attract the largest audience, it could be that it's also related to a trend in our society away from individuality and independence, which is the one characteristic our traditional heroes have had. Also it shows a trend toward realism and away from romanticism. What with the interest in group therapy, group dynamics, group marriage, and group living, there may develop a *group hero* which would embody the qualities we admire. Compare the two great heroic flights of the 20th Century: in 1927, Charles Lindbergh made the first trans-Atlantic flight from New York to Paris *solo* and became a worldwide hero known as "The Lone Eagle." In 1970, three men made the first flight to the moon . . . and became a worldwide heroic *team*.

The Hero in Advertising

Advertising agencies often use American culture heroes to help sell products, and sometimes they create their own heroes. For example, the advertising world has given birth to several "superheroes." Mr. Clean may be magically conjured up by the housewife who is overwhelmed by the magnitude of the dirtiness she faces. And there is the White Knight who may also be called forth to help combat the forces of evil dirt and grime. Perhaps the girl who grew up enjoying the exploits of *Wonder Woman* and *Sheena, Girl of the Jungle,* and who yearned, along with Lois Lane, to have her very own Superman, still believes in the possibility of a magical man, one who will appear in the very nick of time to rescue her from the disasters of dirt.

The classic advertising campaign is one based on the appeal of the Western hero. In 1956, Marlboro cigarettes were marketed for women. They were colored red and were ivory-tipped. Their share of the cigarette market was less than one-quarter of one percent. In those days filters on cigarettes were considered "feminine." Then came the statement by the government that cigarette-smoking was linked to lung cancer. The problem was to make filter cigarettes acceptable to men. The solution (found by Leo Burnett, and which made his agency famous) was simple: consistently picture the most masculine of men smoking a Marlboro. In our society, the most masculine man is considered by both

The Marlboro Man, Leo Burnett Company

Rudolph Valentino as The Sheik

men and women (women smoke cigarettes, too, and they tend to smoke the brand that men like) to be the Western hero. Thus, the Marlboro man was born, and Marlboro cigarettes climbed to among the top-selling brands of cigarettes.

Marshall McLuhan, who was among the first intellectuals to consider the effects of advertising seriously, has said: "In modern ads, you start with the effect. The product that produces the effect comes later. A Forsythe shirt ad shows a field of daisies. There is no sign or mention of shirts, you simply look and feel as fresh as a daisy."

Following this line of thinking, you could say that the message in the Marlboro ads is "Masculine men smoke Marlboros. You are masculine. Smoke Marlboros." Of course, every boy or man likes to think of himself as masculine, and so this kind of appeal works. Part of the appeal, too, is a kind of wishful thinking that goes on at levels so deep we're probably unaware of it. In this case, the message is "Masculine men smoke Marlboros. Smoke Marlboros. Then you will be masculine, too."

The Orpheus Phenomenon

In the history of popular culture (a force in our society which became a major one around 1920 when the growth of electronic media sent the images and sounds of entertainers to a great many people), many men and women have become extremely popular with the public, not only for their talents but for certain aspects about their looks, personality, and life style. It is, in fact, the way celebrities seem to *be* and to *live* (often fabricated by the publicity people) that fills the pages of the fan magazines and even makes newspaper headlines.

Some of these entertainers' popularity may be very short-lived, and others may be popular for very nearly all their lifetime. A few such entertainers made such an impact on the country that they will surely remain a part of our history even if it be merely for sociological and psychological interest. These four entertainers at one time or another created a form of mass hysteria in the country, which could be called "The Orpheus Phenomenon." (Orpheus is the figure in Greek mythology who played the lyre so beautifully that wild animals were soothed, the trees danced, and the rivers stood still. One of the legends concerning his death is that the Thracian women were worked up into such a frenzy by his music that they tore him limb from limb.) When you read the histories of these four entertainers, you will see the similarity to the Orpheus legend. They are Rudolph Valentino, Frank Sinatra, Elvis Presley, and the Beatles (we'll consider them as *one* in number).

Let's look at the history of each.

VALENTINO

VALENTINO, Rudolph (1895-1926), Italian-born American film actor, born Rodolph Alphonso Guglielmi di Valentino d'Antonqueila at Castellaneta, studied agriculture but emigrated to the United States and first appeared on the stage as a dancer. In 1919, he made his screen debut as Julio in *The Four Horsemen of the Apocalypse,* and his subsequent performances in *The Sheik* (1921), *Blood and Sand* (1922), *The Young Rajah* (1922), *Monsieur Beaucaire* (1924), *The Eagle* (1925), and *The Son of the Sheik* (1926) established him as the leading "screen-lover" of the 'twenties. He died suddenly at the height of his adoration in New York and his funeral resembled that of a popular ruler. Besides good looks and athletic bearing he had considerable dramatic gifts.

—*Chambers Biographical Dictionary*

There were by then almost twenty thousand people clamoring to get in [to view the body lying in state in a funeral parlor in New York City]. The sidewalks between the subway stations at Fifty-ninth, Sixty-sixth and Seventy-second Streets were unable to accommodate the influx, and all north- and southbound traffic on Broadway was choked to a standstill, as was crosstown traffic between Columbus and Amsterdam Avenues.

Psychologically blind, emotionally drunk, intoxicated by steamy human contact, increasingly defiant of the impotent police force—the mob, transformed into a human juggernaut, stormed the doors. It shouted and screamed and cried out in a masochistic ecstasy that transmuted pain into joy.

—Irving Shulman, *Valentino*, 1967.

Thousands of people stood in line outside Campbell's funeral parlor.

The author then goes on to explain how the mob pushed the policemen through the glass windows and entered the funeral parlor. People were trampled before the police finally clubbed the mob back. More than a hundred people were injured. The inside of the parlor looked as though locusts had been through it; it had been stripped by souvenir hunters.

By the next day, the police had restored order and had effected perhaps the longest line in history: 30,000 people stood in a relatively orderly line in the middle of New York City in order to file past the body of the movie idol—in a line that moved at 150 a minute! Some people waited an entire day in wet weather for a fraction-of-a-second glimpse of the body of a movie star.

Here is another description of Valentino: "Adagio Dancer," from *U. S. A. (The Big Money),* by John Dos Passos, 1930:

> Wherever he went the sirens of the motorcycle cops screeched ahead of him, flashlights flared, the streets were jumbled with hysterical faces, waving hands, crazy eyes; they stuck out their autograph books, yanked his buttons off, cut a tail off his admirably tailored dress-suit; they stole his hat and pulled at his necktie; his valets removed young women from under his bed. . . .
>
> When he lay in state in a casket covered with a cloth of gold, tens of thousands of men, women, and children packed the streets outside. Hundreds were trampled, had their feet hurt by police horses. In the muggy rain the cops lost control. Jammed masses stampeded under the clubs and the rearing hoofs of the horses. The funeral chapel was gutted, men and women fought over a flower, a piece of wallpaper, a piece of the broken plateglass window. Show windows were burst in. Parked cars were overturned and smashed. When finally the mounted police after repeated charges beat the crowds off Broadway, where traffic was tied up for two hours, they picked up twenty-eight separate shoes, a truckload of umbrellas, papers, hats, tornoff sleeves. All the ambulances in that part of the city were busy carting off women who'd fainted, girls who'd been stepped on. Epileptics threw fits. Cops collected little groups of abandoned children.

Who can say what the reasons were for such a reaction? What we do know is that Valentino did make the tango popular, at least for a time, and did alter the American's notion of what a lover is. Have we ever gotten over the impact of "The Latin Lover" ideal?

It wasn't until 1942 that the United States had another example of "The Orpheus Phenomenon," this time in the person of a skinny little singer named Frank Sinatra.

The following is an excerpt from *Sinatra, Twentieth Century Romantic,* by Arnold Shaw, 1968:

Frank Sinatra

> The scenes at the Paramount, and later at broadcasting studios, were the nearest thing to mass hypnosis the country had seen until then, with girls moaning ecstatically, shrieking uncontrollably, waving personal underthings at him, and just crying his name in sheer rapture.
>
> During his first appearance at the Paramount, as the fever spread among the bobbysoxers, extra guards had to be retained to maintain order. Girls remained in their seats from early morning through Frank's last show at night. Some fainted from hunger, others from excitement. Fearful of losing their previous seats, many would sit through several shows without taking time out for the ladies' room. As his engagement lengthened, the windows of his dressing room had to be blacked out, since the mere sight of him from the street below resulted in traffic jams. Getting him in and out of the theater, his hotel, a restaurant, developed into an elaborate ritual in which his handlers schemed, and not always successfully, to outwit the fans. When they failed, he did not come away with all of his clothes and belongings. On one occasion, two girls caught hold of the loose ends of his bow tie and, in the pulling match for the memento, almost strangled him to death.

The hypnosis continued; adults ridiculed and Sinatra prevailed. He made movies and records and, after a slump in the early '50s, won an Academy Award for his portrayal of Maggio in *From Here to Eternity,* changed his singing style from syrupy to swinging, and became a legend.

After Sinatra, teen girls considered it *de rigueur* to scream over popular singers, but it wasn't until Elvis Presley that the nation was set in an uproar again:

ELVIS PRESLEY

Jacksonville was a turning point in Elvis' career—if not that, a focal point. Teen-agers tore his clothes off, shredding his pink shirt and white jacket, ripping his shoes from his feet, actually putting Elvis in physical danger, although at the time he laughed it off.

—*Elvis,* by Jerry Hopkins, Simon & Schuster, Inc.

This picture of hysteria was not an isolated incident or merely a local explosion. From 1956 on, Elvis was a news event, a social crisis, a censorship controversy, a frequent scapegoat, and occasionally the focal point of a tragedy. In all parts of the country—in places of which he had never heard and in which he would never set foot—and in many parts of the world, people were worrying about Elvis.

—*Operation Elvis,* by Alan Levy, 1960.

As they had thought about Sinatra, the public looked at Presley as a kind of a freaky fad that would soon die away as so many others had. But Presley continues to make records and movies that make money. He now seems to have a permanent place in the American entertainment scene.

Frank Sinatra at the height of his popularity with bobby-soxers.

Elvis Presley

The Beatles

Just when the American public had gotten used to black jeans and shirts, ducktailed and sideburned hair styles, and the guitar-thumping singing known as rock 'n roll, there burst upon the scene—amidst a $50,000 publicity campaign by Capitol Records—four "mop-topped" imports from Britain known by the strange name of the Beatles. "Beatle-mania" had already taken hold of Britain, but that didn't automatically ensure that it would in America. After a couple of their records didn't make it, the Beatles' "I Want to Hold Your Hand" made the number one spot. They were booked on the Ed Sullivan Show and Capitol publicity helped to make that appearance a nationally known event. There were 50,000 applications for 728 seats. The Sullivan show that night had 73 million viewers.

During all the shouting and screaming and boasting of record-breaking tours in Britain and America, the Beatles were crouching somewhere inside the giant piece of machinery which was transporting them round and round the world. They'd retreated inside it in 1963, forced by all the pressures, and remained there, hermetically sealed, as if on a desert island, from all life and reality.

They were trapped in their dressing room during a performance. There was a mad dash, guarded by hordes of police and bodyguards, to the hotel. There they stayed, with the outside world locked out, till the time came for the next move. They never went out in the street, to a restaurant, or for a walk . . . so they all sat in their hotel bedrooms, smoking, playing cards, playing their guitars, putting in the hours. Earning 1,000 or 10,000 or 100,000 pounds (multiply by 2.80 for dollars) for one-night stands was meaningless. Being rich and powerful and famous enough to enter any door was pointless. They were trapped. —*The Beatles,* by Hunter Davies, 1968.

Americans were shocked by the Beatles' hair in 1963.

In each case—Valentino, Sinatra, Presley, and the Beatles—the pattern was the same: the entertainer created a sensation with his (or their) female following. Fans were constantly on the verge of becoming an uncontrollable mob (and sometimes did), putting the object of their idolatry in danger. Then the entertainers became front-page news items, talked about in every circle. Except by their fans, they were ridiculed: Valentino was called a "pink powderpuff"; Sinatra, a "4F draft-dodger" among other things; Presley was known as "The Pelvis" and was actually censored on TV (only shown from the waist up) because of his hip movements; and the Beatles were ridiculed for their clothes and hair style.

Gradually, though, other entertainers, wanting to cash in on the popular style, imitated them, often rather blatantly. The once-jealous male population began affecting their hair and dress styles, until finally they were no longer so outrageously different. Finally came acceptance and ultimately, respect.

Imitation Is the Sincerest Form of Flattery

Valentino's brother had several painful operations on his nose, in a futile attempt to take up where his dead brother had left off.

Sinatra was a tenor of Italian ancestry. There also were Perry Como, Vic Damone, Dean Martin, Frankie Laine, Tony Martin, Tony Bennett, Steve Lawrence, and Bobby Darin. They weren't all Italian, but they all were influenced by Sinatra.

Elvis Presleys are born, not made. Today we know that's true, but in 1959, when Elvis still seemed like another fabulous freak, anybody with an eye to a bank balance was trying to reproduce the phenomenal formula. Get a good-looking boy, teach him to sing like Elvis, to move like Elvis, and wowee, a fortune. Fabian, who came from Philadelphia, was a good-looking boy, and he did resemble Elvis slightly. He wasn't a very good singer but a properly edited tape could remedy that, not to mention some good publicity. It very nearly worked, but in the end, Fabian never did become a big rock star.

—*Rock Encyclopedia,* by Lillian Roxon, 1969.

Where the Beatles were a somewhat spontaneous click, the Monkees are as calculatingly manufactured a product as a TV

dinner. Producers Bert Schneider and Bob Rafelson, both 33, placed an ad last year (1965) in *Variety* announcing auditions "for four insane boys, age 17-21 . . . (who) have courage to work." In four months, the co-producers interviewed hundreds of boys. So frantic was the talent hunt, that Screen Gems studio guards were instructed to send in likely looking lads off the Hollywood streets, and they did—including one bewildered kid carrying a sack of laundry to a Laundromat.

Misspelling: The four finally tapped: Mickey Dolenz, 21, the square-jawed star of TV's *Circus Boy* which he played under the name of Mickey Braddock; Peter Tork, 24, a folk singer with a blond mane; David Jones, 20, an ex disc-jockey who handled the role of Artful Dodger in the Broadway musical, *Oliver,* and lanky Mike Nesmith, 23, a folk-guitarist and singer from Dallas, Texas. The name of the group was chosen by Schneider, and misspelled by Rafelson who, one eye cocked at such concoctions as the Beatles, the Byrds, and the Cyrkle, reckoned it was "contemporary to distort the names of rock 'n' roll groups. . . ." The boys had never sung as a group, so, said Rafelson, "we locked them together in a closet for three months, and they came up with their own sound." —*Newsweek* Magazine, October 24, 1966.

When People Confuse Fantasy with Reality

This story appeared in the *Los Angeles Times,* September 30, 1970: Hollywood . . .

The Superman of Hollywood is dead. Police found him, sitting in his apartment refrigerator—frozen stiff. Since last March, when he moved to Hollywood from Chicago, Arthur W. Mandelko, 24, has waged a never-ending fight against "crime." He used two

guises . . . one, as a policeman he patrolled Hollywood streets at night either on foot or on his small motorcycle. The other was as Superman. He would don his Superman suit: red cape, high boots, skin-tight blue underwear with a big red "S" and jump from roof to roof at the motel where he lived or else jump out at people from telephone booths. He also combined his two identities. He wore his Superman outfit under his policeman's uniform and would enter a phone booth in order to strip off his outer garb to emerge as Superman, often frightening people enough for them to complain to police.

Police took no action against Mandelko because he had no history of dangerous conduct. Also,

after neighbors complained, he seemed willing to give up his nightly roof jumping.

When found in the refrigerator, where he had been for about four weeks, he was fully dressed, although in neither his policeman or Superman clothes, sitting with his knees up to his chin, his hands holding a rope tied to the inside of the refrigerator door.

Who knows what sort of game he was playing?

Although this is an extreme example, there are many people who confuse fantasy with reality and who still are considered perfectly sane. For example, many people confuse an actor or an actress with the role he or she plays.

The following is an excerpt from *Tune In Tomorrow* by Mary Jane Higby, who played the leading role in *When a Girl Marries,* one of the most popular radio soap operas, for many years:

A comfortable, motherly woman approached me one day on the third floor of NBC.

"Your husband has not run away with another woman," she said. "I've walked all the way from the Bronx to tell you."

"Thanks," I said, "but it's just a story. It has nothing to do with me, really. I'm an actress."

"You must go to him. I know where he is."

I gave her my name, my husband's name, and a list of radio characters (about seven) that I was impersonating at the time. She listened patiently, then went right back to the plot of *When a Girl Marries.*

Dolores Gillen came by just then, and I introduced her to the woman.

"You know in the story I have a little boy?" I said.

"Oh, yes," said the woman, beaming. "I love Sammy."

"Well, *this* is Sammy. Miss Gillen plays Sammy. See? We're actors." There was silence. "Dolores," I said, "talk like Sammy."

Standing right in front of the fan from the Bronx and wearing a smart blue suit and a chic feather hat, the finest child imitator in the business obligingly started with Sammy, aged five, and worked back through the years until he was wailing in his crib, gurgling and burping.

The woman frowned, but it was a passing thing, like a shadow cast by a falling leaf. She turned to me, "Your husband still loves you. He's lost his memory. You must go to him."

"OK," I said at last. "I'll go to him."

It was murder being a teen-age idol. You couldn't do anything (without being mobbed). If I had a night off on the road and wanted to see a movie, I'd have to have my manager buy out the balcony.
—Frankie Avalon.

Movie stars affect everyone's lives in ways they don't even know. They even affect people who don't go to the movies. They set styles in clothes. They affect all sorts of behavior. They set life style patterns. The "Hollywood Film" is probably the leading factor in the distortion of values this country has and is now looking at with some perspective. That's dangerous.
—Dustin Hoffman, Oct. 26, 1969.

"A talk-show host will attract a successful amount of involvement, I was told, if he manages to project one or both of the following 'images': The Good Family Man Image and The Little Boy Image. For either to be successful, it must be combined with the Everyman Image. This theory contends that all of the major talk-show hosts are on camera and in real life bland, non-commital, undiscriminating, jelly-fishy or 'plastic' individuals with few, if any, strong personal convictions. They can be all things to all men, so undefined, up to a point, that the viewer can create most of their presumed personality in his head.

"The Sociology of Dumb," by Chris Welles, *Esquire,* May, 1971.

This sort of thing happens all the time to actors and actresses who play radio (or TV) roles. Through letters, telephone calls, and personal confrontations, people speak to the actors as though they were actually the characters they portray. (For instance, there have been several TV series revolving around a doctor: *Ben Casey, Dr. Kildare, Marcus Welby, M.D.* Many people in the TV audience apparently believe so strongly in the actor's portrayal that they write letters to him, asking for medical advice!)

It happens to movie stars, too. Many actors who play "tough guys"— Edward G. Robinson, Bogart, Robert Mitchum, John Wayne, among others—have complained that frequently some patron at a bar or restaurant will accost them with a challenge to prove their "toughness" in a fistfight. So many women wrote actress Claudette Colbert, who played a warm, sensible woman in many movies of the '30s and '40s, that she finally started an advice-to-the-lovelorn newspaper column.

This confusion of the person with the role he plays can be devastating to the actor. Bette Davis states in her autobiography, *The Lonely Life,* that she could never find a man who could see beyond Bette Davis the actress and appreciate her for herself. George Reeves, who played Superman in the movie serial, committed suicide. His friends claimed that he was discouraged because no producer would consider him for any other role.

When Ingrid Bergman, who was married to someone else at the time, became pregnant as a result of an affair with Italian director Roberto Rossellini, the American public was completely shocked. The event was reported in front-page headlines for weeks, and women's clubs took such actions as to recommend that her young daughter be taken away from her, that her films be barred, and that she herself be barred from the country. They were outraged because they had thought that Ingrid Bergman the woman was the same as the roles she often portrayed—a pure, innocent, almost nun-like (she *had* played nuns) girl. Studio publicity helped build this image, too. Miss Bergman was portrayed as a woman who shunned such worldly actions as smoking, drinking, wearing make-up, going to parties, and so on. The public felt that she had betrayed them and so they reacted strongly. As it turned out, Miss Bergman did not return to the United States for over ten years— until such time as she felt she had been "forgiven" by the American public.

Charlie Chaplin actually *was* banned from returning to the United States in 1952. Part of the reason for this exclusion was indignation over his personal life (which was made public by the press). Chaplin

Ingrid Bergman in "The Bells of St. Marys" (1945).

Marilyn Monroe in "Let's Make Love," 20th Century-Fox, 1960

only returned to the United States (in 1972) to accept a special award at the Academy Award ceremonies.

The story of Marilyn Monroe is the most tragic example of what can happen when a person's screen image gets mixed up with what he or she actually is. Norma Jean Baker as a child was shunted from foster home to foster home, encountering people and events that helped her grow up into an emotionally immature, extremely insecure woman. Her beauty, figure, and look of innocent sexiness (plus studio publicity) helped her become a world-renowned Sex Symbol. She was at the height of her career when she committed suicide. Underneath Marilyn Monroe was Norma Jean Baker, who apparently felt she couldn't live as herself.

People's desire for fantasy was well understood by Walt Disney who built a vast empire by appealing to it. The zenith of his creations is Disneyland, where a person can legitimately indulge himself in substituting fantasy for reality. In fact, he is *encouraged* to do so. That is the whole purpose of Disneyland.

It is possible, in a single day in Disneyland, for the visitor not just to see but to enter into time and experience past and time and experience future, to recapitulate not only his own memories and fantasies but those of the race as well. He can visit, impressionistically, every continent of the globe, its mountain heights and ocean depths as well as almost any historical epoch, including the prehistoric. In the revised Tomorrowland he can now even gain an impression of interstellar travel on a ride that simulates such astronautical experiences as weightlessness. It is therefore sometimes possible to feel that Disneyland is best summarized as a model of the "global village" Marshall McLuhan is always talking about, a place where one can literally touch, smell and see, in an instant, and almost as easily as turning around, some representation of the thoughts and experiences that have made us what we are, some representation of the thoughts, traditions and styles that made our fellow villagers.

—*The Disney Version,* by Richard Schickel, Avon, 1968.

As any visitor to Disneyland will claim, it is fun to enter a fantasy world. Indeed, psychologists state that we need an occasional escape into fantasy for our mental well-being. Furthermore, many creative artists transform their fantasies into art in one form or another. The danger is when *all* our experiences are fantasy ones and we no longer experience anything for ourselves. Then we have in a sense stopped living.

Dress and Costume

Imitating dress is the simplest and most obvious way we try to be like others. Pinning a pillow case around the neck of a little boy transforms him into Superman or Batman. Little girls love to put on Mommy's high heels and parade around the house. When we get older, this becoming another person by dressing like him becomes more subtle: we follow the fashion trends set by popular idols.

During the '40s some men wore an outfit called the "Zoot Suit" that has to be seen to be appreciated. The jacket was worn extremely long, and the slacks, belted around the waist, were very wide at the knee. Part of the costume was a long keychain which the young man was able to twirl to display his nonchalance. In the '50s, one of the ways of dressing for boys was dark jeans and dark shirts, with a leather jacket for the "hard" look. The hair was worn (à la Presley) full, meeting at the back of the head in a "duck's tail," with long thin sideburns. In the '50s' era of conformity, young people tended to dress pretty much alike, although they would vary in the extremes they would go to in order to follow the fads.

It was partly due to this tendency toward sameness that made the Beatles so conspicuous when they came to the United States in 1963. In comparison to what they and other musical performers looked like in 1970, they were not so unusual looking. It was mainly their hair. They wore it in bangs over their foreheads and longish in the back. Their clothes were different from the current fashion, too, but it was their hair style that became the focal point of interest. Adults ridiculed it, and young people imitated it. Beatle wigs became big business.

That was the way it began—with the Beatle wigs. And by the end of the '60s, the "do your own thing" attitude was expressed in young

The Zoot Suit

peoples' dress and hair. Now, as far as dress is concerned, anything goes.

With all the variety of dress styles, it has become possible to *communicate* through clothes. When you put on a certain outfit now, you may be saying something to the rest of the world about what you are like, what you believe in, what you like to do. The length of a boy's hair now means many more things than how long it is.

React:

Accumulate several pictures—photographs or clippings from newspapers and magazines—of people in various sorts of dress. (Select people who will be unfamiliar to the class.) Then have the class make some guesses about the people: what are their jobs, what are their general beliefs (liberal or conservative, for example), what are their hobbies, and so on. You will have to select the pictures carefully so that you will be able to tell the guessers whether they're right or wrong.

Create:

Conduct the same sort of experiment using real people. This will take some organizing, but the results should be worth it. Find some people who would be willing to conduct this experiment with you. Try to get a variety of people of varying ages and types. Have them dress in a certain distinct style. Then take them before a group of people who don't know them and have the people guess some things about them. What is their political philosophy? What kind of music do they like? What kind of car do they drive? What cigarette (if any) do they smoke? What is their favorite TV show? And so on. You might then take the same people, have them exchange outfits, and then ask *another group* the same questions about them. You would then be able to determine fairly accurately how clothes transmit a message about the person wearing them.

Create:

Another kind of experiment with dress would be fairly easy. Dress in a certain style popular with young people and go to some stores in the neighborhood. Watch carefully how you are treated. Then, some time later, wear an entirely different kind of clothing, go to the same stores, and see if you are treated differently. You might find that some adults tend to judge young people by their dress and not by their actions.

Create:

Have a costume party. Have each member of the class dress as a certain type of person. You might determine the types ahead of time and let each person select the one he is to dress like. Then the rest of the class could guess what kind of person he's supposed to be. Or, each member of the class might dress as the person he most admires (other than himself).

Create:

Design paper dolls. Name them. Give them wardrobes to match their personalities.

React:

Collect samples of ads in which men are used to sell products. Select ones which are creating an image for the male reader to identify with. Analyze the images projected.

Create:

Do a collage of media heroes—all of a certain type, or a variety.

Do:

Take a certain type of hero (or his opposite, the ordinary man; Charlie Brown and Dagwood Bumstead, for example) and make a report on his existence in the various media: television, movies, comics, advertising, music.

Do:

Investigate the history of a certain type of American hero, such as the cowboy. Compare the historical version with the romanticized version. Trace his popularity from the dime novel through television. (An interesting report would be an investigation of how the American cowboy has become popular in the cultures of other countries, like Japan, for instance.)

Do:

Write a biography of a real hero or popular idol.

React:

Make an analysis of the fan magazines. Who are the people most frequently pictured on the covers? What kind of stories are there? Who reads these magazines? What are their appeals?

React:

Compare American heroes with those of other cultures, with others in our own country, or with those of foreign countries.

Do:

Conduct a survey. To find the most admired men and women in today's world, ask these questions of several members of the following groups: girls and boys the same age as the class; girls and boys younger than the class; men and women the age of the parents of the class; men and women the age between the students' and their parents' ages:
1. What male and/or female from the entertainment world do you admire the most?
2. What about him or her do you admire?
3. Do you try to be like him or her?

4. Do you think you are like him or her in any way?
The results should be revealing. You should be able to determine which qualities are admired by each age group.

React:

Discuss what you would do in each of the following situations:

- The school is on fire. The fire department is there fighting the blaze and evacuating the students. You are one of the last to leave. At the top of the stairs you look back and see that a girl has fallen and can't seem to move. Just then the people cry, "There he is; the last one! They're all safe." The noise is deafening; you can't be heard. The flames are threatening. If you go back to help the girl, you both might not make it out. But if you go down to the firemen on the ground for help, there might not be time enough for them to go up and get her out.

- Some students during lunch time have seriously damaged one of the properties near the school. You happened to have seen them do it, and you're the only one who did. Because of the outraged community, the school administration has decided that, unless the guilty ones are made known, students will no longer be allowed off campus during their free time. The guilty students, whom you know and like, do not confess and seem unlikely to. You and the rest of the student body are very incensed that your freedom has been curtailed. Some students blame the administration; some blame the students for not confessing. It becomes apparent that you are the only one who can make the guilty ones known.

- There's a student we'll call T for thief. T has stolen something fairly valuable from your friend's car, but it can't be proven. Your friend is very angry and decides that, since he can't get back his stolen property or even get the thief in trouble, he'll "teach him a lesson." He plans to beat him up. One day you and your friend and a few other guys run into T, who's all alone. It's the perfect opportunity, which your friend takes advantage of. You have four choices: 1) to help your friend beat T up; 2) to stand by and watch; 3) to help T against the unfair odds; and 4) to go get help for T.

- One night coming home late on a bus, you look out of the window and see a crime being committed. You can see the faces of the culprits clearly, although they don't see you. A few days later you read about the crime, that it is one of a series, and the police have no idea who is committing them. They have some suspects but need an eyewitness to identify them. Later on, you read that no eyewitnesses have come forth and so police are unable to solve the crime.

CREATE:

Play "Hero Charades." Divide into two teams. Each member of each team puts the names of heroes from current or past popular culture or from history on pieces of paper. A member of the opposing team takes a name, then tries to get his team to guess the name within a certain time limit. He can only give hints through his acting.

CREATE:

Will the real hero please stand up? Form a panel of four or five students. Each one is told privately that he is to act like a certain heroic character (the class or certain members of the class may have previously suggested several choices). They may be people from history, from literature, from past or current popular culture: comics, movies, television, advertising—the White Knight, Mr. Clean, the Marlboro man, for example—or from reality. Then the students selected to be the "guest panelists" ask the secret heroes questions, such as "If you were faced with a ferocious beast, what would you do?" The "heroes" may respond with one short sentence about how each would meet the particular situation. After a certain number of questions, the identity of each hero is guessed.

READ:

The Steranko History of the Comics, Supergraphics, 1970, $3.00.
Days of Thrills and Adventure, Barbour, Collier, 1970, $3.95.
The Great Radio Heroes, Harmon, Ace, $.75.
Valentino, Irving Shulman, 1967.
Sinatra: Twentieth Century Romantic, Arnold Shaw, Pocket Books, $.95.
The Beatles, Hunter Davies, Dell, $.95.
Bogie, The Definitive Biography of Humphrey Bogart, Joe Hyams, Signet, 1966, $.75.
His Eye Is on the Sparrow, Ethel Waters, Pyramid, $.75.
W. C. Fields: His Follies and Fortunes, Robert Lewis Taylor, Signet, $.95.
King: A Biography of Clark Gable, Samuels, Popular Library, $.60.
The Lonely Life, Bette Davis, Lancer, $.75.
Long Journey: A Biography of Sidney Poitier, Ewer, Signet, $.60.
My Autobiography, Charlie Chaplin, paperback, $.95.
The Other Side of the Rainbow . . . With Judy Garland on the Dawn Patrol, Mel Torme, Bantam, 1970, $1.25.
Spencer Tracy, Larry Swindell, Signet, 1969, $.95.
Mr. Laurel and Mr. Hardy, John McCabe, Signet, $.95.
Do You Sleep in the Nude? Rex Reed, Signet, 1969, $.95.
Conversations in the Raw, Rex Reed, Signet, 1969, $1.25.
Confessions of a Hollywood Columnist, Sheilah Graham, Bantam, $1.25.

> Clothes are a means of defining the self socially.
> —Marshall McLuhan, *Understanding Media.*

THE PERSONAL MESSAGE

Communicating always involves three elements: the *sender,* the *receiver,* and that which is sent, the *message.* It can be as close as a kiss or as distant and remote as an interplanetary communiqué. In some cases, the three elements can be equally important, as in a kiss; in other words, the sender needs the help of the receiver to keep the message going. At other times, the message is all-important, such as in skywriting, a billboard, a routine weather report tapped out on a teletype machine—the sender is unseen, perhaps unknown, and the intended receiver might be just anybody (or nobody) who happens to be around.

When the communicating is done through the *mass* media, it is, of necessity, impersonal; that is, the sender sends out his message, not to one intended receiver, as with a kiss or a phone call or a personal letter, but to many people whom he doesn't know. The sender really doesn't know whether he has in fact communicated. He sends his message and he hopes that someone gets it: that his printed words are read, that his transmitted words are heard, that his image is seen. He has various ways of checking out receiver reaction: if he runs a newspaper, then he pays close attention to the letters to the editor; if he makes movies, then box office receipts and critics' columns are his gauge; if he is a TV or radio station owner, then he keeps his eye on the rating charts and audience surveys. But the cold fact remains that, at the moment of message-sending, he is addressing an unseen and unknown receiver. It ought to be an uncomfortable situation, for sender and receiver alike; yet each medium, each person within a medium, has his own quirky ways of striking "that warm, personal note."

Perhaps most obvious in his attempt is the deejay:

> It's three bells and bee-utiful in BOSS-Angeles on the tried but true blue show. Don Blue that is. I'm waiting for ya . . . give me a call and I'll spin your favorite record . . . and here we are . . . for Susie and Debbie . . .

This particular deejay is attempting personal connections with his audience at a rate of five per second. He has developed a delivery that highlights himself as a personality; he actively seeks the listeners' involvement in his show through phone-in requests; and when he gets that response, he singles out the girls *by name.* In other words, he has taken extraordinary pains to beat the built-in anonymity of the mass medium in which he works and has tried to reproduce the close connection of a one-to-one conversation. Some listeners will "feel" it; others are repelled by the fast, frenetic pace and high decibel delivery of Boss radio announcers—they feel talked *at* instead of talked *to.* The slow,

rather toneless modulated voice on an FM station; the solemn tones of the announcer on a religious station; the nasal twang of a country music station; the foreign language broadcast—all of them sound highly personal to *someone.*

Distance and objectivity are considered necessities for good newspaper reporting, yet the editors realize that such straight-faced reportage needs to be relieved by human interest stories, opinion pages, and columnists with distinct, personal opinions. They know of the reader's very human need to sense a live human being behind the printed word. Columnists, from the "I'm-a-real-dingbat-around-the-house" type to the sports page commentator, fulfill this need. The casual, free-wheeling style of the following columnist makes it easy to participate in his observation and even to share his opinion:

> The newest directive from the FCC orders the managers of radio stations to examine the lyrics of the records in order to eliminate "the use of language tending to promote or glorify the use of illegal drugs." Most radio station managers I have run across don't even understand the lyrics to the "Star Spangled Banner," so the thought of them straining to understand the Beatles singing "I Get High With Some Help From My Friends" is hilarious.

Casualness, informality, and laughter are used to "personalize" TV shows, too, especially the talk shows. The appearance of the guests, sitting in comfortable swivel chairs, gesturing easily and speaking apparently spontaneously, works to break the ice between TV viewer and celebrity guest who now seems to sit in the viewer's living room. Most people do not realize the rehearsing that goes on beforehand to achieve this effortless, casual, but cracklingly alive impression. Chris Welles, in an article for *Esquire* (May, 1971) called "The Sociology of Dumb," reports that he asked Mike Douglas what would happen if people just sat down on his show and talked as if they *were* in a living room. Douglas looked startled, "The sound of sets being turned off across the country," he answered as if to a child, "would break your eardrums."

Magazine and newspaper ads and TV commercials are full of attempts at "the personal touch," working mainly on the "we care about you" theme and the "we understand how you feel" idea:

- Porsche spent years developing a great competition car . . . so you could have fun driving to work. Take the wheel. It won't fight you.

- There's nobody else exactly like you . . . (insurance ad)

- Brand-name carpets — off-beat, kinky, and uncommonly lush. It's new, thick, sexy, plush polyester—many-tufted, fat and springy — to make it comfortable and your fun uninhibited.

- You deserve a break today . . . so get up and get away.

- Products made with *you* in mind!

- Phone us any time if you have a question or complaint about . . .

The problem with many of these "personal touches" is that they are superficial and their effect is short-lived. We step away and analyze them for a moment, and we feel as though we've been conned, manipulated, softened up so that we'll buy or tune in again or just sit there feeling comfortable. Even if it *is* human nature to enjoy sitting back and being entertained and cajoled and undisturbed, it means, in the long run, a kind of gradual smudging out of the human potential that is in each one of us.

Every so often a message from the media jolts us out of this diminished state. We feel *deeply* affected, sometimes changed or even charged into action. At the least, we feel momentarily alive and stirring, full of our own and others' possibilities. The media we will look at in the remaining chapters have shown, in recent years, the greatest potential for activating these deeper human responses.

CHAPTER 10

Alternate Media - Voices From the Underground

The term "underground" has been associated with rebellion since the early days of our country's history. First, there was the "underground railway," a means of transporting runaway slaves to safety in the North. Then, during World War II, our allies in France formed an "underground" to combat the Nazis who were then occupying their country. Lately, underground has become associated with that which is outside the mainstream of the establishment—whether through illegality or simply rebellion. The term has been used so loosely that there is some

> *underground* adj. Unsanctioned by prevailing social attitudes; anti-establishment. For a long time the public was unaware of the subcultures of drug takers, hippies and sexual swingers. Their existence was kept so quiet that they were called underground. They have influenced mainstream society a great deal: the growth of hair by hippies, beads by the mystic religious sects, clothes by homosexuals and hippies, advertising art by psychedelic art, and the moral code of today by all these groups, to mention only a few of the more obvious aspects. . . . Many underground activities are now successful money-making ventures.*

confusion as to what it actually means. Where better to go for a definition of "underground" than *The Underground Dictionary*?*

"Underground," then, is that which is anti-establishment. In these days of revolution and rebellion, that covers a lot of territory. Those people who consider themselves anti-establishment are many: young people, the blacks and Chicanos, women's "libbers," people who advocate the free use of drugs, and people who believe that our conventional sexual morality is too restrictive. Since the underground people often represent that which is abhorrent to society's mainstream, for the most part, they have been unable to use the communication media of the establishment to express their beliefs or to propagandize. (Still, a few of these "underground" groups *have* used the media to their advantage.) Because these people feel that the establishment media do not speak for them, they have found their voices in the so-called "underground" media. There are *hundreds* of underground newspapers and magazines, a growing coterie of "comix" artists, underground filmmakers, underground radio, and even underground television.

In many cases, the "underground" is less an outlet for radical beliefs than a reaction to the overground media. Thus, the term "alternate media" is used by those people who find the connotations of "underground" inaccurate.

The Underground Dictionary, by Eugene E. Landy, Simon and Schuster, 1971, $1.95.

Whichever term you prefer to use to describe it, however, there is a whole other world of media beyond the one known to most of the American people, the one we have been talking about so far in this book. It is this *other* media world that we will discuss in this chapter.

UNDERGROUND PRESS

The recent growth of the underground press (there are close to 6,000 underground papers being published in the United States today*) is the direct result of two factors: the anti-establishment mood of young people and other dissidents, and second, technological advancements, like offset printing (a simpler and cheaper means of printing than the older *letterpress* method) which have made it possible to publish a newspaper for a fraction of what it used to cost. The average underground paper costs as little as $200 per issue, most of which goes to the printer.

Although there are more underground newspapers than ever before in our country's history, they are by no means the first dissident voices to have found an outlet in an alternate press. The very first newspaper to be published in this country (in 1690), *Publick Occurrences Both Forreign and Domestick,* was banned after its first issue because it criticized the government. Benjamin Franklin worked on what was probably the first underground newspaper in America (in the 1720s), the *New England Courant,* his brother's paper. Franklin wrote a satirical column under the penname "Silas Dogood." There was the Patriot Press of Samuel Adams and Thomas Paine in the Revolutionary War years and the Abolitionist Press of Horace Greeley and Elijah P. Lovejoy in the Civil War period. Whenever people feel that the "overground"—or establishment—press does not speak for them, an "underground"—or alternative—press will develop. The fact that there are so many underground newspapers in the United States today, though, is probably due more to inexpensive printing costs than to the increase in dissidence.

---

*This figure includes an estimated 3,000 underground high school papers. Robert Glessing, in his book *The Underground Press in America,* lists only 456 of the more stable underground papers, which list is by now outdated. (See the bibliographic note on Glessing's book at the end of this section.)

However, the dissidence among Americans today should not be minimized. Even though it is inexpensive to start a newspaper today, there would be no need to do so if the establishment press spoke for *all* of the people. The underground press was developed primarily because the people of the counterculture see the establishment press as a journalistic vacuum.

What has happened to the newspaper in America, a country that cherishes the principle of freedom of the press? For one thing, the newspaper has become Big Business. For another, it has become a monopoly. A few people own a great many newspapers. In many cities, a monopoly of the news exists since there is only one newspaper to serve the city.

One of the most lucrative businesses in the United States today is the small weekly newspaper. The advertiser needs the newspaper to reach his potential customers (80 per cent of Americans read a daily newspaper). Townspeople want a newspaper to read. If there is only one newspaper in town (which is most often the case), then the owner "has it made." He has no other paper to compete with for the reader or for the advertiser (even though he does have to compete with the other media and with the "shoppers"—throwaway papers whose main purpose is to carry advertising).

The newspaper—whether it is a small town newspaper or a big city daily—writes from the point of view of the establishment. It gets much of its news from the large news services—United Press International and Associated Press. What this amounts to is not so much a lessening of the freedom of the press as a failure to *use* that freedom. There is no one censoring the overground newspaper publisher except himself. Since, more often than not, he is motivated by the desire for profit more than by an urge to express his beliefs, he avoids offending his reader and alienating his advertiser. Even though he may have no newspaper competitor, his readers and advertisers would never tolerate his adopting any of the characteristics of the underground press.

He would never, for example, use the term "pigs" to refer to the police, nor would he use any of the other frank language so dear to underground writers. He would never publish nude photos or any other graphic sex-oriented material. He would never advocate the use of illegal drugs, nor would he urge the overthrow of the establishment (of which he may just be a member in good standing). Furthermore, he would never publish his paper in the makeshift way the undergrounds do, nor would he allow the sloppy make-up or the wild use of artwork and color.

In summary, the overground press, both the large city dailies and the small town newspapers, has become the impersonal, standardized, innocuous, profit-motivated voice for only *one* (although by far the largest) segment of the American population. It does not speak for many of the minority groups, which lately have demanded a voice. The need, therefore, for an outlet of expression, combined with the means of providing the outlet, produced the great underground press movement of the '60s.

The *Village Voice* (of which Norman Mailer was one of the founders) and the *Realist* (started by Paul Krassner, who until then had been satisfied with contributing to *Mad Magazine*) were the first of the modern day underground newspapers. They were started in New York City in the 1950s as voices for the "beatnik" generation—the politically left, the artists, poets, writers, the social rebels, who were the radicals of the apathetic '50s. Several other papers were formed before the great surge of underground press growth in the '60s. However, none of them lasted. Only the *Village Voice* (now so successful it is termed "overground" by the newest underground papers, and so conservative as to have inspired its own alternative paper—the *East Village Other*) and the *Realist,* of all the underground papers started in the '50s, have lasted.

In May, 1964, nearly ten years after the birth of the *Village Voice* in New York City's beatnik district of Greenwich Village, the Los Angeles *Free Press* was founded. "Freep," as it is affectionately called, was modeled after the *Village Voice* except that it provided a voice for a new generation of radicals, the people of the rock music world and the people who lived a freewheeling sex life, people who were studiously ignored by the *Los Angeles Times* and other overground papers. Apparently there were enough people who were seeking such a voice (or who at least wanted to read an alternative newspaper), for the *Free Press* has grown from the four-page giveaway it was in 1964 to a 40-page weekly with a paid circulation of nearly 100,000.

Perhaps the most famous, and one of the more financially successful, of the underground papers is the Berkeley *Barb*. It was started in 1965 by Max Scherr, who was then in his mid-fifties, as a reaction to the conservative Berkeley press and the university administration. It was also a voice for Berkeley's "street people." It became an accurate representative for its readers, for it was as garish and as far-out, both in design and content, as the "street people" were in their appearance and life-style.

Tourists, who in 1966 included a slow drive down Haight Street as part of their San Francisco sightseeing itinerary, paid the long-haired paper hawkers a quarter for the *Barb* and got more than their money's worth in shock value alone. People weren't used to seeing such frank language, nude (even obscene) photographs, and sex ads in a newspaper sold openly on the streets. If the *Barb* were mere pornography, it wouldn't have been so fascinating. But it was the strange combination of Christian idealism (peace, love, and flowers), radical politics, and the frankness—plus its unconventional design and layout—that gave the *Barb* its uniqueness. As a result, the paper enjoyed by 1971, twice the circulation of the establishment *Berkeley Gazette*.

The *Barb* grew along with the hippie movement. When the movement died, the *Barb* persisted, as have hundreds of other underground papers. They persist because they are amply supported by establishment advertisers who want to reach the youth market that the underground press attracts. Record companies are the principal advertisers, but other companies who cater to the youth market use the inexpensive undergrounds to advertise their products, too. Also, there are the notorious sex-oriented classified ads, which are a lucrative part of the operation.

Although underground papers have distribution problems (many vendors will not handle the undergrounds), they have no problems finding either advertisers or readers. How long will they be able to attract readers? Probably as long as their viewpoint, their freedom of expression, and their personalness remain an *alternative* to the impersonal, monolithic, establishment-oriented overground press.

As Robert J. Glessing says in, *The Underground Press in America:*

As long as the conditions in (our) society include a war long supported by the overground press, a population allowed to poison the air and water, to kill the cities and to oppress the poor, then this writer believes that the underground press will continue to flourish. And as long as America's leaders offer police repression and harassment as their chief answer to massive youthful unrest, the underground press may prove to be the only medium in the American society with the personal and economic freedom to question and challenge the Establishment—and to record the time historically from a youthful point of view.

Read:

The Underground Press in America, Robert J. Glessing, Indiana University Press, 1970.

Dennis Kiernan works on a paste-up for *Rolling Stone*.

Underground Magazines

If *Playboy* is the success story of the "overground" magazine world (and ironically, *Playboy's* success stems from founder Hugh Hefner's making the underground nudity-and-sex-oriented material acceptable to the overground), then *Rolling Stone* is its counterpart in the underground magazine world. Started in 1967 in San Francisco by Jann Wenner with a mere $10,000 (compared with the $1,000,000-plus figure needed to launch the slick magazine *New York*), *Rolling Stone* is now operating well into the black. On its fourth birthday (November, 1971), it had a yearly income of two and a quarter million dollars and a circulation above 300,000 readers. *Stone* has started a book division, The Straight Arrow Press, and plans to publish at least 10 books each year, and has gone international with an edition in England.

What are the reasons for *Rolling Stone's* success? One probable reason is that, with the exception of a few issues which ventured into radical politics, it has kept its focus on rock music. Through specialization, it has built up a following among rock music fans (a good portion of today's young people). Today *Rolling Stone* is considered the definitive magazine of popular music. With a solid readership and financial success, *Rolling Stone* now has enlarged its scope. It covers not only the rock music scene, but every aspect of the counterculture.

Some of *Stone's* staffers felt that the rock music format was too limiting. They left the magazine in the early 1970s to join *Rags,* a magazine that was just getting started. Although *Rags* is presumably a "fashion" magazine, it is closer to the *Whole Earth Catalogue* than it is to *Vogue* or *Harper's Bazaar*. It does not confine itself to fashion alone, but will discuss any subject that is related to the underground scene. You might say that it is the woman's magazine for the *hip* woman, the ones who are repelled by the artificial slickness of the establishment woman's magazine.

Rags' circulation is increasing. It may become as successful as *Rolling Stone*. It, like *Stone,* specializes in providing material of interest to its readers. Also like *Stone,* it avoids the blatant sex-oriented material and ads that make up such a large part of the underground press.

Another offshoot of *Stone* is *Clear Creek* which, as *Earth Times,* was started by Wenner in 1969 in the flush of his success with *Rolling Stone*. After four issues, though, Wenner dropped *Earth Times* as a poor venture. The magazine's staff, however, managed to get enough money to start the magazine again. They changed its name to *Clear Creek* and plan the magazine to be a platform for the environmental movement.

Like the underground newspapers, the underground magazines such as *Rolling Stone, Rags* and *Clear Creek* are much cheaper to publish than their overground counterparts. First, they use newsprint rather than the more expensive "slick" paper. (Newsprint, or "pulp," has until now been associated with magazines that have exploited the sensational: confessions, sex, violence, gossip, etc.) Second, the magazine is stapled or simply folded together rather than glued. Third, inexpensive offset printing methods are used instead of letterpress. Fourth, staff members take on all tasks of producing the magazines, avoiding hassling with unions and many other orthodox and costly business procedures. (*Rolling Stone,* though, has gotten so big it has had to farm out some of its printing.)

A magazine hybrid is *Earth* magazine, which was started by veteran magazinist Jim Goode in December, 1970, as a bridge between the establishment and the underground worlds. Since Goode had some substantial capital with which to start the magazine, he prints *Earth* on glossy paper rather than on newsprint and uses four-color photography, far more costly than black and white photography used by the penurious underground mags. *Earth,* although it may look like an establishment magazine, devotes its content to counterculture topics. It has developed Earth News Service, which provides underground radio stations with news items from the emerging culture.

Because an underground magazine is less expensive to produce, it doesn't need much advertising to support it. A slick must devote 60 percent of its pages to advertising to make money, whereas an underground needs only 30 percent. Being less dependent on advertising than its overground counterpart, the underground magazine has more freedom to print what it wishes.

> The prospect is that the alternate press may be much reduced in size and may change in content and tone, but it will survive. And that is a good thing, because the diversity of the press in a democracy is one of the best guarantees of the system's good health.
> —John Tebbel, *Saturday Review,* November 13, 1971

UNDERGROUND COMIX

The Berkeley *Barb* was founded in 1965; the *Rolling Stone,* in 1967. Haight-Ashbury was in flower; and San Francisco was thought to be "where it was at." Many people, attracted to the culture that San Francisco and Berkeley represented, flocked to the area. Among those who came was a former greeting card illustrator named Robert Crumb. The atmosphere was ripe for Crumb's kind of self-expression. Here were the kind of readers who would dig his stuff (although the police probably wouldn't). He was right. The first issue of his comix magazine, *Zap,* which he and his wife sold on the streets of Berkeley, was popular with the "street people" but not with the police (some dealers were busted for selling a couple of *Zap* editions). The first issue, which featured Mr. Natural, declared "Fair Warning: FOR ADULT INTELLECTUALS ONLY!"

Although there had been a couple of underground comics published before *Zap,* it was Robert Crumb's work that actually started the underground comix movement. Other comix artists drifted to the Bay area and began to put out books. Jack Jaxon and Gilbert Shelton started Rip Off Press, a cooperative for comix artists, to avoid being exploited by the middle men. Other artists who joined the burgeoning comix movement were S. Clay Wilson, Rick Griffin, and Victor Moscoso who, with Crumb, became the nucleus for *Zap Comix. Yellow Dog Comics* was published by Berkeley's Print Mint, which now publishes different underground titles. Other comix publishers have formed the San Francisco Comic Book Company, Last Gasp Eco-Funnies, Krupp Comic Works, and The Company & Sons.

It is impossible to give the exact number of underground comix titles, since new ones are being published all the time. However, there are over a dozen different titles on the stands (of the dealers who are willing to handle them) at any given time. And apparently the movement is still growing; new titles are being planned as this book goes to press. It would seem that, far from leveling-off, the underground comix in 1972 are still in the early growing stages.

"The proper and traditional realm of comics [is] to indulge people's fantasies," claims Jaxon, one of the founders of Rip Off Press. Artists are able to render their fantasies into colorful graphics and the reader indulges his fantasies by immersing himself in the comic book artist's fantasy world. Underground comix have developed because the establishment comics do not allow artists complete freedom to reflect their basic obsessions, which seem to be with sex and violence. In 1955, Senator Estes Kefauver's committee began investigating juvenile delinquency and took to heart Frederic Wertham's book *The Seduction of the Innocent* (which claimed that violence in comic books was contributing to juvenile delinquency). The committee recommended that the comic books do something about the excessive violence contained within their colorful pages. The Comics Code Authority resulted, which maintained strict control over comic book content during the next 15 years.

Zap and the other underground comix have reacted to this control by taking the comic book to the very extremes of sex and sadism. Although some comix are "adult" only by virtue of the subject matter and the use of four-letter words, there are some comix which are simply pornographic. The quality that keeps them from being classed as mere pornography is the artistry of the rendering. Some comix artists are extremely talented. They do not work in the underground because they are waiting to break into establishment comics; they do so because they enjoy the freedom of expression the underground provides. Not only are they able to draw their fantasies of sex and violence, but also they are able to attack everything about middle-class America that they don't like: sadistic police, hardhats, army officers, authority figures, machines, war, and much of what middle-class Americans cherish.

It is not only the freedom of subject matter that attracts the comic artist to the underground, though. He also enjoys artistic freedom. In the establishment comic world, the artist is an employee. His work is controlled by the editors and publishers he works for. In the underground, he draws what he wishes, makes his own deadlines, helps with the printing and publishing of his book, and also profits by the success of his work (the cooperative comix publishers divide the royalties— half goes to the artist and the other half to the publisher).

With sales of establishment comics going down and those of the underground going up, one would expect that the overground would adopt some of the characteristics of the underground in order to recapture its readers—or, at least, to subsidize a comix publisher in order to cash in on the underground comix success. So far, they have not. Perhaps they really believe that their superheroes can overpower everything, even the anti-heroes from the underground.

Created by Jack Jaxon of Rip-Off Press, San Francisco

Underground Radio

Many people are confused about the differences between underground and FM radio. Many people feel they are synonymous. FM (frequency modulation) is a wave-length frequency band which is an addition to the standard AM dial. Since a relative minority of existing radios in the United States have FM capability* FM is not the Big Business operation that AM radio is. Because there are fewer listeners to an FM station, the station attracts fewer advertisers. It is this format—more music, fewer commercials, plus the better fidelity—which draws listeners to FM, whether it be to an underground, a classical, a country and western, or an "easy listening" station.

An FM station, then, is far from the multi-million dollar business operation that an AM station is. In fact, many FM stations are merely automated adjuncts to a profitable AM station. In visiting AM station KYA in San Francisco, you see a door marked KOIT-FM. Opening the door, all you see is a small room containing several large machines. All the programming—announcements, commercials, as well as music—has been pre-recorded. The only movement in the room is the silent, slowly-revolving reel on one of the huge tape decks.

Because FM is a low-power financial operation, it was as FM stations that the undergrounds were first heard. The first underground station is said to have been KMPX-FM in San Francisco, founded by AM-dropout Tom Donahue in 1967. Donahue developed his kind of radio as an alternative to the tight AM format, as exemplified by the Drake stations. (Donahue formerly was a deejay on the Drake-programmed KFRC in San Francisco.) Instead of a tight playlist of the best-selling singles, an underground station plays long-playing albums uninterrupted by jingles or announcements. Instead of a restrictive format which is as precisely planned and as carefully monitored as a spaceship-launching countdown, the underground "format" is freeform and undisciplined. Instead of the fast-talking, frantic pitch of the Top-40 AM deejay, the underground deejay's tone is "mellow"—mellifluous and low-key. In-

stead of a strict adherence to the principles of profit-making, the underground station broadcasts not only the music but the *culture* and the *politics* of its listeners. An underground station may, for example, refuse to accept or offer to alter a commercial which it feels is ecologically unsound. An underground station may, as KSAN did during a recent oil spillage disaster in San Francisco Bay, become the center of a counterculture *cause célèbre*. Such un-businesslike practices scare away many advertisers who are fearful of being associated with "revolutionists." However, the popularity of such underground stations as KSAN in San Francisco, with its audience of young listeners, easily alleviates such fears. Therefore, ad agencies that want to reach the pocketbooks of the affluent young must buy time on the "revolutionary" underground stations.

Many people predict that underground radio of today will be the standard radio of tomorrow—along with a few other types of stations on the FM dial—and that AM will be devoted to news and information. Whether this prediction comes true or not depends on whether the people underground radio speaks for remain part of a subculture or whether they emerge as the dominant culture-bearers.

How does an FM deejay feel about his job?

Phil Buchanan, deejay and programming manager for San Francisco's KMPX-FM, declares that his present job is the most satisfying one he's had in the field—and he has been in all kinds of radio. Although he could easily make a great deal more money in AM radio, he appreciates the freedom he now has to play the kind of music he likes. He feels that this freedom is worth more than a higher salary.

"A good disc jockey must have a genuine love of music," Phil claims. For someone with a strong interest in music to restrict himself to the tight playlist dictated by the Drake type of format is extremely dissatisfying. As program director for the freeform format of station KMPX*, Phil may play any music he likes—rock, classical, jazz, or whatever. To keep up with what's happening in the music field, he goes to concerts, talks to musicians, reads the trade magazines, confers with other deejays. He believes that he's obligated to his listeners to share with them what he feels is the best of the newest music, although, in the final analysis, he says, "you have to satisfy yourself."

---

*Of the 230 million plug-in and portable home radios, only 69 million have FM. Of the 80 million car radios, only 6 million have FM . . . according to the June 21, 1971, issue of *Broadcasting* magazine.

---

*KMPX was converted in 1972 to an "easy-listening, swing-music" station.

Underground Film

"For good or bad, the underground filmmaker is a man alone. But he is a man free to decide. This is a prerequisite for the making of art."
—Sheldon Renan, *An Introduction to the American Underground Film*

Since the time when movies were first developed, around 1900, there has been a conflict over whether movies are primarily a commercial enterprise or an art form. Because a motion picture is so expensive to produce (the average movie costs about one million dollars to make, and a "big" movie may cost as much as twelve million), the "business" side of movies cannot be ignored. People who invest thousands and perhaps millions of dollars wish to be assured not only of getting their money back but also of making a profit. Therefore, since the outset of filmmaking, "business" interests in the industry have collided with the artistic ones—those filmmakers who want to create art. From D. W. Griffith on, movie makers have fought the "money men" to retain their artistic vision. Some of them have succeeded.

When a director produces enough box office successes to prove that he can do both—that is, create a film that satisfies both his artistic integrity *and* the profit-making interests of the film's producers (one of whom may well be himself)—he gains the power to rise above this conflict of business vs. art. Stanley Kubrick, for example, who has proven both his artistic ability and his ability for box-office success in such movies as *The Killing, Paths of Glory, Spartacus, Lolita, Dr. Strangelove,* and *2001: A Space Odyssey,* will be entrusted with millions of dollars to make a movie out of his own artistic vision. Thus, he has the power and freedom to make the innovative *A Clockwork Orange.*

On the other hand, when a director does not have this power and freedom, he may have to relinquish his artistic control to the business side of moviemaking—the producers, the financial backers, or the parent studio. For example, several directors have disclaimed their films as not being the films *they* made. The producers took the footage they had shot and had it edited and arranged according to what they, the producers, thought would be most successful at the box office. (The head of a major film studio was once sued by several directors for having "butchered" their films.)

There are, of course, people who make movies and could care less about art. They make "exploitation" films—films that try to cash in on a certain trend in popular appeal. This kind of movie-maker is probably best exemplified by the producer of pornographic films, which are notoriously lacking in artistry. By the same token, there are people who eschew the idea of making money from films. They create a film as one would write a poem, to express their own feelings, attitudes, or ideas. These are the underground filmmakers.

The "underground" film goes back to the early days of the movies, in the '20s. Those people who were experimenting in film without any thought of commercial success (in those days, all filmmakers were experimenters—some of them, like D. W. Griffith, simply worked within commercial confines) were the *avant-garde,* who, like those practitioners of Modern Art, tried to create the "far-out." In the '40s, with the development of cheaper and more portable 16mm film equipment, there was another surge of experimental filmmaking, when filmmakers tested the limits of the 16mm format.

In the late '50s, Hollywood, the center of commercial filmmaking, was undergoing an upheaval. Television had dislodged it from its complacent position as a fantasy factory for the public. Many people in the industry, attuned to the fact that the time was ripe for experimentation, divorced themselves from dependency upon the parent studios and formed their own companies. These independent producers, though, still were primarily commercially oriented.

During this same time, around 1955, the underground film movement had a new surge of creativity, which has lasted to the present day. This movement is made up of artists who are devoted to the idea that their films be made and seen despite all the economic and legal barriers* placed before them.

Since underground filmmakers are bound by limited budgets, they have had to improvise. Their improvisations, then, are what make their films "experimental." Just as the most inventive cuisines have developed within the poorest societies, so the most innovative techniques are created by filmmakers who lack large money resources. The underground

---

*Legally, film is a business and not an art form. Certain taxes and legislation are discriminatory against the non-commercial filmmaker and distributor. There is a law, for example, which states that projection booths must be made from cinderblock as a safeguard against possible fire, even though safety film was developed as far back as 1930. Having to comply with this law imposes a huge financial burden upon the underground filmmakers, who aren't particularly interested in showing films for profit.

filmmaker has taken the film medium to its farthest extremes. He has experimented with movement. One filmmaker may have a different shot in each individual frame. Another, such as Andy Warhol, may shoot the same motionless subject for as long as eight hours. A filmmaker may experiment with the film itself. Some filmmakers paint images directly onto the film; others scratch images onto it. One filmmaker went so far as to project clear film. Another ran a projector with no film at all.

These are extremes, of course, but between these extremes lie films that are experiments with any or all of the dimensions of film: form, color, movement, plastic space, time, and sound. There are experiments in any one or several of the stages that film goes through: direction of action, photography, developing, printing, editing, and even projecting and viewing.

Whatever the experimental techniques used (and there are as many kinds of underground films as there are underground filmmakers), there is one thing that underground films have in common: each film is the personal creation of the filmmaker.

Underground Television

"The differences in regular broadcast TV, educational TV, and guerrilla television are these:

"The networks are run by people who operate the camera in their own interest. Educational TV is where Liberals demand the cameras to operate in the people's interest. And guerrilla television gets cameras to the people to let them do it themselves."*

Guerrilla television is another name for underground television, television production which is the antithesis of commercial television. Commercial television consists of a few very powerful people who own some complex, highly expensive equipment and who send out images to a great many people in order to make a profit. Underground television, on the other hand, can be produced by anyone who can borrow or buy a portable, videotape camera. (When Sony came out in 1968 with a $1,500, 21-pound, battery-powered VideoRover, underground

---

*Guerrilla Television by Michael Shamberg, Holt, Rinehart & Winston, 1971

television became possible.) The operator of this equipment is not wedded to a studio; he becomes the studio. Video can be produced and played back wherever he can carry his camera. Some underground TV producers, in fact, set up a media bus, a van with video equipment which becomes, at once, a home and a studio. The mobile producer is interested not so much in video for profit as in using his camera to communicate or to allow others to communicate. In some cases, he wishes to report his own antiestablishment beliefs and/or to videotape scenes to support his theories. Other times, as artist he experiments with video to create new forms.

One experimenter, Eric Siegel, has developed a device that takes images from a portable TV camera and transforms them into variations of the color spectrum for the TV screen. The results rival the stargate corridor scene from *2001* in sheer beauty of color and form.

Whether his motives are political or artistic, the underground TV producer uses his camera unlike the commercial TV producer. Commercial TV is rooted in the tradition of the theater; what we see on TV is either vaudeville or stage drama. The underground TV producer, on the other hand, tries to use his TV camera as a unique instrument.

Some underground television production centers are Raindance, Videofreex, and People's Video Theatre in New York and Video Free America in San Francisco.

Read:

Radical Software, published by Raindance in New York City

Guerrilla Television by Michael Shamberg, Holt, Rinehart & Winston, 1971

Expanded Cinema by Gene Youngblood, E. P. Dutton, 1970

An Introduction to the American Underground Film, by Sheldon Renan, Dutton, 1967, $2.25.

See:

For rental of underground films, contact: Canyon Cinema Co-op, Room 220, Industrial Center Bldg., Sausalito, Calif.

Vickie Jackson and Jon Goodchild work on a book for Straight Arrow press.

Chapter 11

The Special Message of Songs

Of all the media, popular songs are undoubtedly the most personal self-expression . . . for both the singer and the listener. The single human voice, in motion on the waves of a melody—nothing can compare to its expressive power. For some singers, the songs they perform comprise an autobiography of feelings and attitudes (James Taylor, for example, selects the songs he sings according to his current feelings toward life and love). For the listener . . . the record-buyer or the dial-turner . . . a song's worth depends on how well it expresses *his* current feelings and attitudes. Couples talk about "their" song; girls are moved to tears over the sentiments of a certain song; groups of people select a song to give voice to their beliefs. Songs are the poetry and the philosophy of the people, and particularly of young people.

It is the time of youth—between the carefree years of childhood and the carefraught years of adulthood—that one thinks the grand thoughts: what's love, what's the meaning of life, what's it all about (Alfie?). Later, it's "Is that all there is?" These thoughts seem to be most movingly expressed when they are sung. A person may forget many people and places and events of his life, but he will remember the words of the favorite songs of his youth.

Dig:

Try testing this theory. Ask a parent, grandparent, or anyone whose adolescence was "yesteryear" to tell you the favorite songs of his youth (try to pinpoint the exact years the songs were popular). Ask him to write (or sing) the lyrics for you. And be tolerant. Just remember that while "Mairsy doats and dosey doats and little lambsey divey" may be absolutely ridiculous to you, it *was* a popular song of its time (although it didn't express any special sentiment of belief other than liking for sound and words and nonsense) and that some song that *you* now like may seem equally ridiculous to someone ten or twenty years from now. Get as many lyrics as you possibly can, and try to cover each ten-year period, beginning with the 1920s. If possible, bring old 45s and 78s to play in class, so that the class can become familiar with the "sounds" of yesteryear, as well as the sentiments.

React:

Listening to these old songs, can you see whether they served any purpose (you'll have to draw on your knowledge of history here), such as . . .

- being silly for a change during hard times (such as the Great Depression or a world war);

- reaffirming moral principles during a period of national despair and deprivation;

Joni Mitchell

- bolstering pride in the U.S.A.;
- searching for the truth, telling it "like it is" in the face of hypocrisy or over-idealizing;
- creating dream worlds into which to escape a harsh reality;
- commiserating, in blues fashion: "I know how bad, sad, etc., it is";
- cheering up by stressing the positive, light-hearted, optimistic view of things?

REACT:

What kinds of love are most of these older songs about? romantic? family? country? pets? To what, in other words, did people attach their affections? Are the causes of love different in today's songs?

One of the great changes in popular music within recent times is the rise of the performer who composes his own music.

A song's complete message cannot be read in the lyrics, however. In fact, writing down the lyrics of your favorite song can be an embarrassing experience—how could *anyone* in the 1950s have loved "You, you, you. I'm in love with you, you, you. I could be so true, true, true. . . . to someone like you, you, you." The power of song to communicate goes beyond the words—it lies in the singer's voice, sense of phrasing and "feel." Compare a Tom Jones recording with a page containing just the lyrics of his song. There's a world of difference. In the case of Tom Jones, there is the additional dimension of *seeing* him in your mind as he sings, thanks to his wide TV exposure. Or consider the entirely new message Barbra Streisand sends when she sings "Happy Days Are Here Again"; no one looking at the hopeful, jaunty lyrics and melody line of that 1940 song would imagine that it could take on the bittersweet tone Streisand gives it.

And then there is the matter of accompaniment and musical arrangement affecting a song's message. A lone guitar, a trio, a sitar, an autoharp—each instrument and combination of instruments has its own evocative power, its own message "between the lines" of the song's lyrics. The revival and popularity of the musical instruments of the Appalachian region are proof of this point.

React:

Compare different recordings of the same song. Why is one better than the other? For example, compare Bob Dylan's recording of his song, "Just Like A Woman" to those of Richie Havens and Roberta Flack. Compare an "easy listening" recording of a Beatles song to the original Beatle rendition. Compare Joni Mitchell's recording of her song, "Both Sides Now," to the popular version—that of Judy Collins. Both Carole King and James Taylor recorded "You've Got a Friend." Which do you prefer?

Take a song that has been recorded by several artists. Collect all the recordings and play them for the class. Have the class determine which is the best rendition.

Did you have the feeling as you listened to the songs of past years that the songwriters couldn't have been *serious*? Other than the *blues* of the blacks and the *folk* songs of the poor and oppressed, which were blatantly honest in their expression of the way things are . . . in love and in human relations, was there a song that seemed to you to explore an important subject seriously? It has been noted by psychologists that the overly-idealized viewpoint of romantic love that most of the songs of the '30s and '40s and '50s expressed is part of the cause of the marital discontent today, among those people whose impressionable adolescence was during those years. They were prepared for nothing beyond flowers, fun and happiness-ever-after.

In the 1960s, however, song lyrics stopped being meaningless generalities about idealistic love (otherwise known as the moon-June-spoon school of writing) and became expressions of the songwriter's deepest feelings, his attempt to fathom life. This poetry-as-song way of writing was new to American song-writing, which up to this time was strictly a commercial undertaking aimed at satisfying the public's superficial needs.

What kind of magic brought about the transformation? Perhaps the Magic Music Muse decreed on the eve of the year 1960 that "hereafter all songs will be sincere expressions of honest feelings and ideas"? No, it doesn't work that way. Changes are gradual and more complex in origin. There is no split-second when, and no simple reason why, one phase ends and another begins. It is only in looking back that we see shifts in emphasis and the reasons for them. Let's be the historian for a moment and see how the medium of song came to be the one the young people trust.

James Taylor

Frankie Avalon

Why, in the 1950s, didn't songs such as "Dream . . . that's the thing to do . . . Dream . . and it might come true," appeal to the public any more? Why did the songs begin to insist that reality be confronted? One reason, certainly, was that television was beginning to bring the nation's problems to the attention of the mass public. "A television image is worth a thousand printed words" may not be fortune-cookie material, but it has proven to hold some truth, to the good and ill fortune of us all. The omnipresent eye of the TV tube shining its image into nearly every American home allowed few secrets. In the '50s, social injustices, economic disparities, political shenanigans, and war were sandwiched in between Milton Berle and the local wrestling matches, and like it or not, the people couldn't avoid becoming educated about the world's problems. By the 1960s the generation which had grown up with TV knew too much to accept insipid ballads; they wanted truthful expressions of the way things are.

Television, though, was not the only technological factor of the music "revolution." Another was radio. When TV arrived on the scene, radio entertainment format was similar to what television is today (soap operas, detective stories, situation comedies, mysteries, etc.). Television's take-over of this programming forced radio to take on a new role—that of providing recorded music to specialized segments of the public—those inclined to listen and those inclined to buy. The segment of the public most inclined to listen and to buy (now that it had the money to spend) was the teenage market. By 1955, radio had dropped almost all people-shows, which were all done by TV now, and devoted its time to music shows . . . a guy playing records. Thus, popular music had acquired a voice—many voices, in fact, for nearly every kind of music was provided an outlet by radio. What's more, the "play it again and again if it's a hit" programming made songs the loud and persuasive voices they have come to be today.

The situation was ripe for a music revolution: there was a large teenage population with money to spend. They had portable radios, radios in their cars, and record players in their rooms. They felt vaguely disillusioned and dissatisfied and yearned for outlets through which to express these feelings. No longer would the croon-a-tune style of Frank Sinatra, Perry Como, Eddie Fisher, and Tony Bennett satisfy these yearnings. Nor did the baby-faced innocent image projected by Frankie Avalon, Ricky Nelson, Paul Anka, and Pat Boone inspire imitation.

The first stirrings of the music revolution were made to the raucous sounds of "Rock Around the Clock," by Bill Haley & the Comets; the top record of 1955, it introduced the *big beat*. The next year a singer named Elvis Presley was introduced, and the nation experienced the first pop-singer hysteria since Sinatra. Elvis contributed much toward the revolution which was to reach its full power in 1965. First, he gave young people practice in defying their parents. He was disliked by the adult world because of his vaguely "evil" image: he had long dark side-burns, wore what looked like a "motorcycle outfit," and moved his hips in a sexy way. He symbolized rebellion; and the young people, particularly the girls, took to him in a big way. Second, he combined three musical styles that until then had been completely separate . . . pop, rhythm and blues, and country and western. His record, "Heartbreak Hotel," produced in 1956, was bought by people who liked pop, blacks who liked rhythm and blues, and the farm folk who liked country/western. It was the first time that a record had made it all three markets, each of which had its own hit parade. Listening to Elvis was not just listening to words; it was an experience in feeling, movement, and aliveness. This appeal to basic emotions overcame (and will always overcome) social class and geographic region. Elvis hit upon a universal language.

Popular music had a new gut-level beat and a new idol, but "can you dance to it?" The next giant step toward the development of rock was the Twist, introduced by Chubby Checker. It became a dance craze which swept the nation in 1962. Maybe Elvis had prepared white America for it. Once shocked by Elvis' pelvic gyrations, the adult world, particularly the sophisticated and arty jet-setters, liked the idea of "letting themselves go" and tried the dance whose instructions were "Move like you're drying your back with a towel." Actually, what the Twist did was to give a lot of publicity to what the young people were doing. And what they *were* doing, the adult world discovered, was enjoying themselves in a way adults couldn't. The older generation had been taught self-restraint and control. Dancing for them meant the waltz or the fox-trot, both rigidly controlled in rhythm and movement in order to achieve the refined, flowing grace that was the goal of all serious ballroom dancers. Even the supposedly casual, boisterous dances of the older generation—like the square dance—were exercises in following someone else's instructions. The Twist, in addition to being uninhibited, was 90 per cent improvisation, or "doing your own thing" as your feelings-of-the-moment dictated. Dance, as well as song, became self-expression. Formula-dancing and formula-singing were out, because they communicated only the formula, not the person.

A revolution needs a leader and although, in looking back, one can see that "Rock Around the Clock," Elvis Presley, and the Twist were

Chubby Checker doing the Twist.

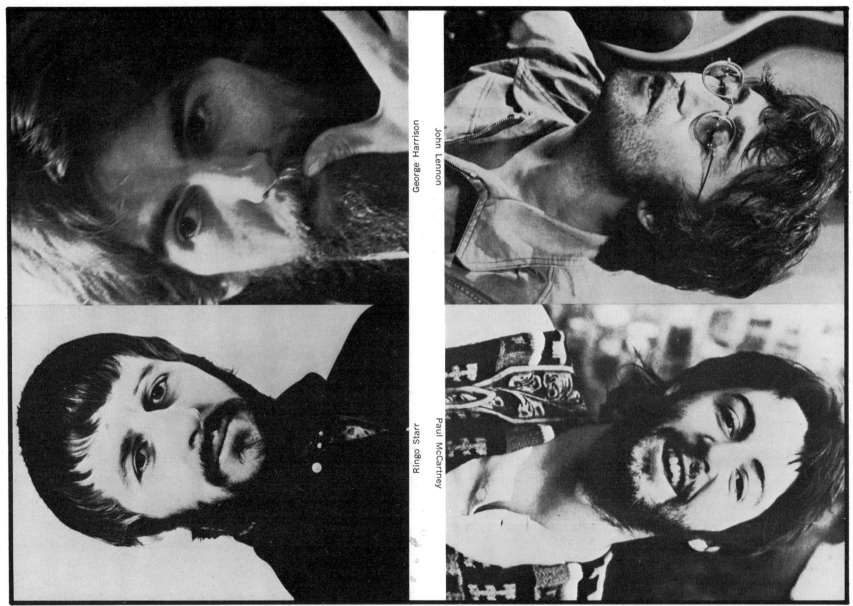

George Harrison

John Lennon

Ringo Starr

Paul McCartney

The Beatles

steps, the great change in music during the Sixties' never would have happened without the Beatles. They had their first hit record in 1964: "I Want to Hold Your Hand." They appeared on the Ed Sullivan show. Then all hell broke loose. Boys started to let their crew cuts grow out until, inch by inch, what was considered acceptable hair length got longer and longer. Hair became one of the issues of the decade. Clothes went from conforming to creative. The admired attitude changed from conforming to creative. The smooth sound gave way to the Big Beat; the rhythm section—the bass, guitar, drums, and piano—became the whole band. Four roustabouts from Liverpool, England, set the young life-style and the music style for the '60s.

There was another, quieter leader who achieved great popularity in 1964 and whose influence on the rock revolution is barely second to that of the Beatles. In 1963 Bob Dylan's song, "Blowin' in the Wind," sung by Peter, Paul and Mary was a hit: and Dylan himself was introduced to the folk music fans by Joan Baez at the Newport Folk Festival. In 1964 Dylan's "The Times They Are A-Changin'" was published; and his name made *Life* and *Newsweek,* which dubbed him "the spokesman of his generation." Although his records never achieved the great popularity of the Beatles, and he was never a performer girls screamed and cried over, he was a major innovator in the rock movement. When he used an electric guitar at the Newport Folk Festival in 1965, for example, he was booed off the stage. However, whether he effected the change or merely foresaw it, folk and rock came together to form a new musical style. Then he made a record with Johnny Cash, merging folk with country and western. He also introduced in this album his "new voice," less harsh and nasal than what he used in his "protest period."

What made both the Beatles and Bob Dylan the great innovators that they were was their refusal to settle down with the sound and style that made them popular. Instead, each took musical steps that shocked their fans, and they did so in the face of followers who were crying for "more of the same." They had the courage to experiment and change, right in front of their listeners' ears; and their redirections were, in the end, accepted. The innovative songs and albums they did were just as popular as the previous ones, and sometimes even more popular. The final proof of acceptance came—they were *imitated*.

What the Beatles and Bob Dylan helped achieve is what probably accounts for the tremendous impact of rock—the amalgamation of various musical styles. No longer was it *my* music and *your* music—it was *our* music. The white teens accepted rhythm and blues, and the blacks accepted pop. The city's young people liked country and western, and the

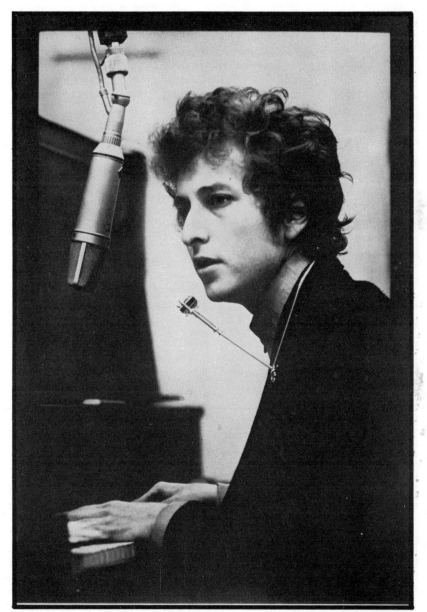

Bob Dylan

Johnny Cash

country's young people bought Beatle records. Musical styles blended into one another. Although what was happening in American society belied the myth of America as a "melting pot," in terms of popular music that truism took on new meaning.

Whereas musical *styles* began to blend and to influence one another, *lyrics* began to reflect the splits that had developed in American ideology. Dialogues in song were conducted between various philosophical and political splinter groups: *Okie from Muskogee* was answered by *Hippie from Olema. The Ballad of the Green Berets* contrasted with Country Joe and the Fish's *I'm-Feeling-Like-I'm-Fixin-to-Die-Rag.*

The trend toward realism and honesty in songs was reflected in various political and personal philosophies singers and songwriters expressed. The pacifist philosophy of Joan Baez, for example, contrasted with the national militarism of a country and western singer like Merle Haggard. Singers such as these were true spokesmen for their fans and followers.

What was true of popular music of the '60s was that songs became the true outlet for the feelings and thoughts of the people, especially of young people. It was the poetry and philosophy of the time: obscene and spiritual; patriotic and revolutionary; sincere and satirical; lay-on, put-down, and put-on; raw and tender. It *was* the times. An accurate history of the heart and mind of the '60s could be written using the lyrics of popular songs.

THEMES of the '60s, CHANGIN' TIMES

If one were to choose one song to reflect the decade, it would be Bob Dylan's *The Times They Are A-Changin'.* The '60s were a time of change, of rebellion, of a replacement of old values with new ones. The popular song, as no other vehicle could do, reflected these turbulent times. Not only did it reflect the spirit of rebellion, it helped to spread revolution. Certain songs became rallying cries for revolutionary movements. *We Shall Overcome,* for example, was sung by those people who worked and marched for civil rights. The black people, perhaps in reaction to the continual television barrage of "Buy, buy . . . have, have" were no longer content with their lot. They strove for a new image—

Say It Loud — I'm Black and I'm Proud —hoping that Black Pride would aid in their struggle for equal opportunity.

Many young people—white, brown, yellow, red, or black—felt sympathy for the oppressed, whether a racial minority or a soldier fighting in an unwanted war. Many worked for the freedom of others, recognizing that *There, but for fortune, go you and I.*

War and Peace

In the '70s, the issues stirred up in the '60s are still aflame—the antiwar movement, for example. For the first time in American history, a widespread reaction came against a war being fought by the United States. Young people, especially, mistrusted the political and military authorities and reacted violently to involvement in Vietnam. This reaction was expressed early by Bob Dylan in *Blowin' in the Wind.* Old-time folk singer Pete Seeger's songs were sung by popular folk singers. *Where Have All the Flowers Gone? Turn! Turn! Turn!* and *Waist Deep in the Big Muddy* all cry of the waste of war and of a need for peace.

Values and Beliefs

Young people, balking at the idea of war, also began in the '60s to question other American values, those of their fathers who were reared to believe that all good things come to the man who works—the good things being a nice home, sundry electrical appliances, a car or two, and possibly a boat or a weekend retreat. Growing up in the nice home, replete with appliances ("Live better electrically" and "Progress is our most important product" go the advertising slogans), and taking advantage of the car, the boat, and the weekend place, this was the good life. But some youths believed that their parents had not been made happy by achieving their goals. They determined that happiness might come about through other means, not through *having* so much as *loving.* Malvina Reynolds, the older-generation folk singer and songwriter, was struck by the mass-produced, sterile sameness of rows of suburban houses in the fog-bound outskirts of San Francisco and wrote *Little Boxes,* an explicit put-down of the middle-class American value system.

In reaction to this system, the children of middle-class suburbia left home *(She's Leaving Home)* and went to San Francisco's Haight-Ashbury district, where young people had settled in a community held

Neil Young

Simon and Garfunkle

together by a hope for love and peace and a desire for freedom from the rat-race pace of their parents' lives. The song which served as the Pied Piper's call was *San Francisco (Be Sure to Wear Some Flowers in Your Hair)*. These young people were dubbed "flower children" and members of the "love generation." Then the term "hippie" became standard. More often than not it was used as a derisive term.

The flower children were introduced to the "outside" world in the rock musical *Hair* which at first shocked the nation with its frank language, its emphasis on sex and drugs, and its nudity. (Later, the increasing liberalness within all entertainment forms would transform *Hair* into an expression of idealism and innocence.) The troupe sang of *The Dawning of the Age of Aquarius,* a time of "harmony and understanding." They closed the show with the rousing *Let the Sunshine in,* passing flowers to the audience, and inviting them up on stage to dance with the cast.

While the long-haired, bare-footed flower children were trying to spread love and peace, the "plastics" and the exploiters moved in. After a rash of murders and other acts of violence, the flower children left San Francisco, some to form quiet communes in the country. Haight-Ashbury came to be a symbol for just another wilted dream.

Loneliness

All over the country, though, the American society was discussed in terms of "fragmentation," "splits," "gaps," "polarization"; people seemed farther and farther away from the "harmony and understanding" that the Aquarian Age was to bring. Alienation was deemed the malady of the '60s. Simon and Garfunkle expressed this ailment in two beautiful, poetic songs: *The Sound of Silence* and *The Dangling Conversation.* The Beatles sang about "all the lonely people" in *Eleanor Rigby.* Joni Mitchell wrote and sang about love and life's illusions in *Both Sides Now.* People longed for a time past when things seemed better. *Those Were the Days,* one song claimed; *Try to Remember,* another urged. *Yesterday* ("all my troubles seemed so far away") went the beautiful Beatles' ballad.

As the decade ended, none of the issues which had put the country into turmoil had been resolved. Hate and violence seemed to outweigh whatever sincere pleas had been made for love and peace, and everyone had to agree with the popular song that philosophised, *What the World Needs Now Is Love, Sweet Love.*

Do:

- Then & Now: *The Songs of My Youth*. Using lyrics dug up in the assignment at the beginning of this chapter, prepare a workbook page in which you contrast the lyrics of yesteryear with those of today, matching them according to the subject sung about.

- Opposite a drawing or cut-out of the instruments currently popular, give the names of the artists who perform on them well.

- Reserve a few pages for recording the complete lyrics of songs you find particularly good.

- Do a dummy of a rock concert program. Give a location you think would be good. List the music and performers in order of appearance; provide for change of pace as you plan this. On the back, review the concert; that is, tell "what happened" as it would appear in a traditional newspaper, as it would be told by word of mouth, and as it might be written up for *Earth News*.

- If you had a complete music library at your disposal, which records would you play for which occasions? In other words, choose music to _____by.

- Show your understanding of various musical styles by giving the songs (and the recording groups) that illustrate 1) folk-rock, 2) acid rock, 3) hard rock, 4) jazz rock, 5) soul, 6) pure jazz, 7) blues rock, 8) pure blues, 9) folk, 10) blue grass, 11) funky jazz, 12) "Jesus" music, 13) combinations (rockability, etc.)

- Take these subjects: friendship, love, sex, a good time, the good life, happiness, being a good person (or a bad one), and ways to face

David Cassidy

Joan Baez

troubles. Opposite each, give lyrics from popular songs which express young peoples' attitudes towards the subject.

Do:

Take a poll and find out who the favorite groups and singers are with each age group: 14-17, 18-24, 25-35, 36 and older. Show the number of votes and distinguish between male and female voters.

Create:

- Write some song lyrics of your own. (Then find someone who can write music and you're in business!)

- Illustrate a song in one of the following ways: a) do a collage—a past-up of magazine cutouts—based on the theme of a certain song; b) illustrate the lines of a song with photographs; c) make a movie of a song (you can act out a song that tells a story or do an impressionistic move with tape recording accompaniment); d) make a videoatpe with music as the audio portion.

Do:

- Interview people (use a portable cassette-recorder), preferably of the "older generation," asking them what they think of young peoples' music.

- Try to "turn someone on" to the music you like. Try sitting your parents down one night and playing some of your records for them (perhaps with the volume turned down a bit). You may end up lessening the generation gap a bit.

- Sing or play for the class. Get your band to play for the faculty and students. Arrange for a hootenanny or musical variety show.

CREATE:

Review rock concerts for the benefit of the class. Write a review for the school newspaper. Make a documentary film or videotape of a rock concert.

Do a simulated radio show (on tape) either following or parodying a certain type of radio station, its announcing style and programming format.

DO:

Supposing you decide to give someone you love an hour-long tape cassette of your favorite music. What would you include on it?

DIG:

Research popular songs and do a study of how they reflected their times. For example, get the words to *Brother, Can You Spare a Dime?*, a popular song during the crisis year of the Depression, 1932, and those of *Happy Days Are Here Again,* the campaign song of Franklin Delano Roosevelt, who vowed to bring American people out of the Depression. Compare the attitudes expressed by popular songs during wartime. How do the popular songs of World War I, World War II, and the Vietnam War compare to one another in patriotic attitude (surely things have changed since *Praise the Lord and Pass the Ammunition!*)? If the songs you choose are also dance songs, describe the dance and comment on the amount (kind) of self-expression the dance allowed.

REACT:

If you were joining a group taking a space flight to colonize another planet and were limited to taking only three albums with you as your *only* recorded music to listen to, which ones would you take?

Neil Diamond

Roberta Flack

Read:

Some books you might find useful:
Great Songs of the Sixties, edited by Milton Okun, Quadrangle, 1970.
Something to Sing About!, collected and arranged by Milton Okun, Macmillan, 1968.
American Folksongs of Protest, Greenway, Octagon, 1971.

References which would give you concise histories:

Facts on File
World Almanac
Reader's Digest Almanac
Information Please Almanac
Whitaker's Almanac
The New York Times Almanac
Statesmen's Yearbook
Webster's Guide to American History
A Short Chronology of American History, Kull, Rutgers, 1952.
The World Book Encyclopedia Yearbooks

Records of the pop songs of yesteryear:

The Swing Era, Time-Life, several albums of the songs of 1936 through 1942.
Songs of Our Times, Vocalion (Decca), VL 3628-3656, an album of the popular songs for each year—from 1916 through 1944.

Books about rock music:

Rock from the Beginning, Nik Cohn, Pocket Books, 1970, $.95.
The Rock Revolution, Arnold Shaw, Paperback Lib., 1970, $.95.
The Rock Story, Jerry Hopkins, New American Library, 1970, $.95.
The Poetry of Rock, Richard Goldstein, Bantam, $1.00.
Age of Rock, vols. I and II, edited by Jonathan Eisen, Vintage, $2.95 ea.
Rock Encyclopedia, Lillian Roxon, Grosset & Dunlap, $3.95.

Books about special types of music and about certain singers and groups:

Outlaw Blues, Paul Williams, Dutton, $1.75.
The Jefferson Airplane and the San Francisco Sound, Ralph J. Gleason, Ballantine, 1969, $.95.
The World of Soul, Arnold Shaw, Paperback Lib., $1.25.
The American Folk Scene, David deTurk and A. Poulin, Jr., Dell, $.95.

The Electric Kool-Aid Acid Test, Tom Wolfe, Bantam, $1.25.
Daybreak, Joan Baez, Avon, $.95.
The Beatles, Hunter Davies, Dell, $.95.
Our Own Story, by the Rolling Stones, Paul Goodman, Bantam, $.75.
Bob Dylan, Kramer, Paperback Lib., $.95.
The Rolling Stone Interviews, Paperback Lib., 1971, $1.50.
Goldstein's Greatest Hits, Richard Goldstein, Tower, 1970, $.95.

Books about old-timers:

Lady Sings the Blues, Billie Holiday and W. Dufty, Lancer, $.95.
Lena, Lena Horne and Richard Schickel, Signet, $.75.
Satchmo, Louis Armstrong, Signet, $.95.
Raw Pearl, Pearl Bailey, Paperback Lib., $.95.
Yes, I Can, Sammy Davis, Jr., Paperback Lib., $.95.
Sinatra, Twentieth Century Romantic, Arnold Shaw, Pocket Books, 1969, $.95.

Arlo Guthrie

> The way I like it, pop is all teenage property, and it mirrors everything that happens to teenagers in this time, in this American twentieth century. It is about clothes and cars and dancing; it's about parents and high school and being tied and breaking loose; it's about sex and getting rich and getting old; it's about America; it's about cities and noise. Get right down to it, it's all about Coca-Cola.
>
> —Nik Cohn, *Rock from the Beginning,* Pocket Books, $.95.

> In the sixties, this new generation of writers overturned the commercial restraints on subject matter and taste, and created an art form that is one of the most important cultural revolutions in history.
>
> —Milton Okun, "The Sixties: Songs and Sound," *the New York Times Great Songs of the Sixties,* Quadrangle Books, Inc., 1970, $17.50 (hardbound).

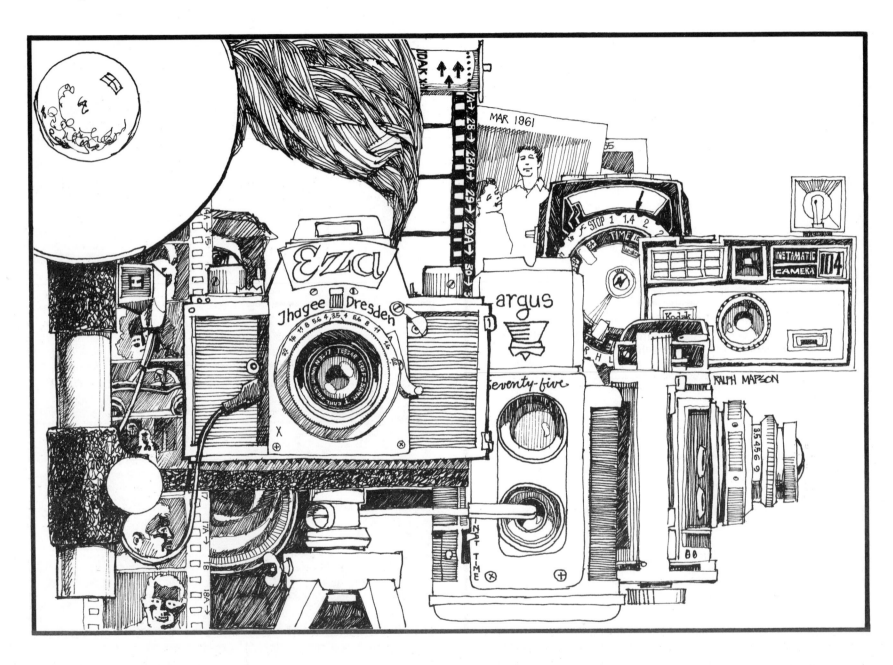

Chapter 12

Still Photography - Frozen Images

by Alan Oddie

"Photography is an extraordinarily absorbing, challenging, and uninhibited way of relating to the universe."

Arthur Goldsmith, Director & President of Famous Photographers School

"In viewing a still photograph you can enter a world of frozen time, where all the clocks have stopped and nothing ever changes. You can see things with a greater clarity than you usually can in the shifting, confusing world of physical reality. You can study an expression, a gesture, or a play of light and shadow that is transfixed forever. This is one of photography's greatest gifts."

Arthur Goldsmith

"Pick a theme and work it to exhaustion. Pictures are a medium of communication, and the subject must be something you truly love or truly hate."

Dorothea Lange, professional photographer

"Often your response to a photograph may be one that's quite impossible to put into words—a kind of electrical disturbance that makes the back of your neck tingle, a sensation of peace, a complex blend of sadness and elation, a feeling of completeness because all the elements in the photograph are exactly right."

Arthur Goldsmith

"Don't let a camera intimidate you. . . . It is nothing more than a sophisticated cigar box. You're not in awe of a cigar box, are you?"

Arthur Goldsmith

Goldsmith, Arthur. *The Photography Game.* New York: Viking Press, 1971. Very readable; contains short, interesting history of the early developments in photographic technique; well presented "how to" information; interviews with great photographers; advice on turning professional.

A telephoto lens throws the figure in the background out of focus so that most of the attention goes to the man with the paper. At the same time, the older man's presence is very much a part of the total feeling expressed.

For most of us, still photography means "snapshots" of important occasions—moments and events that we think we will want to look back on some day. A "click" and we have captured a fragment of our experience, to be gazed upon later and remembered with all the warmth that nostalgia brings. Used for this purpose snapshots communicate in a very special way: from our older self to our younger self and back again.

But do these quick snaps communicate with anyone else? If you've ever been held captive by a returning traveler showing his boxful of slides or handful of pictures, you know that the enthusiasm is *not* contagious. In short, very little is communicated. It is rare indeed to see a photographer who uses fresh approaches to his subject and who takes care with the composition of his picture. It is even more rare to find a photographer who is able to communicate more than his own day-to-day past history; who is able, in other words, to bridge the gap between his and your experiences as human beings and engage your mind and emotions.

That is what still photography as a *communicative art* attempts to do; and the great photographers spend a lifetime perfecting and refining the message-sending power of this wordless and soundless and motionless medium. The "Great Photograph" that results from this dedication involves more than a lucky flick of the index finger, it engages at least three human faculties simultaneously:

the human eye, which has sensitized itself to the play of light, the arrangements of shapes, the expressions of the face;

the human heart, which can *feel* the importance of a moment, even though it isn't the kind of moment that historians or scrapbook-makers would think of capturing; and

the human brain, which can concentrate all its attention on manipulating the camera's controls to get the best picture at the best moment.

It is the sensitivity and interplay of this extraordinary human eye/heart/brain combination that turn a snapshot into a communicative medium.

Because knowing how to take a still photo helps you "get the message" when you look at another person's photos, we will be concentrating in this chapter on picture-taking technique. As you gain in skill and awareness, you will probably come to understand more and more the communicative power of still photographs such as those interspersed throughout this chapter.

The Still
Camera

Although we're putting this first, the kind or cost of the camera used isn't nearly as important as the kind of *you* that's holding the camera. A sensitive, imaginative, careful *you* can make great pictures with a $5.00 or even a 50¢ camera. An uncaring, unobservant, sloppy looker stands very little chance of making worthwhile pictures even with that Rolls Royce of cameras, the Leicaflex. So don't get carried away about equipment. Buy only what you can afford and what you'll use. To help you hold your own with salesmen (live or in print), here are some basics.

Camera Size

Cameras are classified by size of film they're designed for. The great majority use film that's 35mm wide, so they're called (reasonably enough) 35mm cameras. This size has several advantages: (1) it's small and compact and can be used to make prints or slides; (2) you have a wide range and price of camera types to choose from; (3) if you can afford it, you can buy a camera with two or three different interchangeable lenses, giving you an opportunity to try for striking and unusual effects which a standard lens alone cannot achieve.

The second most popular size, but trailing a long way behind 35mm, is 2¼ x 2¼ in. Top of this class in price and prestige is the Swedish-made Hasselblad which astronauts take to, and sometimes leave on, the moon. More down to earth in this format are the Rolleiflex and Mamiya-flex. If you look around for a while, you can probably find a good buy in a used Rolleiflex.

Big advantage of this size is just that—the size. The large negative these cameras produce gives you a better quality picture, other things being equal. You can blow up a 2¼ x 2¼ without everything going grainy on you. And if you should be just a little off in your focus or just a little shaky when you fire the shutter, this size is more forgiving than 35mm. There are a couple of disadvantages: (1) the camera is heavier and bulkier; (2) you cannot make slides with this size of film.

Single or Twin Lens?

The 2¼ x 2¼ comes in the single lens variety or in the less expensive, but slightly less convenient, twin-lens style. With the first, known as SLR, or "single lens reflex," you compose and focus your picture by looking through the same lens that admits light to the film. There's never any doubt that what you see when you press the shutter release is what will be on your negative (give or take a bit of blurriness, distortion of color, and minor details like that!).

With the twin lens reflex, you compose and focus your picture through the top lens, but light is admitted to the film through the bottom lens. This can be a problem when you're very close to your subject. There's a danger that you may cut off the top of the subject's head unless you make the proper allowance for the different points of view taken by you and by the film.

All 35mm cameras are the single lens type, but not all let you focus and compose through the taking lens. Some have range finders. When you look through a range finder and don't have the subject focused, you see a double image. As soon as the focus is correct, the double image moves together and becomes one. You may find this a little tricky at first, but many photographers prefer it to the reflex method of focusing.

Camera Controls

A camera is not much more, really, than a light-tight box with two "doors" behind the lens that admit exactly the amount of light you specify. The first "door" is the shutter. This is always closed except at the moment when you press the shutter release. Depending on where you set the speed control, the shutter stays open for a period of time varying from one second to perhaps 1/1,000th of a second.

The second "door" through which light passes on its way to the film is the diaphragm. The hole or aperture in the diaphragm is open all the time, but the size of the hole can be varied to let more or less light through. All films are designed to respond to a certain amount of light, so your purpose in adjusting the two "doors" is to ensure that this same amount of light reaches the film regardless of time of day, weather, location, etc. Too much light will "overcook"—overexpose—the film. Too little will leave it raw, or underexposed. How you juggle the two controls to keep the light constant will be dealt with a little later. First, there's another function which the variable aperture in the diaphragm performs, and it's an important one for the quality and artistry of your picture.

Depth of Field

Suppose you stand with your camera at the front of a class. You want to photograph the girl in the second row. You don't want the boy in the first row, or the writing on the chalkboard in the background, to distract attention from that long-haired girl you want in your picture. What do you do? You could climb on a step-ladder and photograph her from above. Or you could lie on the floor and take a low-angle shot with the ceiling as background. A quicker, and often more artistic, solution is to use as wide an aperture as possible which will give you a shallow depth of field and, hopefully, ensure that everything except your favorite girl will be out of focus.

Just remember, then, that the bigger the aperture the less the depth of field. The smaller the aperture, the greater the depth of field. As an example of what this means, suppose you are standing six feet from that girl in the second row. You focus the camera at six feet. With a small aperture, things will be more or less in focus all the way from a point four feet behind the girl to a point one and one half feet in front of her. With the lens wide open (a large aperture) the depth of field may extend only a matter of inches.

Setting the Shutter Speed

In a 2¼ x 2¼ camera, the control for the shutter will probably be around the barrel of the lens. On 35mm cameras, it's more likely to be in the region of the shutter release. It's easily recognized because it will be marked with the letter 'B' plus some (or all) of these numbers:

1   2   4   8   15   30   60   125   500   1000   2000

By setting the control to 'B' you can make a time exposure for as long as you keep the shutter release pressed in. Set the control to 'l' and the shutter will automatically stay open for one second. All the other numbers are fractions of a second from ½ to 1/2000th of a second.

Setting the Aperture: The Mysteries of the 'f' Stops

You can easily tell which controls on the barrel of the lens change the size of the aperture. The barrel is marked with various strange-looking numbers which may include the following:

f/1   f/1.4   f/2   f/2.8   f/4   f/5.6   f/8   f/11   f/16   f/22   f/32

The numbers are actually fractions, so the higher the number, the smaller the size of the aperture and vice versa. The numbers are easy to work with because, each time you move from one number to the next, you exactly halve, or double the amount of light that reaches the film. If the control is set at f/11 and you change it to f/8, twice as much light will pass through the aperture. If you alter the control from f/2.8 to f/4, half the amount of light will reach the film.

How to Select Shutter Speed and Aperture

If in doubt, use 1/125 as the shutter speed and then set the aperture at whatever opening is needed to give the correct exposure at that shutter speed. Many cameras now come equipped with a light meter which will automatically set the right aperture to go with the shutter speed you select. If your camera does not have a built-in meter, you can buy a separate meter. Having a meter is well worth the money. Many more pictures will be correctly exposed than if you try to guess the exposure. A meter is particularly necessary if you are using color film.

Whether you have a built-in or a separate meter, the first thing to do is set the meter for the speed of film you are using. Film speed, measured in units known as ASA, is simply an indication of the sensitivity of the film to light. Kodak Tri-X is a fast film with a speed of 400 ASA. If you want to take pictures indoors without additional lights, this is the film to use. Kodak Plus-X is a medium speed black and white film with a speed of 125 ASA. It's about the best all-round film for everything except indoor work.

The photo shows how the dial of a Gossen Luna-Pro light meter will look after you've set a film speed of 125 ASA, pointed the meter at your subject, and got a reading of 18. (The needle at the top of the meter points to 18 on the dial.) Around the outside of the circle below the needle are 13 possible shutter speeds from 1/4000 to one second. Below these shutter speeds are 13 possible aperture settings from f/1.4 to f/90. Any one of those 13 combinations, 1/4000 at f/1.4, or 1/250 at f/5.6, or 1/8 at f/32, or any of the others, would give you a correctly exposed picture under these lighting conditions. Which combination do you choose?

As we already mentioned, if in doubt, 1/125 is a good average shutter speed that will handle most pictures in which the subject is not moving. So, look for 1/125 on the meter and set the aperture called for at this speed: f/8. If your subject is moving, you might want to increase the shutter speed to 1/500. At that speed you would have to open up the aperture to f/4. On the other hand, you might want to make sure you have a wide depth of field, in which case you would choose f/16 or f/22 which would call for shutter speeds of 1/30 and 1/15 respectively. You could only take pictures at those very slow shutter speeds, however, if you mount your camera on a tripod.

A low camera angle makes a powerful and striking face even more striking. A high sun, shining towards the camera, silvers the man's hair and clearly separates it from the background.

By waiting until almost sunset and shooting towards the sun, a photographer can capture lengthened shadows and silhouetted figures. A high camera angle frames the picture interestingly with branches of a tree and reveals the balance of the composition.

Focus

The third control on all except very simple cameras is focus. This is usually marked in feet from perhaps one foot to 100 feet. Most cameras have a mark just beyond the 100 which looks like this: ∞ , and means infinity. It's the place to set the focus if you're photographing a landscape or some other distant vista or object.

The arrow shows the markings on a typical focus control. Notice that the smaller the camera-to-subject distance is, the wider apart the numbers on the lens are; which means that if a close subject moves just a little, you have to change the focus quite a lot to keep your picture sharp. Once the subject is more than 10 or 12 feet away, focus becomes far less critical. Just remember this: the closer you are to your subject, the more careful you must be with focusing.

What to Photograph

It really doesn't matter what you photograph as long as your finished picture touches other people with your own unique viewpoint about whatever you freeze on your film. Margaret Bourke-White, who became *Fortune* magazine's first photographer in 1929 and later toured the world as a staff photographer for *Life* magazine, got the job on the strength of the dramatic pictures she made inside the steel mills of Cleveland. Maybe you are turned on by the shiny convolutions of motorcycles, by the spontaneity of small children, or by the bare, black branches of trees in winter time. Record what fascinates you, but translate onto film your reaction to what you see, also. That way, what might be just a picture becomes a personal statement that communicates with others.

Pointers to Personal Statements

The first and practically the only rule is to *simplify*. A sculptor was once asked how he turned a great big block of stone into the likeness of a man. He replied that he simply chipped away everything that didn't look like the man. You have a similar challenge in picture-making (and for "picture," read "personal statement that communicates with others"). Decide what the *essence* of your subject is. Try to exclude everything that isn't part of that essential something.

To do this, get close to your subject. A great many pictures are less than they might be simply because the photographer was afraid to move in close. And sometimes this does take nerve. Do it anyway; you'll soon find yourself so absorbed in getting the very best view of your subject that any initial embarrassment will be forgotten.

Watch Out for the Background

If the subject has a gorgeous head of black hair, don't stand her up against a dark oak door; all that beauty will vanish into the woodwork. Photographs taken in the backyard call for special care, because of unsightly overhead wires and the ever-present possibility that what you thought was a great picture of your brother Jeff will be ruined by a tree that appears to be growing out of his head.

There are a number of ways of ensuring an un-cluttered background for your subject. (1) Take a higher or lower viewpoint. Take the picture from above and you'll have grass or floor as background. Take a low angle and—if you can avoid those tiresome power cables—you'll have the sky or ceiling as background. Remember, too, that a wide open aperture (a low 'f' number) gives you minimum depth of field, softly and artistically blurring out unwanted distractions.

Water almost always looks best when photographed into the sun. Here, the hands appear to be reaching for diamonds even though the surface of the water is 30 or 40 feet from the hands. This picture called for a lengthy depth of field, so a medium lens was used.

A yellow filter on the lens darkens the blue sky to make the cloud stand out dramatically. Sun behind the cloud spills out around its edges to make the effect more striking.

There are times, however, when a particular background adds a dimension to the mood or story you want to tell through your photograph. A row of books adds an element to a portrait of a teacher. A picture of a boy who likes to surf would be enhanced if you include at least a portion of his surf board, or maybe a curling wavetop.

Painting With Light and Shadow

Light and shadows are the brush and the paint you work with on the canvas of your film. Get to know the fantastic things light can do. Go out in the early morning. Lie down in the grass with your face to the sun and watch the light sparkling in the diamonds of dew. Put a river or a lake between you and the sun. If you're there at the right time, it will seem as if some benevolent giant is scattering handfuls of gems across the water.

Hair that looks distressingly ordinary when photographed with the sun shining directly on it turns to threads of gold when it's backlit. (That is, when the sun is shining through it, towards the camera.) In fact, almost everything looks more striking with back lighting. The bark of a tree, a dandelion puff, cobblestones, icicles, clouds, water, railroad tracks, leaves and blossoms—all are transfigured when viewed or photographed with the light behind them. So don't be afraid of pointing your camera towards the sun—nine times out of ten you'll probably like the result better than the conventional sun-behind-the-photographer's-shoulder lighting.

To protect your film against sun streaming straight through the lens, invest a few dollars in a lens hood, which is a kind of hat or shade that fits securely over the end of the lens. Another worthwhile extra is a close-up attachment. This will let you get within inches of blossoms, dew drops, toy soldiers, and all manner of miniature things that look fantastic in a close-up shot.

Save for a Rainy Day

There's an old saying: "Mad dogs and Englishmen go out in the noonday sun." Actually, high sunlight is one of the least interesting kinds of light for a photograph. Save some film for a rainy day. The softly diffused light, the raindrops glistening on windshields, and the slick blackness of pavements make stunning pictures.

Vanishing Clouds

Black and white film is great stuff, but it doesn't see the world in the same way as our eyes do. One of its peculiarities is that it's over-sensitive to blue, seeing it as having the same brightness as white. So you may be surprised some day to find that the pictures you took of a blue sky dotted with white clouds came out with blank skies. You can bring back the vanishing clouds with a yellow filter over the lens. The filter removes some of the blue rays, making the sky darker and the clouds visible. For an even more dramatic, moonlight effect, use a red filter. It makes blue sky appear almost black. Remember that a filter removes some of the light, so you have to compensate by opening up the aperture (or reducing the shutter speed) by a point or two.

Do:

Illustrate, by clipping ads and pictures from magazines (or by rummaging through some of your own photos), the photographic techniques described in this chapter so far.

Examples:
- angle shot (from below subject);
- with effective use of contrast;
- angle shot (from above subject);
- large aperture, shallow depth of field (blurring of material in front of or behind a sharply defined subject);
- effective use of soft, diffused light;
- high shutter speed (necessary to capture motion without blurring);
- slow shutter speed (time exposure; use of tripod, probably).

Do:

Collect examples of "beginners' mistakes" and make a large display poster for the classroom. Some of the mistakes which might come up:

A careful choice of angle in this picture puts the man's white shirt against a dark background, and his dark trousers against a light background. Timing is good, too.

An into-the-sun shot and use of extra contrasty paper in the printing, emphasize the lights and darks in this San Francisco street scene.

- aperture too large, too small;

- distance misjudged (focus off);

- shutter speed too fast, too slow;

- subject not given enough importance: background too cluttered, subject too far away, freakish, intrusive background object;

- where have all the white clouds gone?
  or, forgetting that blue and white photograph the same on black and white film;

- high-noon sun-blanched picture.

Leave space for pictures which show skill in each of these respects (for instance, the use of back-lighting to avoid the sun-baked scene; the use of a yellow or red filter to bring back the clouds dramatically).

Do:

Keep a record of f/stop, distance, and shutter speed for each black and white picture you take on a roll of film. Mount the photos and label each with the photographic information you've kept. Decide what you would change (if anything) if you had a chance to take the picture over again. See if the rest of the class agrees.

Do:

Get a magazine or book devoted to photography. Look for pictures you find particularly good and study the photographic information given for them. Go out and try for the same effects.

Do:

Study the works of a great photographer and get to know his (her) style.

The shape of the car window through which the picture was taken acts as a frame to keep the eye on the action. A telephoto lens was used in order to achieve a shallow depth of field, throwing the raindrops out of focus for a more interesting effect.

CREATE:

Give a report (with photos) to the rest of the class. Some suggestions for the subject:

> People in love;
> Someone you like;
> Hands;
> Spring;
> Wind or rain;
> A friend who's flunked math;
> A local businessman who's done something for ecology;
> A teacher you think is great;
> Part of your town that needs improvement;
> Part of your town that people should be proud of;
> People who enjoy their jobs;
> Textures (cobblestones, old rubber tires, bread, the bark of trees, a pineapple, newly-washed hair, the surface of a phonograph record).

CREATE:

- Take a word, or phrase, or favorite quotation and match it with a still, black and white photograph that expresses the same feeling. Do this with four subjects and see which one "says it" better, picture or words. Does the *combination* of picture and words say it best?

- Tell a story or explore a theme through a sequence of still, black and white photographs. No words allowed. Show it to your classmates and see if your meaning is understood by having *them* put it into words.

Color Slides

To make slides you must use a 35mm camera. Other than that, the procedure is much the same as for black and white photography. There

Sometimes, as with this shot of a very temporary police officer, success is partly a matter of being in the right place at the right time. The other part is focusing and exposing correctly and making sure there is no distracting background.

are just two precautions: (1) Be even more particular about measuring the intensity of the light and setting your camera accordingly because color film has a little less latitude than black and white. (2) Be sure to move in close to your subject. In black and white photography you can take your negative into the darkroom and work some minor miracles before you show the world your finished print. You can crop out empty spaces around the subject. You can print different parts lighter or darker than the rest. When you make a slide, you can't do this. Everything you put on the film when you fire the shutter release will be up there on the screen when you project the slide. Be careful!

Types of Color Film

Daylight tends to be somewhat blue. Artificial light tends to have more red in it. Our eyes automatically adjust for this, but film does not. Consequently, you should buy daylight type film for outdoor work and artificial light film if you'll be working indoors with artificial light.

CREATE:

Make a Slide-Song

An interesting way to make a personal statement with color slides is to combine them with a song. Since you'll want to show the finished production to other people, choose a song that's not too long and one in which the lyrics come across very clearly. From three to five minutes is a good length.

The most effective way to present the program is to use two slide projectors linked by a dissolve control. In this way, instead of slides flashing on and off—which is quite tiring for people watching—one slide literally dissolves into the other, giving a very smooth, almost movie-like show.

Before you shoot any slides, listen to the song a dozen times or more. Write the lyrics down. (You'll probably want to mimeograph them and pass them out to the audience.) Study the lyrics. Translate them into mental pictures. If the mood of the lyrics seems to be one of loneliness, for example, would a picture of a child playing by himself in an empty playground say what you want to say? What about a single, leafless tree in silhouette? Color and lighting can be very eloquent. Bright sunlight would tend to match a happy, lively feeling. Shades of grey and blue are more somber than red or orange.

Just because you have color film in your camera, don't feel that you have to photograph only subjects that have lots of color. A single small patch of yellow or green in an almost colorless area can speak more eloquently than a jumble of different colors all competing for attention. Color and lack of color are much like the juxtaposition of sound and silence. A few softly spoken words surrounded by silence can be far more striking than a roomful of loud sound.

How many slides do you need? If you use a Kodak dissolve and two projectors, the maximum speed at which you can run the dissolve puts a new slide on the screen about every 2.2 seconds. At this rate (assuming you don't vary the rate during the song), you would need about 100 slides for a four-minute song. But to get that many slides that you're really happy with, you should probably shoot at least 200. This will be fairly expensive since one slide—including the cost of film and the cost of processing—comes to about 17¢. If you really want to do it, you'll find a legal way to raise the cash. But just be aware before you get in too deep that photography is not the cheapest art form in the world.

There are way of cutting your cost: (1) choose a shorter song; (2) share the project with a friend; (3) run the dissolve unit slower. One way *not* to cut costs is to take your color film to cut-rate processors. Their quality matches their price, and you won't be happy with it. Photography is something that's only worth doing if you do it to the best of your ability. Done that way, it's a fantastic medium through which to share yourself with others.

Chapter 13

Film: How It Works Its Magic

A box of popcorn in one hand and a soft drink in the other, you settle into the comfort of the theater seat, awaiting the darkening of the lights and the appearance of the images on the large screen in front of you. It is a moment of pleasant anticipation. During the next few hours you will be in the delightful situation of being able to experience without actual physical involvement. In the comfort and security of your theater seat, you can enter any world in time and space. You may feel any number of emotions: fear, joy, sorrow, love, triumph, horror; you may even go through a mind-wrenching experience that causes you to look at the world in a new way.

The moment when the first image appears on the screen is much like the initial lurch of the car in a Disneyland ride. You leave the real world and enter a "magic kingdom"—a fantasy world. If the movie is good, you won't be conscious of the real world again until the "ride" is over—when "The End" appears on the screen and lights go on again. The more completely you forget your surroundings, the better the "trip" is said to be. On the Disneyland Submarine Ride, when you're down in the sub and the captain shouts his warning, "Sea serpent ahead!", you peer apprehensively out through the porthole into the mysterious sea depths. When the monster suddenly appears on the other side of the porthole glass, you can't help but catch your breath and draw back in fright (even though you've already looked down into the shallow moat and seen the artificial "sea monsters").

In a well-directed movie, like a good Hitchcock film, no claim of "It's only a movie!" can stop you from feeling the goose bumps or from reacting to the sudden appearance of danger. Furthermore, you don't *want* to stop feeling and reacting—that's why you went to the movie. It's only when Disney or Hitchcock or any other master of fantasy fails to make you react that you become disappointed. When you go on a Disneyland ride or attend the movies, you *expect* to experience as fully as you can.

Why are some movies more successful than others at enabling us to experience? Why do some movies allow a great number of people to experience while others reach only a relatively few? Why are some movies appealing to a specific audience—children, women, young people, for example? Watching a movie can become an experience only when it has some element through which we can attach ourselves personally. That element may be the *story* or the *situation*. For example, a situation involving a group of people in an isolated community whose lives are suddenly put in danger (as in *Airport* and *The Birds*) is one with which most of us can identify. We can identify with this situation because it touches a fear that we all carry with us—that our snug little world may become endangered by the murderous intruder—a stealthy burglar, an invading army, or an alien being from outer space.

Some movie situations, though, are not meant for all of us. Mom might get a lot of thinking done while she sits through the latest Disney film with the kids; Dad will snooze while his wife wipes away her tears during the big musical melodrama; parents stay home and watch TV while the young people stand in line to see the latest "black humor" flick.

Sidney Poitier, star of the Mr. Tibbs series.

The situation may be one in which we can place ourselves, but usually there is also a *person* in the movie who appeals to us. He may appeal to us because we secretly feel we're the same kind of person he is. Or we may like him or admire him because he has traits or qualities we admire. On its simplest level, this process of identification may occur when the moviegoer identifies with the character who is physically most like him. Thus, in a movie like *Airport,* the children will identify with the child on the plane, the teenagers with the young couple, the older people with the stowaway woman, and so on. (Television producers, sensitive to criticism about all-white casts, are careful to include characters for the non-white viewers to identify with. The '70s saw the creation of a new movie hero—the black hero—who appeared in such pictures as *Cotton Comes to Harlem, Shaft,* and the *Mr. Tibbs* series. The black hero is the answer to the black man's demand for a strong character to identify with.)

At a more subtle level, we identify with a character who fits our subconscious image of ourselves. (For a more thorough discussion of this process, see Chapter 9.) It could be that the test of a happily married couple is that when they go to a Clint Eastwood movie, they *both* sit there thinking how much the husband is like the movie star.

Another element that may draw us into a movie could be the human *emotion* it explores. Although the events and the people may be far removed from our life, the movie may be concerned with an emotion which touches us: love, for example. You don't have to be a ten-year-old boy to cry with a boy in a movie over the death of his pet. Anyone who has experienced the loss of a loved one will be able—in some degree—to feel the boy's pain. On the other hand, a movie about the frustration of a middle-aged American man may have a limited audience. In fact, it may be limited to frustrated middle-aged American men, or recently liberated ones. When the emotion emphasized in the movie is one we recognize, however, we are able to become involved.

Finally, the *idea* in a movie may be the main reason the movie becomes an experience for us. The movie may have no other element with which we can identify except that it is about an idea which intrigues us—like man's relationship with God or with the universe. *2001: A Space Odyssey* is a good example. The movie has only the barest outline of a plot, and no character is made sympathetic to the audience; yet it is a fascinating film because it involves us in an idea. It suggests another step in man's evolution—an evolving of a universal consciousness, as expressed by the image of the "star child" in the last scene in the film.

A great movie, though, will provide us with more than one way to become involved. We may identify with a character, with the emotions he feels, with the situation, and with the idea behind the film all at once. In fact, the more levels on which we become involved, the more memorable the film.

The Magic of Film

Earlier we compared seeing a movie to taking a Disneyland ride. It can also be compared to watching a television drama, seeing a stage play, or reading a comic book. In each instance, the participant is letting himself in for a vicarious experience. The process of identification we've spoken of could happen in each of these activities. There is, however, the experience that is uniquely the film experience. A film may draw us into it in ways no other medium can. Let's try to see what it is about film that is unique. How does film create its own special image?

> Every movie sequence is like a deck of picture cards, and the significance of a film experience lies in the arrangement of shots. The alert filmgoer who is interested in story must become shot-oriented, aware of moving forms and moving camera, of angles, of contrasts between foregrounds and backgrounds, of playing areas of the screen in which actors are placed.   —*The Film Experience*

The arrangement of shots

The basic unit of film is the **shot,** or one single camera operation. It may take from four to 40 seconds. You might compare the shot to a sentence in a short story. A series of shots make up a **sequence,** just as sentences go together to make a paragraph in a story. A sequence is often like a scene in a play, in that it shows one continuous action.

Take, for example, the egg-eating scene in *Cool Hand Luke.* To win a bet, Luke, played by Paul Newman, must eat 50 hardboiled eggs in an hour. A series of shots make up this sequence. The first one lets the audience take in the situation: the excited inmates are gathered around

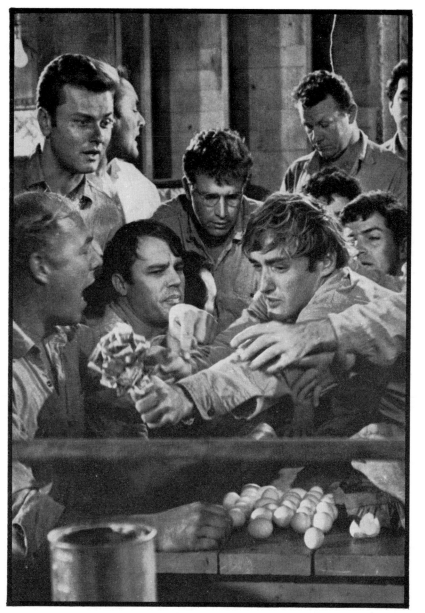

The prisoners place their bets on Luke's egg-eating contest.

A close-up shot emphasizes the situation.

Paul Newman as Cool Hand Luke, a Warner Bros.-Seven Arts release.

the prison dining room table on which lies the huge pile of eggs; we see Luke's confident warming-up exercises. A second shot—closer up—shows Luke popping the eggs into his mouth, in rapid-fire succession. Later on, a shot—a close-up—shows Luke's friend easing the eggs into Luke's slowly churning mouth. The final shot in the sequence is a boom shot—when the camera pulls up toward the ceiling and looks down on Luke lying in a stupor on the table.

There were many more shots in this sequence, carefully selected by the director to accomplish many tasks. First, he had to show you the event itself—to convince you without actually showing it that Luke was eating 50 eggs. Second, he had to show you the feelings of the men without making them too obvious. Third, he had to keep your sympathies with Luke. And fourth, he wanted to draw the parallel between Luke and Christ, which he did in the last shot by showing Luke in the Crucifixion position.

In obtaining the results he wants, there are special factors the director must consider with regard to a movie sequence. First, *how long* should the shot be? If the camera lingers too long on a subject, the audience's interest flags. Too long can be a matter of a second or two. After 20 years of television, people have become "speed watchers"; it doesn't take them as long as it used to to take in an image. (See for yourself. Compare a movie of pre-television days to one of today. Count the seconds in the shots in each. You'll see that the average shot in today's movie is shorter.) People are now able to perceive an image which appears on the screen for even a fraction of a second.

Second, the director must consider the *order* of the shots. The audience will assume that what happens in one shot has caused the action in the next. If you see a man firing a gun in one shot and another man falling in the next, the conclusion is obvious. However, there are more subtle effects that can be achieved by **montage**—the juxtaposition of shots of not-so-obviously connected material. In the film *Bonnie and Clyde,* for example, there is an early scene when Clyde proudly shows Bonnie his gun. The director sets up a symbol. The gun represents Clyde's masculinity. There are several subsequent scenes which reinforce this symbolism. Shots of lovemaking are juxtaposed with those involving a gun. In the film *Easy Rider* there is a scene in which the director shows the parallel between the motorcycle and the horse. The young men have stopped at a farmhouse to fix a tire on one of their motorcycles. One shot shows the farmer shoeing his horse and the next shows the man fixing the tire. (For a more thorough discussion of this symbolism, see Chapter 9.) The order of shots, then, may suggest some parallels or make symbolic comparisons.

Clyde shows Bonnie his gun. Warner Bros.

Also, the order in which the director places the shots may add to the suspense of a film. In Hitchcock's film *The Birds* there is a scene in which the young woman (played by Tippi Hedron) is waiting outside the schoolhouse. She sits on a bench, alone in a deserted schoolyard. The film cuts to a shot of a few crows perched atop the bars of the schoolyard gym. By alternating shots of the vulnerable woman with the gathering restless crows, Hitchcock prepares us for the scene of horror which is to follow. In another film, Hitchcock deliberately sets us up to be thoroughly shocked. In *Psycho* we are made to identify with the woman, Janet Leigh, by being let in on her unhappy predicament—having a love affair with a married man. We see her steal the money and her awkward attempts at a getaway. By the time she makes up her mind to return the money, we are rooting for her. Feeling relieved at having made a decision, she decides to take a shower. We relax—perhaps a love affair will develop between her and the nice young man she has just met at the motel. The cut from the showering woman to the shadowy figure of the murderer as seen through the shower curtain is one of the most famous in movies. We are thoroughly shocked because Hitchcock has arranged the shots so as to relax us completely. The order in which shots are arranged may build up a tension or they may relax us sufficiently so that we are scared out of our wits. A director like Hitchcock knows how to make us feel the emotions he wants us to feel. He does so through the arrangement of shots, among other movie techniques.

Closely related to the technique of montage is the technique of **cross-cutting:** when the director cuts from one scene to another and then back again. We see cross-cutting in the traditional chase scene. The stage-coach is rattling along the plains; cut to whooping Indians . . . back to the stagecoach, then to the Indians again. A good example of cross-cutting occurs in the final sequence of *Bridge on the River Kwai,* which was directed by David Lean. The British commandos have made preparations to blow up the bridge at the moment the Japanese troop train crosses it. The scene cuts from the British commander, Alec Guinness, who sees the demolition wire and sets out to stop the bridge's destruction—to William Holden, who is plunging across the river to get Guinness—to the soldier hovering over the plunger awaiting the moment when the train is on the bridge—to Jack Hawkins, who is watching the commander from across the river—to the bridge itself, awaiting the train's crossing. The director cuts from one to the other, in ever-shortening shots. The tension build-up is tremendous.

Today's movies use **intercutting**—interrupting a scene with bits of

Rod Steiger in "The Pawnbroker"

Schoolgirls are terrorized by birds in the Universal picture.

"Bridge on the River Kwai," Columbia

"The Last Picture Show," Columbia

another scene—when the director wishes to show a flashback or a flashforward—to take you back or forward in time. In the film *The Pawnbroker,* for example, the emotionally bankrupt pawnbroker, played by Rod Steiger, begins to recall his tragic past. His recollections are called forth by events in his present life: a date on a calendar, his meeting with a sympathetic social worker, his relations with his eager young apprentice. Cuts to past events—a few seconds of a scene—interrupt the scene taking place in the present. A cut into the scene between the pawnbroker and a prostitute, for example, shows his wife in a room with a Nazi officer. The cut serves two purposes: we draw the conclusion that his wife was used as a prostitute in the concentration camp and we see one of the past events that has contributed to the pawnbroker's state of mind.

This technique of showing a **flashback** by intercutting works because audiences are visually more sophisticated than they were 20 years ago. Watching television, particularly the commercials, has made them so. Commercial-makers, having to get across a message in 60, 30, or even 20 dearly-paid-for seconds, devised speedy and efficient ways of presenting images. Movie directors, in attempting to appeal to hip audiences, replaced the old techniques with the new ones.* For example, the old-fashioned way of showing a flashback is to show a close-up of an actor's dreamy face; then blur the scene. When the camera focuses in again, the flashback scene is shown. At the end of the flashback, blur again. Then we see the actor's face again, as he supposedly comes out of his reverie. Directors no longer feel the need to use such an obvious technique; audiences are used to straight film cuts for showing changes in time and place.

Some directors have even intercut **flashforwards** into their films. That is, there is a cut to a scene from a future event. In *Easy Rider,* before the final fiery scene, there is a barely perceptible image from that event cut into a scene. The film *They Shoot Horses, Don't They?* shows flashforwards of Robert's trial intercutting the present action. An interesting alternative to the intercut flashforward is used in *Butch Cassidy and the Sundance Kid.* Butch and Sundance go to the movies and see a film about themselves. They see their own deaths; they are shot by the Superposse in this movie within a movie, foreshadowing the film's final scenes.

Cutting to flashbacks or flashforwards is not the only way a director

*Some young directors (Peter Bogdanovich in *The Last Picture Show* and Francis Ford Coppola in *The Godfather*) eschew TV-commercial film techniques and follow the style of cinema masters like Howard Hawks and John Ford.

Peter Bogdanovich directs Timothy Bottoms in a scene from "The Last Picture Show."

Tony Perkins, the star of "Psycho."

may alter the normal flow of time in a film. He may shorten the time it takes for an event to occur, or he may prolong it. There are many actions which must be shortened by the director if he wants to keep his audience interested. For example, suppose he wishes to show an actor searching a house and finding nothing. He will show him looking in one room, then jump cut to him in another room, keeping the **continuity** of the action by showing the actor moving in the same direction in each shot. The sequence may be completed in five or six shots. On the other hand, suppose the director wants to show an actor moving through a house in which a murderer is hiding. If he wishes us to feel the full extent of the tension of this situation, he will prolong the action —to make it last longer than it would normally. How does he do it? As the actor moves stealthily and slowly up a darkened flight of stairs, the director may cut to an ominous statue in the room, to the darkened hallway at the top of the stairs, to the actor's frightened eyes, to his foot touching a creaking stair, and so on. Hitchcock is a specialist at this kind of scene—of prolonging an action in order to have his audience *experience* rather than just watch an event. The famous shower-murder scene in *Psycho,* for example, lasted forty-five hair-raising seconds on the screen and involved a complicated montage of quick cuts which took seven days to film. In reality, a stabbing murder would have lasted only a few seconds. It is prolonging of the action, of showing the audience just what he wants to show them in a certain order, that is like "taking them through the haunted house at the fairground or the roller-coaster" . . . which is how Hitchcock himself explains what he does to audiences.

The punctuating of shots

A movie is made up of shots as a short story is made up of sentences, and a poem of words. The director tries to make each shot a perfect creation, just as the short story writer labors over each sentence and the poet over each word. The shots, however, must go together in such a way as to make the movie more than just a collection of well-executed shots. One shot has got to lead in to the next, according to the action being filmed. In filming a conversation between two people, for example, the director will cut back and forth between them—the angle from which he shoots depending on how involved he wants the audience to become. He may shoot from behind the shoulder of one of the actors, if he is the character with whom the audience is to identify, or of both characters, if the director wants the audience to become deeply involved —as in a conversation between two lovers.

When the conversation sequence ends, though, the director must decide how to lead into the next sequence. There are several techniques he can use. The simplest and most common is the straight **cut.** Suppose that when the conversation comes to a close, our hero leaves. The next shot might show him in another place, involved in another action. The connection between the shots is simply the hero himself. So as not to jar the audience, however, the director will make sure the two shots—the final shot of the conversation sequence and the first shot of the next sequence—will have some relationship to each other. Perhaps the hero has slammed a door, or gotten into his car, or hopped onto his horse— then the next shot could show him opening another door, getting out of a car, or riding on his horse. The transition between shots, in this case, is the action and perhaps also the distance between the hero and the camera.

A director would probably not end one sequence with a **long shot** and open the next with an extreme **close-up.** He might, though, end a sequence with a close-up and begin the next with the same kind of shot. Rather than have the hero leave at the end of a conversation, for example, the director might end the sequence with an extreme close-up of the drink the hero is holding. The next shot could be another extreme close-up of a drink. The camera would pull back to show the hero in another place at another time. The director can connect sequences, then, by close-up shots of objects: a glowing lamp, a swishing windshield wiper, the shining spur of a boot.

Suppose, however, there is a radical shift in time and place between two sequences. The director can show this shift in two ways: by dissolving or by fading out. A dissolve is less abrupt than a fade-out. A **dissolve** shows two images on the screen at the same time; the final shot of one sequence fades out while the superimposed first shot of the next sequence becomes dominant. The dissolve may last a few seconds or be a long, slow dissolve of 10 to 15 seconds, depending on the effect the director wishes to achieve.

For example, suppose the movie is a Western and the director has to show the hero traveling alone for several months. He might use a sequence of shots, dissolving from one to the other, to show the passage of time and the change of location. (By the way, if the hero is moving toward the left, we assume that he is traveling west. Movies treat the screen as though it were a map, so as not to confuse the audience.) A director might also use a sequence of dissolving shots to show a man and a woman falling in love. A few minutes of such a sequence can compress time and place and situation.

On the other hand, the **fade-out** is like the closing curtain after a scene on the stage. A fade-out ends a sequence with a second or two of a blank screen. The director then fades-in to the next sequence. (There are other, less frequently used techniques for "punctuating" shots. One is to blur the final shot of a sequence and then to focus in on the first shot of the next, as when the hero loses consciousness and then comes to. Another is the **wipe** shot, when one image is "wiped" from the screen by the second, usually from left to right. A variation is the **flip wipe,** when the image seems to spin around to reveal another image. The rarely used **iris** shot blanks out all of the image except that part in a small circle in the middle of the frame; then the small circle will widen out to reveal a new scene.) Today, directors do not use the dissolve and the fade-out as much as they used to. Today's audience is used to quick cutting from image to image; the dissolve and the fade seem to slow down the action. The fade-out, however, is used frequently in television, mainly as a separation between programming and commercials.

Of moving forms and moving camera . . .

A movie is an arrangement of shots, punctuated by cuts and sometimes by dissolves and fades. But what of the shot itself? What goes into the making of a good shot? Basically, all movie-making follows the same principle. Whether he is using a Super 8 or a gigantic 35-mm Hollywood-studio type of camera, a director puts on film what he points the camera at. To keep his audience interested, he must have movement. To get movement, he can do only two things: move the subject or move the camera . . . or both. The most boring films ever made are the typical "educational" films. They are boring because they are so static; they lack movement, or at least a variety of movement. They look as though they are filmed from one spot; the camera never moves. Or, if the camera moves, it moves in an uninteresting way. For example, let's imagine such an educational film. We'll call it *San Francisco: Golden Gateway to the West.* After the "establishing shot" (the film's opening shot to let you know the location of the action) of the city from the air, you will see various shots of what the city is famous for: the Golden Gate Bridge (a 10-second pan), Alcatraz Island (a four-second shot), the San Francisco-Oakland Bay Bridge (a ten-second pan), dissolve to a close-up of the clock on the Ferry Building (two seconds), dissolve to outside elevator on the Fairmont Hotel (two seconds), dissolve to . . . and so on. In the background the music and the voice of the narrator alternate, neither of them distinctive enough to add interest to the static film.

Steve McQueen in "Bullitt," Warner Bros.-Seven Arts

It isn't enough for the director just to film moving objects, or move his camera. To *involve* the audience, to get you to *experience* the film, the director must achieve movement that is both varied and appropriate to the subject of the film. For example, the film *Bullitt* contains a sequence that is one of the most involving ever filmed. Rather than film the chase (between the detective, played by Steve McQueen, and the criminals) from a distance, the camera got right in on the action. The audience alternates between the positions of onlooker (you're right on the street as the car careens, squealing, around a San Francisco street corner) and driver (you become Steve McQueen as the camera shows the chase from his viewpoint). As the car speeds up and down and around corners of San Francisco's steep streets, your stomach flips over and you clutch the arms of your theater seat (or your companion) for support. *Bullitt* involves us in the atmosphere of San Francisco more than an educational film like the one described ever could.

Movement doesn't have to be quick to be involving. In *Butch Cassidy and the Sundance Kid,* for example, when the two outlaws arrive at the Hole-in-the-Wall Valley, Butch remarks how the first sight of the place always affects him; then the camera cuts to a **panoramic** shot of the beautiful, desolate valley surrounded by high rocky cliffs. A slow pan is usually used to let the audience see the beauty of such a location. However, a pan shot may also be used in a close-up. For example, the camera turns away from a heroine as she searches through a desk, pans slowly across a darkened room, to a close-up of a turning door-knob.

At the opposite extreme of the slow pan, there is the **swish-pan,** in which the camera is turned so quickly that the image is blurred. The swish-pan might be used to draw the audience's attention to a certain object or person. For example, suppose the director wishes to show us a certain character as he walks through the busy city streets. He could swish-pan through the crowd and stop his camera to focus on the man. A more common shot, though, is the **zoom,** when the lens enlarges a segment of the frame, bringing it closer to view. The zoom is used more frequently in television than in movies; movie directors prefer cutting to zooming in. They also prefer moving the camera itself to simulating movement with a zoom lens. Therefore, to keep our attention on the man walking through the crowded streets, the movie director could call for a **tracking shot,** in which the camera moves along with the man, the lens adjusted in such a way as to keep everyone else on the street out of focus.

To get closer to a subject, instead of using a zoom lens the director moves the camera closer in. For example, suppose a movie sequence

"Butch Cassidy and the Sundance Kid"

"The Graduate," Embassy Pictures

involves a man and a woman meeting in a restaurant. One shot might be a long shot taking in the interior of the place, with the man walking into view. The next shot might be a pan shot, with the camera **dollying** in closer, showing the man as he walks through the restaurant. The next is a medium shot of the woman sitting at the table. Then, a cut to the man standing beside the table. With these shots, the director has brought us to the table, too, so that during the conversation the couple is about to have, we can eavesdrop. (A skillful director will involve us even further by allowing us to become either the man or the woman for a moment, by showing close-ups as each speaks.)

Suppose the director had used a zoom-in shot to the couple sitting at the table, instead of the moving camera shots described. It would have called our sudden attention to the couple, as though we were looking at them through binoculars or through the telescopic sight on a rifle. They would look closer to us, yet we would lack the feeling of being near them. Perhaps that is the effect the director wishes: to make us feel as though we are watching rather than participating. If he wishes us to feel as though we have moved in closer to what's happening, he will dolly in with the camera. The camera dollies in closer as we would walk in, and the lens sees as we would see. We have, in effect, become the camera.

As a matter of fact, there are many instances in movie-making when the camera moves for us and sees for us. In addition to the ones already mentioned, there are other special techniques of **subjective camera.** A handheld camera moving jerkily through a crowd lets us feel what the jostled actor feels. A spinning camera simulates dizziness. A fisheye lens distorts perspective as our eyes and mind do when we are disturbed.

In *The Graduate,* for example, Benjamin, played by Dustin Hoffman, looks at his parents through a snorkel mask. The distorted images we see and the voices we hear let us feel the frustration Benjamin feels over his parents' attempts to "reach" him. In *2001: A Space Odyssey,* we become the astronaut as he hurtles through a timespace warp in his space pod. In *Vertigo* we experience along with Jimmy Stewart the horrible sight of a man plunging to the sidewalk hundreds of feet below. These are scenes that involve us completely. The director has involved us by creating effects with special cameras and lenses, often at great financial expense.

Many effects, though, can be produced with the simplest of cameras. A **low angle** shot looking up at a person will make him seem larger than he is. Conversely, a **high angle** shot looking down at him will em-

phasize his insignificance. The opening shot of *Gunsmoke,* for example, is a low angle shot of Marshal Dillon (played by James Arness) walking slowly down the main street of town. That camera angle emphasizes the marshal's physical and moral stature. Compare that shot to the one in *High Noon* when we look down on the marshal walking up the deserted street to meet the gunmen. This camera angle reinforces the vulnerability of the actor (Gary Cooper) who must go to meet the men alone and without help. (See Chapter 9 for a discussion of *High Noon.*)

Even slow and fast motion can be achieved with an ordinary camera. By running the film through the camera more slowly than is normal, a director gets fast motion; and by running it through more rapidly he gets slow motion. Conventionally, fast motion creates a comical effect, and slow motion, a beautiful, poetic one. Recently, movie directors have used fast and slow motion ironically. In *Bonnie and Clyde,* Arthur Penn filmed the machine-gunning of the outlaw pair in slow motion, which made the killing seem all the more horrible. In *A Clockwork Orange,* Stanley Kubrick filmed a sex orgy scene in fast motion, rendering it comic rather than erotic. The danger of using such unusual special effects, though, is that they will be imitated. Overdone, an effect becomes a cliché. After *Bonnie and Clyde,* for example, other directors used slow motion in killing scenes with a lesser impact.

It is unlikely, though, that a creative film director will ever run out of ways to make viewing a film a fresh and involving experience for us. There are so many factors involved—many of which we have not even mentioned in this chapter: sets and locations; script and dialogue; casting and acting; sound and music; lighting and color—that the possibilities are nearly infinite. Film is a medium that can work magic. What we have talked about here are only some of the ways that the magic is created.

Do:

- Write a movie (or movie for TV) review, describing the movie in terms of shots and discussing film techniques.

- Make a list of film techniques discussed in this chapter (crosscutting, flashback, flashforward, the camera movements, camera angles, and so on) and describe *one* effective use of this technique that you have seen.

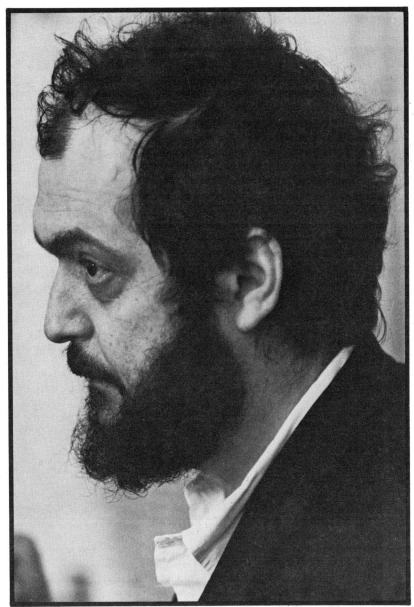

Stanley Kubrick, director of "A Clockwork Orange," Warner Bros.

CREATE:

Sketch and write up a storyboard for the filming of a nursery rhyme.

Example:
> *Humpty-Dumpty sat on a wall,*
> *Humpty-Dumpty had a great fall;*
> *All the king's horses and all the king's men*
> *Couldn't put Humpty-Dumpty together again.*

Others to use:
> *Little Jack Horner*
> *Sat in a corner*
> *Eating a Christmas pie*
> *He put in his thumb,*
> *And pulled out a plum*
> *And cried, "What a good boy am I!"*

> *Hey, diddle, diddle,*
> *The cat and the fiddle,*
> *The cow jumped over the moon;*
> *The little dog laughed*
> *To see such a sight*
> *And the dish ran away with the spoon.*

> *Jack and Jill went up the hill*
> *To fetch a pail of water.*
> *Jack fell down and broke his crown*
> *And Jill came tumbling after.*

REACT:

"The Godfather" promises to become one of the most popular movies ever made, rivalling "Gone With the Wind" and "The Sound of Music." What are the appeals of the film? Is its popularity due to its violence? To its subject matter? To the fine acting of its principals? Why do many people go to see the movie for a second time?

"The Godfather," Paramount Pictures

CREATE:

Make a movie. One roll of Super 8 film costs four to six dollars and runs close to four minutes. If you plan ahead and shoot carefully, you can end up with a fine film. (Some of the most interesting films are under 10 minutes.)

Here are some suggestions:

1. Film several commercials. Make up your own or parody existing ones. Commercials are 20, 30, and 60 seconds long, so four minutes can involve a lot of creativity.

2. Select a popular song and use it as your "script." A song that tells a story like the Beatles' *Rocky Raccoon* can be enacted; whereas a song that doesn't follow a story line can be given an impressionistic treatment. Record the song on a cassette tape; then carry a portable player with you when you go out to film. You can then film an action while you play a line of the song. This way you end up with film and sound synchronized. (But *plan ahead;* you save time and a lot of editing.)

3. Go to a place where you'll find lots of interesting subjects, like a zoo or a popular tourist spot or big shopping center. Decide upon a way to give your film continuity and go to it! You can give your film continuity by filming people doing a certain action, like walking or eating. Take a friend with you. Have your friend hold up a sign that says, "SMILE!" Then film everyone who complies.

4. You don't need a complicated script or elaborate sets to make an interesting film. For example, film people's hands in various actions: at hard work, at rest, showing strength and gentleness, expressing love and hate, and so on.

5. Make a film which parodies current film clichés. For example, a slow motion shot of two lovers running toward each other in a sunlit meadow has already been parodied in an amusing television commercial.

6. Make a film of film techniques. For example, use montage (cross-cutting of different subjects) to create a visual symbol. Film a scene using flashbacks or flashforwards.

DO:

• Watch a 15-second TV commercial and analyze it as a film sequence; that is, distinguish each *shot* and what the camera does in each (angle, movement, distance from subject); if you can catch any of the transitional devices mentioned above, indicate which ones were used. Then write it up in *storyboard* fashion.

• Describe a movie or a TV story in terms of shots and other movie-making terms. For example, here is how a "print-oriented" person would describe *Welcome Home, Johnny Bristol,* a movie for TV aired in January, 1972.

Basically, the story is about a man named Johnny Bristol (played by Martin Landau), who has undergone the extreme torture of "the cage" (a tall bamboo structure through which the enemy views him and jeers at him constantly) in Vietnam. He is returned to the States for treatment, physical and perhaps psychological rehabilitation as well. He talks incessantly and with great fondness about his first home, Charles, Vermont—a perfect, serene community nestled in the hills; and how just thinking about it kept him sane while in "the cage." His first weekend off he goes to visit the town, and it isn't there. He accuses the army of a giant conspiracy involving the destruction of his town, and the army answers by putting him in the psycho ward.

He escapes, of course, to track down his own past, to find the people whose faces he remembers as a part of Charles, Vermont. He goes to Philadelphia, to the home he lived in with his parents before they died; and to the orphanage in the same city, where he was placed after their death. Each place triggers memories of his past, but he can't piece things together until the psychiatrists force him to remember how his parents were killed— the victims of a street mugging right in front of their house in Philadelphia, with all the neighbors looking on, helpless. The reason no one has helped him remember is that he shouted the night of the murder that he would "come back and kill all of you" for not saving his parents' lives. Once Bristol realizes that he has been refusing to think about his real past, he understands why his mind invented Charles, Vermont. It was a lovely safe substitute for the horror of reality.

Now here is how to describe the movie in visual terms:

The movie begins with *shots* of Bristol being recovered in Vietnam and embarked on a transport plane headed back to the States. The next shot is of the ambulance, rushing down a freeway (American car models, road signs, etc.). One efficient shot and we now know where we are, that Bristol is still in extremely critical condition, and that the next stop will be the hospital.

The next shot is important—Bristol finally regaining consciousness in the hospital. The director used a *subjective camera* technique; that is, he has the camera act as Bristol and simulate the awakening process. Blurred shapes of figures bent over and looking down toward the camera come gradually into focus.

To emphasize that Bristol's mind could still play tricks on him, and to do so dramatically, the director showed *flashbacks* to the horrors of "the cage." He used *crosscuts* in the following manner: In the Boston hospital ward, the nurse sets up screens (with vertical rods and curtains) all around the bed for privacy. When he wakes in the night and sees them, he thinks he is back in the cage. The resemblance in shape and form is made obvious in the series of crosscuts comparing them. The shots get shorter and shorter, building up the tension and pace until finally he screams and the nurse takes the screens down.

The rest of the film is told mostly through flashbacks to events of his youth. Two techniques are used in order to make it clear to the viewing audience that these scenes are from his past: in the flashback scenes which contain incidents he only imagined, the voices all sound hollow. In another series of flashback events intercut with present events, those from the past are tinted pink.

And finally, the director has kept the panic in Bristol's mind uppermost in our minds by using many scenes of flight and putting many screams, sirens, strident bells on the *sound track.*

> The black man will have arrived in the movies when they cast him as a villain. Black can be good and bad as well as beautiful. We just ask you make us human.
> —Jim Brown, July 10, 1969.

Read:

On Movies (collections of reviews and essays):

Private Screenings, John Simon, Berkley Medallion Books, 1967, $1.25.
On Movies, Dwight Macdonald, Berkley Medallion Books, 1969, $1.50.
The Private Eye, The Cowboy, and the Very Naked Girl, Judith Crist, Paperback Lib., 1970, $.95.
Kiss Kiss, Bang Bang, Pauline Kael, Bantam, 1969, $1.95.
I Lost It at the Movies, Pauline Kael, Bantam, $1.25.
Going Steady, Pauline Kael, Bantam, $1.95.
A Year in the Dark, Renata Adler, Berkley Medallion, 1971, $1.50.

On Directors:

Interviews with Film Directors, Andrew Sarris, Avon, 1967, $1.65.
The Film Director as Superstar, Joseph Gelmis, Doubleday & Co., 1970, $3.50.
The American Cinema, Andrew Sarris, Dutton Paperback, 1968, $2.95.
Hitchcock's Films, Robin Wood, Paperback Lib., 1970, $1.25.

On Film Theory:

The Film Experience, Roy Huss and Norman Silverstein, Delta, 1968, $1.95.
An Introduction to the American Underground Film, Sheldon Renan, Dutton, 1967, $2.25.
Film Culture Reader, edited by P. Adams Sitney, Praeger, 1970, $4.95.
The Contemporary Cinema, Penelope Houston, Penguin, 1963, $1.45.
Man and the Movies, W. A. Robinson, editor; Pelican, 1969, $1.95.
Renaissance of the Film, edited by Julius Bellone, Collier, 1970, $2.95.
Expanded Cinema, Gene Youngblood, Dutton, 1970, $4.95.

On Making Your Own Movies:

Behind the Camera, William Kuhns and Thomas Girardino, Pflaum/Standard, 1970, $3.50.
Guide to Filmmaking, Edward Pincus, Signet, 1969, $1.50.
Creative Filmmaking, Smallman, Collier, 1969, $3.95.
How to Make Good Movies, Kodak, $1.00.
Young Filmmakers, Roger Larson and Ellen Meade, Avon, $.95.

CHAPTER 14

THE HUMAN TOUCH

At first blush, it seems ironic that the era of the mass communication overload should also be the time of experiments with new forms of communication like encounter groups and sensitivity training. But perhaps it's not ironic, simply indicative of a need for the human touch. Although we may be surfeited with being talked at, we are hungry for personal communication.

This hunger has resulted in what's known as the "Human Potential Movement," a search for intimacy in a time of alienation. It is a curious social phenomenon that the more crowded together people are, the more lonely they become. Think of what might be a typical day: bumper to bumper, you drive to school or work over crowded roads and freeways. Elbow to elbow, you are jostled along busy streets, or hallways, or store aisles. At work or school, you are just one of many engaged in the same activity; you join the assembly line. Back home in your own "little box" or apartment "cell," you turn on the TV. For escape? Companionship? "Human" contact?

Aside from exchanging a few pleasantries and banalities, a person may spend his entire day without talking to anyone although he may come in "contact" (bumper to bumper and elbow to elbow) with hundreds of people. Whatever the cause—whether it is a reaction to over-crowdedness, an antidote to an excess of impersonal communication, or because we've been "massaged" by television for 20 years and have become sensory in place of logical (a McLuhan theory)—the effect has been the emergence of experimental "schools of communication," where people go to learn how to achieve contact with other people.

This new interest in group communication may affect nearly everyone in one way or another. Let's take one family as an example. The father may become involved in a group at work, whether he be a high-powered executive or an ordinary worker. More and more businesses are hiring human relations counselors to give training sessions to their employees—not out of some altruistic motive to help make better people out of them, but from the very practical one that it might help business. Due to increased automation, employees are dealing with people more than they are with things, so management may decide that they need some people training. The purpose of this kind of training is to help a person become more aware of the point of view and the needs of the other person—to become more empathetic. Whether empathy is a skill for which one may be trained is a debatable point. But what is obvious is that the conventional, middle-class world has become aware of the need for human communication.

The mother, if she doesn't work and become involved in a group training session there, may become involved in a group in her role as parent. Even though her children may be very young and without apparent problems, a woman may attend a group whose purpose is to help its members become "better" mothers. The women may simply exchange their notions on such subjects as toilet-training, thumb-sucking, and bed-wetting, actually doing what women in another society would do over the wash at the river bank or at the town's central washing well—they're sharing their problems and their techniques for solving them; and they're learning from each other.

The children of the family may become involved in a group at school, at church, or at some youth organization they belong to. Although they are in a minority, there are some leaders at these institutions who recognize that young people are no longer satisfied (if they ever were!) with the traditional approach to education—the approach whereby an "expert," the adult vested with some kind of knowledge the young person may need, imparts that knowledge while the child is expected to absorb it. This process used to be called writing on a "blank slate," a metaphor to explain the absence of knowledge in the child's brain. Now it's called programming. What these experimental leaders recognize is that young people do not need programming as much as they need an opportunity for communication, for interaction, and for self-expression. They need to work with one another in the learning process. They need a chance to react to all the data and stimuli that have been fed into them by such impersonal forces as the mass media. Group discussion replaces the lecture or the sermon, and projects demanding involvement replace the test.

These are examples of an individual's becoming involved in group communication within his ordinary activities. However, he may also become involved in a group when he has a special problem. Then the purpose of the group may be therapeutic, and the members do more than talk . . . they *encounter*. In an encounter group, which should be led by a trained professional, participants are encouraged to be honest and frank. The barriers people usually put up to protect themselves from hurt are deliberately removed. It is a painful process, but the goal is that the individual gains strength from having to deal with himself and his problem honestly.

Suppose the family members have a problem getting along with each other, a problem which will usually manifest itself in one person—let's say a teenager who may become a truant. The family, or part of it, may seek (or be recommended to join) an encounter group. Such a group, which may be under the auspices of the city mental health department, will bring together parents and children with similar problems who, under the guidance of a trained leader, will be encouraged to express how they feel about each other. It is a comment upon our times that people of the most intimate relationships—parent and child, husband and wife—may live together as strangers and are only able to talk with one another under these artificial conditions.

In another possible case, suppose the mother seeks psychiatric care for depression. The psychiatrist may recommend group therapy for her, where she is brought together with others with a similar problem, again under the leadership of a professional. Here, she may learn to face her particular strengths and weaknesses, her fears and anxieties, and better learn to cope with them. She faces them because, perhaps for the first time in her life, people tell her the truth about herself and force her to do the same. (I'm afraid . . . I'm lonely . . . I can't love anyone . . . I can't *feel* anything.)

Meanwhile, suppose the father is an alcoholic or a drug addict. He may seek help from one of two very successful self-help organizations which are based on the group therapy structure, Alcoholics Anonymous or Synanon. Alcoholics Anonymous was founded in 1934 and is an organization run by alcoholics for alcoholics. In AA, there is no such person as a former alcoholic. The basic premise upon which the AA philosophy rests is that alcoholism is a permanent condition which can only be kept dormant. The AA goal is simply: Don't take a drink *today*. What AA offers is moral support; the emphasis is on facing blunt facts. "Hello, I'm Joe, and I'm an alcoholic," is the standard opening to any talk. Joe may not have taken a drink for a couple of thousand days, but in AA, there is no hierarchy of alcoholism.

The meetings are conducted by alcoholics and are structured along the lines of group therapy. Each person is given a chance to tell his story. One group meeting may bring together a derelict drunk, his body and brain ravaged by alcohol, and an articulate and attractive member of the upper social strata who has recognized his (or her) dependence upon alcohol. Each may gain strength from being able to share his problems honestly with the other. That is the principle upon which AA is founded, and it has been very successful for many people.

One person for whom AA was not completely satisfactory is Chuck Dederich, who started Synanon in 1959. Synanon is basically for "dope fiends," although people with other "hangups" may take part. Synanon is more involving than AA, for persons do more than attend a weekly meeting; for some people Synanon may become a way of life, almost a religion. As far as group therapy is concerned, Synanon is known for its brutally honest session called "The Game," where the only rules are that everybody takes part and that there be no physical violence. Verbal violence, though, is the name of The Game; and emotions run raw and basic. The growth of Synanon can only prove the need for this kind of outlet; it now controls millions of dollars' worth of real estate, has branches in eight major cities, and sponsors some 80 tribes that practice the Synanon Game in encounter groups.

These are but a few of the kinds of encounter groups now being conducted throughout the nation, which may range from an informal "truth" session conducted after a buffet supper by some amateur psychologist in his apartment to a highly sophisticated (and highly expensive) weekend at Esalen Institute in Big Sur, California.

Esalen, which has become for the encounter-inclined what the Golden Door and Main Chance are for the weight watchers, was founded in 1962 by Michael Murphy and Richard Price, who were classmates at Stanford. Esalen* is 62 acres of seacoast land at Big Sur, an area known for its primitive beauty, located on California's Highway 1 north of the Hearst Castle at San Simeon and south of Carmel-by-the-Sea. Satirized in the film *Bob & Carol & Ted & Alice,* Esalen has become famous for its most salient virtues—the fabulous beauty and romantic remoteness of its location and its ritual steam baths, where you slip nude into a hot tub peopled with your awareness confreres. For some, it is really just a Super Motel; however, for the knowledgeable, Esalen is truly an authentic innovator. There have been many outgrowths of the center, whose goal is "growth of the human potential."

What Esalen and groups like it really strive for is an increasing awareness for the human being. What they recognize and try to overcome in people is a stultification of feeling. We have either suppressed or have never developed our abilities for full sensory awareness and feeling, they believe. (Marshall McLuhan holds this same theory, only he talks about it in terms of the effects of mass media.) Therefore, the workshops consist of training sessions to develop awareness, popularly called "sensitivity training." A more accurate term is "sensory awareness."

Sensory awareness training, very generally, consists of exercises which are intended to heighten awareness of stimuli we are not used to responding to. We are used to responding to that which we hear and that which we see, but we suppress the stimuli to the sense of touch particularly, awareness trainers believe. The training, therefore, is that of learning to recognize and respond to tactile stimulus, that of touching.

Sensitivity training has become a focal point of controversy between educational innovators and the general public. Because touching is also used for erotic stimulus, sensory awareness training may become associated with sexual experimentation in the minds of some people who are ignorant of training techniques. While the teacher may be motivated by the sincerest of intentions, he may be seen as some kind of perverted monster by fearful parents. What may have been a classroom session in holding hands and/or achieving eye contact may become, via rumor, a sexual liason in a darkened room. This kind of unreasonable rumor can only be believed in a society that equates touching with eroticism and sensitivity with sex. And it is these limitations of our viewpoint that the practitioners of sensory awareness are trying to break through.

Contrary to the philosophy of this book, this is one time when we recommend that the student *not* experiment. In discussing the techniques of visual or print communication, we have advocated that the student experiment with making films, producing newspapers or magazines, conceiving his own radio or television programs, and if possible producing one. In this case, the medium—the encounter group or the sensory awareness training session—is of an experimental nature. So we strongly advocate not experimenting. Because each deals with the very delicate area of the human psyche, we would no sooner recommend that the encounter group or the sensory awareness training session be tried without professional guidance than we would encourage amateur heart surgery.

READ:

We can recommend these books, however, which are first-hand accounts of people who experienced much of what the "Human Potential Movement" has to offer:

Please Touch, Jane Howard, Dell Publishing Co., 1970.
Turning On, Rosa Gustaitis, Macmillan, 1968.

You may also be interested in:

Games People Play, Eric Berne, M.D., Grove Press, 1967.
I'm OK, You're OK, A Practical Guide to Transactional Analysis, Thomas A. Harris, Harper & Row (hardbound).
Man the Manipulator, Everett L. Shostrom, Bantam, 1968.
Body Language, Julius Fast, Pocket Books, 1971.

"See Me, Touch Me, Feel Me"
—song from the rock opera "Tommy" by The Who

---

*It was originally run as a mineral springs resort, Big Sur Hot Springs, although it was too remote to be successful. When Murphy inherited it, he saw the chance to put into practice some of the theories of Eastern mysticism in which he believed.

Chapter 15

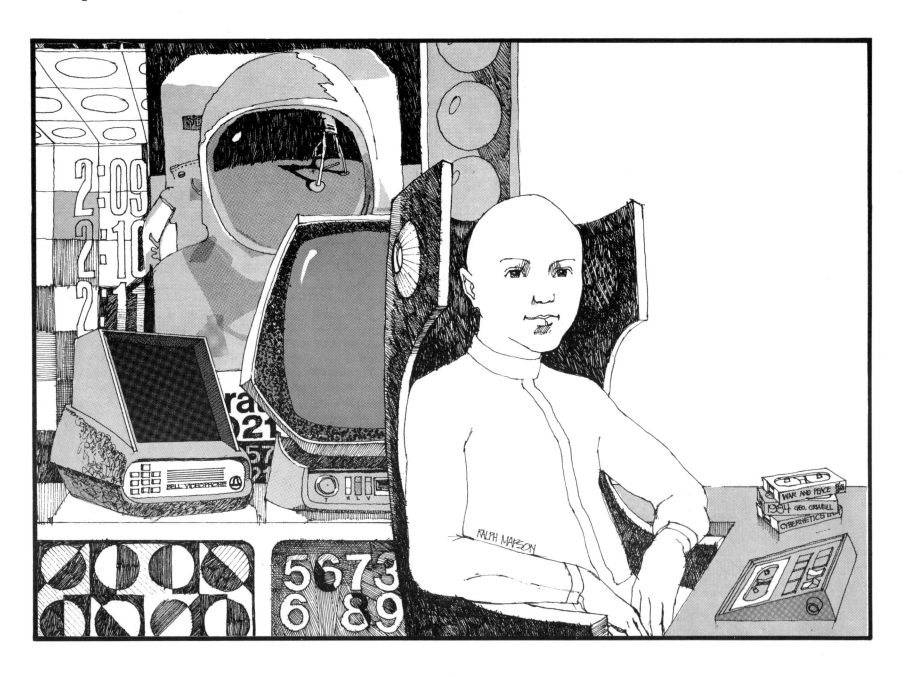

Tuning in Tomorrow

In Chapter 4 we traced the development of the modern media. We went back one generation, to the early 1940s, and saw that people lived without television, transistor radios, and easy music recording and playback devices. Yet at that time, before vinyl records and inexpensive tape recorders, people seemed quite happy with what they had—bulky, breakable 78rpm records. They had to be careful not to drop them, of course; and they had to stack a lot of them on the spindle (a seven-inch record played only one three-minute song on each side) to get a half-hour of the Sinatra, Glenn Miller, and Stan Kenton sounds they enjoyed.

We went back to the generation before that, to the time of World War I (around 1920), and saw radio and movies in the first stages of their development. Yet even in 1920, as poor as the sound quality of radio transmission was, and as imperfect as the movies were (movement was jerky and there was no sound or color), people accepted with delight the entertainment the radio and the movies brought them. Knowing no better, they enjoyed the radio and the movies as they were.

People generally are contented with the entertainment forms they have, yet each new development is enthusiastically welcomed. As soon as the improvement is available, everybody wants to replace the old with the new. Who wants black and white TV when he can have color? Who wants monaural when he can have stereo or even quadra sound? Who *doesn't* want an 8-track stereo tape deck in his car?

When we consider what we have now—color TV, transistor radios, portable tape recorders, tape decks—we feel pretty satisfied. How could any of these devices become obsolete? Each seems as good as it can possibly be. It is difficult to imagine what could make the newest, best-made color television set as old-fashioned a piece of furniture as a 1940 model radio console is today. Yet it is inevitable that we will someday discard each wonderful entertainment machine we have for a newer model . . . or for a different entertainment machine. Will your children grow up with something that you now can't even imagine? (Before 1945, no one imagined that he would soon have the instant entertainment of television.)

How can we predict what changes will come about? We can't foresee exactly what the future will bring, but we can make some educated guesses. That is, knowing what technological experiments are now being made gives us a basis for safe prediction. Also, knowing the history of the development of radio and recording and movies gives us a good idea of future development of television.

Let's look at some of today's technological experiments and newest developments in communication.

No longer in the experimental stage, the *picture phone* exists and will soon be available to the general public.

Easier and less expensive means of *copying* material are being developed all the time. For instance, it is possible to transmit photographs which can be printed in a quality better than that of *National Geographic* magazine.

Computers are being put to greater use.

Holography is in the experimental stage . . . comparable to the state of the motion picture in 1900. (Holography is a means of photographing and projecting images in three dimensions. The images are projected in space and look quite as real as the objects and/or people they represent.)

Video cassette playback machines are the newest device to hit the mass market, and it is expected that video cassettes will someday be as plentiful and inexpensive as paperbacks or record albums.

Cable television, now in nine percent of American homes, is on the brink of enormous expansion. Experts predict that within 20 years, 95 percent of American households will be wired for cable television reception.

Cable television will make it possible for a household to receive 20 or even 40 channels with the additional feature of sending back a simple response. Some people feel that cable television will change our way of life. Television itself has had a tremendous impact on our lives. With cable television making it possible for so many more channels to operate, it is not hard to imagine that video communication will replace many kinds of print and personal communication.

What will life be like when these new forms of communication become a part of our lives? Let's try to imagine. Here is what your day *might* be like if it were thirty years from now . . . in the year 2001 PLUS . . .

A Day in the Year 2001 Plus

John woke up at 7:30 as usual. He reached over to his night stand and picked out the video cassette he had just bought and put it on. As he listened to the music, he gazed sleepily at the colors bursting rhythmically on the screen. As he did every morning, he wished he had a wall screen for his room. They were so expensive, and first he had to pay for his car. He had hinted to his parents that a wall screen might make a nice Christmas present for him, but his father had said that one in the house was enough. 7:45. He'd better get up and get something to eat before his first class came on. He wished he could watch in bed, but then he couldn't reach the response button. They always thought of something!

He went into the kitchen, got some toast and a glass of milk and was back just in time for his first telecourse. He pulled out the cassette, turned the set to "Cable" and switched to Channel 27. He just made it. There was Mr. Cross telling everyone to push the response button. Another boring lecture on Marine Biology. He kept his finger poised over the button. Mr. Cross had a clever habit of sneaking calls for a response into his lectures. He wouldn't even change his tone of voice, so you couldn't tell he was asking a question unless you were listening. Twice John had missed responding. Once more and he'd have to repeat the course. Just the mere thought made him nervous. He put his headset on so he could tune in better.

He was right. Cross put in five response questions, each one worded in a different way. He probably stayed up all night dreaming those up, John grumbled to himself. He ought to spend his time trying to make his course a little more interesting. Why couldn't he show a cassette once in a while?

8:55. Cross tuned out at last. John took advantage of the break to get another glass of milk. A telecard showing some changes in the schedule was on when he got back. Just at 9 Mr. Allison's course came on. Not Mr. Allison, though. You hardly ever saw him. He used more visuals than any teacher. That's why his courses were so popular. Also, he never put in any response-calls like Cross did. The screen showed a photograph of some funny-looking *hairy* men as Mr. Allison's voice told everyone to signal in.

With Allison, after you signalled in for attendance, you could take a nap or something. The only problem was you might miss something; his course was usually pretty interesting. Besides, what else was there to do? If the school computer didn't monitor everyone's set, you could watch some other channel or play a cassette. He couldn't use the picture phone 'cause his mother would know. So, he stayed tuned to Mr. Allison.

John put his headset on again. Allison was explaining who the four weird-looking guys were. They were a musical group called The Beetles. He said that they were more or less responsible for the Rock Age. How could four creepy-looking *hairy* guys like that have so much influence? Now the screen was showing a film cassette of a few scenes from a movie these guys had made. It was called "Help!" They *were* sort of funny, John thought, especially the way they talked.

When the cassette was over, Mr. Allison put a visual on again. It was an old cover, he explained, of The Beetles' best record album.

It was called "Sergeant Pepper's Lonely Hearts Club Band." Then he played the record on his old-fashioned "stereo." He must have kept everything he ever had! He's always showing us his old stuff. He played a cut called "A Day in the Life" that was really weird. While he was talking about the meaning of the song and showing another picture of The Beetles, John's mind wandered. He was thinking of how boring it was to have music without video. He was trying to imagine how people back in those days could even have enjoyed their music . . . like this Beetle music. Mr. Allison's voice cut into John's thoughts; he was announcing the next day's program. He was planning to show a movie cassette. It was a film of one of the big events of the Swinging Sixties (that was the name of his course), a music festival at a place called Woodstock. Then he called for the signal and tune out.

Next, John had Computer Programming. He got his portable computer out of his desk drawer and braced himself for Ms. Silver. Silver's course was really hard and it was all John could do to keep up.

At 11, John felt hungry, but he decided to view the video cassette he'd taken out of the library for Cross' course. He had to go to the school center today anyway, so he might as well turn it in. He wanted to take out "Help!"; he liked the scene he had seen today on the Swinging Sixties. He took the cassette off the shelf, put it on and switched the set over to "Playback." There was Mr. Cross again. It was a cassette he had made in California on crustaceans. At least the scenery was pretty to look at; and John enjoyed watching the crabs scuttling behind the rocks. If only Cross wouldn't talk so much and use all those big words, he might enjoy this cassette. When it was over, he put it back in the case and went out to the kitchen.

John's mother glanced at him as he opened the refrigerator door to see what he could find for lunch.

"There's some leftover hamburgers," she said. She was sitting at the console teleshopping. He glanced at the screen. It was on fruits and vegetables. There was a close-up of a sliced orange. It looked so good that it made him want one. He looked into the fruit bin. Rats! No oranges. "Hey, signal for oranges!" he told his mother.

"I did," she answered, absorbed in watching the vegetable girl squeeze a head of lettuce.

John made himself a hamburger sandwich and watched the console as he ate. Every once in a while when he saw something that

he liked, he asked his mother to signal for it. "I guess I'll have to pick up the groceries on the way home from the school center," he thought.

He finished his lunch just as his mother switched off the supermarket channel and turned the console to Channel 17. 17 was her favorite channel; the host played all her type of music cassettes. Like now, he was playing some bubbly stuff. The screen showed a smiling long-hair singing and playing the piano. Humming along with the music, his mother got up and busied herself at the kitchen counter.

"I gotta go to the school center now, Mom," John said, "Do you want me to pick up the groceries?"

"Yes, please, Johnny," she answered, "and stop at Sears. I signalled for some things on their channel. Okay? Take my identity card with you."

"Okay, Mom. Hey, tell Dave if he phones that I'll be home around 5."

"Tell the console. I might forget."

John went over to the console and picked up the recorder. He pressed "Phone record" and stood in front of the camera lens. "Dave, I'm at the center. I'll be home around 5. Call me back because I want to go to the holographs tonight. It's got Flint Westwood in ' Moon Patrol.' Yaaaaahhg." He made a face and switched off.

"Do you always have to do that?" his mother was saying as he went out the door.

As soon as John got into the car, he put a cassette on his car video and drove to the school center. By the time he got there, he'd gone through three cassettes. The center was twenty-five miles from where he lived, and the traffic was as thick as usual. He parked in the underground parking lot and took the elevator to the library level. He put the California crustaceans cassette in the return slot and looked up "Help!" in the electronic catalog.

It was out. Somebody had gotten there before him. He noticed there was another Beatles' (he noticed how they spelled their name, too) movie cassette, "A Hard Day's Night," so he punched for it. It was there. He got it and headed down to the level where the studios were.

He was supposed to meet Mark and Steve at Studio 7 at 2 o'clock. They had to videotape a discussion on some aspect of the Swinging Sixties for Mr. Allison's course. They had decided to talk about hair, which Mr. Allison considered one of the great issues of the

Sixties. When John got there, Mark and Steve were already in the studio goofing off.

"Hey, let's get this over with. I gotta run 10 laps for P.E. before I go home," John said as he went into the studio.

"Okay, you got anything? I got some print-outs from the library," Mark answered. He held up some color prints.

"Yeah, and I got some print-outs from some history book. What've you got?"

John grinned at Steve. He pointed to his shiny skull. "I got it all up here."

Mark put a blank cassette into the recorder and switched on the automatic camera. The boys managed to fill a half-hour tape. Steve read from his print-outs, and Mark held up the photos. John felt that he contributed the most. It was easy for him, though; it fascinated him how hair—which was now considered freaky—could once have been such an important thing.

When they were finished, John left the library and headed for the track. Every student was required to run a certain number of laps a week to fulfill his P.E. requirement. John had been doing his home exercises fairly regularly; if you didn't, it showed up in the check-up.

John did the laps easily; he was glad, though, when he was finished. In the gym, he took a shower, and went into a booth for his check-up. He sat in the "hot seat" (they called it that after the electric chair of the olden days) and stuck his identity card into the computer slot. While the computer checked his blood pressure, respiration, pulse, and so on, John thought about that evening. He had a date with Nancy, a friend of Dave's girl. He hoped she liked Flint Westwood.

Flint was John's idol. He saw every one of his holographs. "Moon Patrol" was the latest in a series in which Flint played a space detective. Space was a popular subject at the holographs, probably because it was such an effective setting in full dimension. John's card popped up; his check-up was finished. He left the gym and got his car.

John forgot all about the groceries and Sears until he was almost home. He had to go back about five miles to pick up the food and stuff his mother had ordered. By the time he got home, his father was already there. As usual, his dad was sitting in front of the console, having a drink and going through the print-outs.

"Hi, Dad, did Dave call?" It was way after 5, so he must have.

"Yeah, and I had to look at the hairless wonder. He probably couldn't grow hair if he wanted to . . ." He must have just viewed a loss on the stock market, John thought, if he was zeroing in on the irresponsible younger generation at this time of day.

"Okay, Dad," John grinned, "what did the hairless wonder *say*?" John always tried to humor his dad when he got on this subject.

"He said to pick him up at 8:00. He said he heard that 'Moon Patrol' was just 'infinite' . . . and that going to the holographs was an 'infinite' idea." John's dad loved to tease him about the way he and his friends talked.

"*Infinite!* Hey, Mom, when's dinner?" John started toward his room to call Nancy.

"In about half an hour . . . Dad wants to view a cassette he got from one of the salesmen. I'll call you," John's mother answered.

John glanced into his mirror before he called Nancy. He noticed a bit of hair growing in, so he sprayed it and wiped it off. He spray-powdered his skull so that it wouldn't shine while he video-phoned. He punched Nancy's number; her little brother answered. There was a pause while the kid switched over to Nancy's phone. Then John saw her picture on the screen.

"Come on, let me see *you*; I don't want to look at your picture," John said into the phone. He was joking, but he *did* feel funny talking to a picture.

"No, I'm not ready yet. What time are you picking me up?"

John didn't even look at the picture as he answered. He tuned out and got dressed before his mother called him for dinner. He put on his blue tunic, blue-striped pants-sox, and his new plasto-shoes. He spray-powdered his head a little . . . not too much or his father would get so mad he'd burn out his vidicon tube.

When John came out for dinner, his mother smiled. She liked to see him dressed up, even if she didn't entirely approve of the way he dressed. She was pretty good; she never said anything about his clothes or his head. His dad, though, couldn't accept John's spraying off his hair. He thought it wasn't masculine not to have hair down to your shoulders!

His dad wasn't through with the cassette yet, so John watched it while he waited. It was a demo on a new kind of plastic wall lining. The salesman was showing how durable it was; he tried to scratch it and mark it up but it wouldn't show anything.

"Look at this, honey, what do you think of it?" John's dad always asked John's mother about any new product before he would try it on any of his building projects.

John's mother came over to the console and looked at the screen for a few minutes.

"It looks okay, but what if you want to hang pictures?" She went back to setting the table.

"Hmm," was all Dad said, and he switched off the console.

At dinner, John asked his parents if they remembered the Beatles. That started them off reminiscing about when they were his age. John thought it was pretty interesting all this stuff about the olden days. He was almost sorry when dinner was over and his parents went into the viewing room to watch the screen. This was "Eureka!" night and they never missed that. John looked at his watch; he had a few minutes so he went in and viewed for a while.

John's mother and dad settled into their respective recliners and turned on the screen. It covered nearly one entire wall of the room. It was about six feet square and came out about four inches from the wall. Some people had them built in, but John's dad said you never knew when they'd come out with a new model, so he just attached it to the wall. He did put up corner speakers, though, so they'd have surround sound. "Eureka!" came on, and there was the old West in three dimensions and color. John still liked the holographs better; it was so much more *real.*

John was just getting interested in the story when he had to leave. His parents were completely absorbed in the program and didn't even look up when he left. At least he didn't get teased about his clothes. He played a cassette of some electronic music on the way to Nancy's to put himself in a good mood.

By the time he waited for Nancy and picked up Dave and his girl, it was late. He hoped there would be a box left at the holographs. They were lucky; there was one available box for four. John hurried everyone into the box and soon they were peering through the small window into holographic space. Flint's space pod was hurtling through the universe; soon he'd meet up with a ship from the Negative World and the fight would begin. All Flint's holographs were pretty much the same, but John liked them.

As John looked through the window into the holograph area, it was as though he were on a space pod himself . . . traveling through a time warp into the Negative World. . . .

CREDITS

Photos

The Cinema Shop, San Francisco 58, 59, 61, 72, 73, 74, 100, 109, 120, 121, 123, 134, 135, 136, 137, 154, 157, 159, 160, 164, 167, 170, 175, 176, 178, 183, 184, 187, 199, 200, 225, 232, 235, 252, 253, 254, 255, 256, 257, 258, 259, 260, 261, 264, 265, 266, 268, 269

Alan Oddie 68, 151, 162, 238, 241, 242, 243, 244, 245, 246, 247, 248

NBC 84, 97, 103, 141, 142, 143, 143, 144, 144

ABC 138, 139, 140, 145, 188, 231

The Museum of Modern Art/Film Stills Archive 179, 180, 181, 190, 194

Hal Kataoka, Creative Photography, Redwood City, California 24, 81, 86, 212, 219

Warner Brothers Records 222, 223, 229, 235

Columbia Records 227, 228, 230

KCBS Radio, San Francisco 14, 45, 46

Culver Pictures, Inc. 192, 201

KQED-TV, San Francisco 21, 26

Atlantic Records 234

Batjac Productions, Inc. 182

Leo Burnett Company, Inc. 189

Capitol Records 226

Cinemabilia, New York 195

Larry Edmunds Bookshop, Inc., Hollywood 196

Fawcett Publications 149

Gray Advertising, Inc., New York 129

KRON, San Francisco 19

KYA, San Francisco 15

MCA Records 233

Tandem Productions 96